THE QUALITY OF PUPIL LEARNING EXPERIENCES

THE QUALITY OF
PUPIL LEARNING EXPERIENCES

Neville Bennett
Charles Desforges
Anne Cockburn
Betty Wilkinson

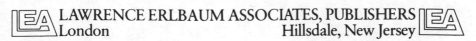
LAWRENCE ERLBAUM ASSOCIATES, PUBLISHERS
London   Hillsdale, New Jersey

Lawrence Erlbaum Associates, Ltd., Publishers
Chancery House
319 City Road
London EC1V 1LJ

Reprinted 1986

British Library Cataloguing in Publication Data

The Quality of pupil learning experiences.
  1. Learning 2. Education, Elementary—
England
I. Bennett, Neville
372'.01'9   LB1060

ISBN 0-86377-010-X
ISBN 0-86377-011-8 Pbk

Typeset by Preface Ltd., Salisbury, printed and bound by A. Wheaton & Co. Ltd., Exeter.

Contents

Foreword   vii
Acknowledgements   ix

1. **Introduction**   1
2. **Research Design**   9
    The Matching Study   9
    Pre-task Interview with Teacher   14
    Transfer Study   19
3. **Task Demand**   21
    A Theory of Complex Learning   22
    Intended and Actual Task Demands   28
    Intended Demands, Actual Demands and Levels of
        Attainment   35
    Summary   39
4. **Matching**   41
    Assessing the Degree of Match   41
    Judging the Appropriateness of Practice Tasks   42
    Judging the Appropriateness of Incremental Tasks   43
    The Appropriateness of Enrichment Tasks   44
    Matching: The General Picture   45
    The Teacher's View of Matching   48
    The Child's Experience   50
    Assigning and Working Tasks in the Classroom   57
    Summary   65

5. The Number Curriculum   67
   The Teachers and Their Approach to Number   67
   Content Covered   68
   Case Studies in Curriculum Coverage   77
   Differentiation in the Curriculum: A Quantitative
      Assessment   83
   Performance on the Curriculum   85
   Test Construction   86
   Providing Quality Maths Experiences   93
   Summary   96
6. The Language Curriculum 99
   Overview   99
   Teaching Children to Write   101
   Progress in Writing   104
   Teaching Language Comprehension   115
   Summary   128
7. Transfer from Infants to Juniors   129
   The Process of Transfer   129
   The First Week in Junior Classes   135
   Task Demand   138
   Matching   146
8. Classroom Groups   153
   Types of Talk   154
   Categories of Talk   159
   The Nature of Instructional Input   163
9. The Quality of Teacher Diagnosis 185
   Materials Used in Training: Example 1   191
   Materials Used in Training: Example 2   193
   Interviews following Language Tasks   208
   Children's Responses to Diagnostic Interviewing   211
10. Conclusion   213

References   223
Appendices   225
      Appendix A: Curriculum Cover: Mathematics   227
      Appendix B: Language: Stimulus Stories   245
      Appendix C: Classroom Groups   249

Author Index   255
Subject Index   257

Foreword

This book concerns the quality of the learning environments provided by 16 able teachers of 6- and 7-year-old children. Decisions regarding the quality of such environments rest on many factors. The study reported here has broken new ground by considering the whole task process in classrooms. Consideration has thus been given to the planning and presentation of classroom tasks, their curriculum content, the intellectual demands they make on children, their appropriateness or match to the children's attainments, their continuity across change of school and the nature of teachers' explanations, diagnoses of children's work and classroom management strategies.

The book is written for teachers and those involved in the training of teachers. This audience has been deliberately chosen since although one crucial role of research is to inform and initiate change it is the members of this audience who will implement it. As such the findings are reported in the form of detailed case studies and descriptive tables.

The findings reveal that despite the conscientious efforts of able teachers a number of serious issues are apparent, some of which appear to be hidden from teachers. These issues are clearly specified in the book, not for the purpose of criticism, but as a necessary basis for improvement. As such these findings will pose challenges both for those who currently teach this age group and for those who train them.

Acknowledgements

This book reports the outcomes of a study funded by the Social Science Research Council. It could not have been written without the unstinting help and cooperation of a large number of people. It is not possible to mention them all by name but the following deserve our special thanks.

Our particular gratitude is expressed to all of the participating teachers, and their headteachers, in the schools studied. They allowed us unlimited access to their schools and classrooms and remained uncomplaining despite our continuous demands on their time and resources.

A special word of thanks must also be extended to our band of overworked and underpaid fieldworkers. These were—Jack Bentley, who also ran the in-service course, Rowena Ardern, Joyce Churchill, Gill Cohen, Helen Miller, Millie Pearson, Jill Pilkington, Mavis Rangeley, Eileen Williams, Brenda Young, and, for the study on classroom groups, Sheila Garbutt. Their experience and commitment were central to the success of the study.

Others made significant contributions in areas of data analysis. Special mention must be made of Liz Roth's contribution to the quantitative analysis of the data on classroom groups; to Liz Shaw for work on the transfer study; to Dorothy Anderson, Brenda Chesworth and Julie Massey for analyses of the number and language curriculum; to Annette Goldsmith for work on the in-service course; to Anne Desforges for her invaluable professional guidance; and to the staff of the Centre for Applied Statistics for their valuable help and advice.

Finally no acknowledgement would be complete without reference to our secretarial support. Our thanks thus go to Joanna Smith, the project secretary, and to Pauline Cross on whom fell the arduous task of typing endless drafts and the final report. As always she undertook these with speed, accuracy and good humour.

1 Introduction

Dan is a bright 6-year-old in his third year of infant schooling. In his number work he has been proceeding through the mathematics scheme, dealing quickly and easily with assignments on capacity, weight, volume and length. His current work is on area and he has already completed six work cards on this topic. In the observed session he began work on card seven for which the teacher's stated intention was that Dan should gain experience with irregular shapes.

The work card is reproduced below (Fig. 1.1). No teacher instructions were provided; he simply took out the card and commenced work. His first concern was what to call the oval shape on the extreme left of the card, and

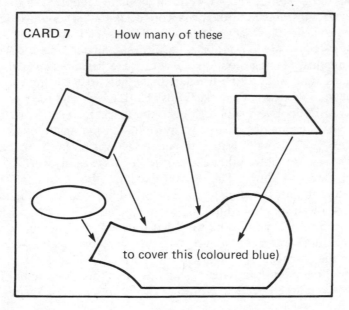

FIG. 1.1.

therefore he asked the teacher. She told him that she thought it was an ellipse and asked why he wanted to know. He replied that he wanted to write it down. Because his teacher was unsure she asked another teacher who, after perusing the maths book, told him to call it a segment.

Satisfied, he returned to his task, roughly tracing over the minor shapes and, equally roughly, cutting them out. He fitted them over the shape one at a time to see how many fittings it took to cover it. He then asked the teacher the name of the extreme right-hand shape—a trapezium. She told him it was a rhombus. He wrote it down.

At this point he was called out to read to the teacher and returned 7 minutes later to continue work on his card. His answers were as follows:

    11 segments cover the blue thing
    6 rhombuses cover the blue thing
    4 diamonds cover the blue thing
    8 oblongs cover the blue thing

In another third-year infant classroom Alan was given a writing assignment. His teacher showed him a set of cards, each of which illustrated people at work, and suggested that he write about one of them. He selected the card showing a bus driver and took it to his desk.

He paused for 5 minutes, apparently thinking about what to write. Eventually the teacher approached and asked him what his first sentence was going to be. He replied, "I went on a bus to school." He started his writing and then searched through his word book for "school." He failed to find it and consulted his teacher. She helped him spell it and then explained about the "sleepy c." He went back to his desk and continued to write for several minutes, reading aloud as he wrote. He hesitated over the word "sometimes" and went to the teacher to ask how to spell "times." There was a queue at the teacher's desk. Whilst waiting he found the word under "t" in his word book and shouted out to the teacher, "I've found it, Miss. It's here." A few minutes later he went to the teacher again to ask how to spell "gives." After a brief wait in the queue he was given the word. Later he went out again, showed the teacher the "f" page in his word book and asked for the word "fing." The teacher gave him the spelling of "thing." After 5 more minutes' writing he took his word book again to the teacher. After a brief wait he showed her the "i" page and asked her how to spell "eat." In the next 2 minutes he went out to check that "going" ended in "ing," that "am" was spelt "a-m-e" and that sleep was spelt "s-e-e-p." In each case the teacher responded with the correct spelling.

Twenty-three minutes after choosing the work card Alan took his story out to have it marked. He had written, "I went to school on the bus and I went home on the bus sometimes the bus driver gives me something to eat Im going homs I am going to sleep til morning."

These two brief sketches are tiny portions of the classroom lives of Dan, Alan and their respective teachers. They were observed in the process of the research to be reported in this book. They are, of course, grossly selective. Missing from the descriptions is any sense of the classrooms and their inhabitants, any hint of the bustle, the background noise and the aura of the classroom. Also missing is any account of the general learning environment provided by the teachers surrounding Alan and Dan. The experienced reader may have superimposed on these descriptions images of wall charts, word lists, tables, boxes of apparatus and 30 or more children clamouring for information and willing to give assistance. It will also have been recognised that although Dan and Alan were not told what to do they knew the rules of the classroom. Despite being presented as disembodied events, the tasks assigned were small elements in large programmes of work.

Selective and disembodied though these descriptions undoubtedly are, they capture significant aspects of the learning experience of children in the infant classroom. Children predominantly work on their own on tasks assigned and structured by their teachers. Examination of the pupil and teacher behaviour on these singular tasks raises a number of important questions regarding the quality of pupil learning experiences. What did the children achieve from working on their respective tasks? To what extent was Dan's knowledge of area extended? Did Alan's written expression improve? What did they each learn about learning and the use of the resources available to them? Did they know what their teachers intended? Were they equipped to make the best of their learning opportunities? Or, put another way, were the learning opportunities well matched to the attainments and capacities of the children? How did the teachers rate the children's work? What did the teachers learn about Dan and Alan that would help them select suitable subsequent learning experiences?

These questions are not concerned with how much the children learned but with the quality of their learning experiences. They are concerned with the nature of learning and the manner in which the environment provided by the teacher fosters or inhibits the business of learning.

Very little is known about the quality of learning experiences provided for pupils in schools, although some doubts have recently been expressed about some aspects of them. Both in Britain and the United States studies have concluded that in some parts of the primary school or early grades curriculum, large percentages of the work set are not well matched to pupils' attainments (Anderson, 1981; HMI, 1978). The consequences of such provision, it is suggested, is that high-attaining children are "not stretched" (HMI, 1978) and that low-attaining children are mystified (Anderson, 1981).

This situation is apparent despite the availability of an abundance of advice for teachers, particularly from psychologists who have been energetic in offering teachers prescriptions on how to design ideal learning environments. This advice is very familiar to educators. In the Cockroft report on mathematics education, for example, it was recognised that in specifying good mathematics teaching "we are aware that we are not saying anything that has not already been said many times and over many years (Cockroft, 1982, p. 72)."

It is now very widely recognised that such advice has had very little impact on the practice of teaching (Atkinson, 1976; Ausubel & Robinson, 1969; Glaser et al., 1977). There are, no doubt, many reasons for this. Some arise from the manner in which those who have studied teaching and learning have oversimplified the lives of classroom participants (Bronfenbrenner, 1976). Until recently, research on learning had largely ignored the processes of teaching and research on teaching had neglected the processes of learning. Consequently, some of the advice to teachers emanating from research was consistent only with theories of cognition, which did not attend to the constraints on the teacher.

The approach to generating advice to teachers from theories of cognition has been adopted by Ausubel (1969), Bruner (1964), and Posner (1978), among others. It is also manifest in most of the attempts to generate teaching implications from Piaget's theory (Duckworth, 1979; Schwebel & Raph, 1974). However, the impracticality of this approach to improving teaching has long been asserted (cf. Sullivan, 1967), since it typically ignores, for example, the teacher's limited resources of materials and time, and the attention she must pay to the social and emotional needs of her pupils. Also, the teacher's autonomy is generally overestimated. Class teachers have little choice in the teaching materials at their disposal and the timetable and other organisational features of the school are generally imposed on them.

In contrast to the generation of prescriptions from cognitive psychology a vast literature from classroom-based research documents the relationships between pupil achievement and many aspects of the classroom setting (cf. Haertel et al., 1983, for a recent summary), and these, too, have been used to provide prescriptive advice to teachers. A recent, and typical, example is that reported by Denham and Lieberman (1980) who, among other things, exhort teachers to make tasks clear, obtain and sustain pupil attention, assign appropriate reinforcements and feedback and cover the material which is to be tested. That these processes are important has never been in contention. Indeed, it has been considered that such research findings have barely caught up with common sense

(Jackson, 1967; McNamara, 1981). If teaching were so simple, it is difficult to understand why teachers behave otherwise in classrooms. Additionally, the dangers of adopting such tactics, such as spending disproportionate amounts of time on accounting and testing activities, and a concentration on those parts of the curriculum which are to be tested, have been ignored.

In attempting to account for the limited effect that research on teaching and learning has had on classroom practice, some researchers have suggested that classroom life is much more complex than researchers have imagined. In this view, attempts to change practice must be based first on an understanding of this complexity (Bronfenbrenner, 1976; Doyle, 1979a, 1979b).

Doyle has developed a model of classroom learning processes which attempts to capture some of the subtle processes involved as teachers and learners adapt to each other and to the classroom environment. In order to understand these processes he argues that the main features of the classroom environment and the resources of those who inhabit it must first be described.

Doyle suggests that classrooms are potentially rich sources of information. They are laden, for example, with books, charts, displays and verbal and non-verbal behaviour. However, these sources are not consistently reliable as instructional cues. Teachers and pupils can, for instance, easily misinterpret each other's intentions and thoughts. Additionally, in Doyle's view, classrooms are mass processing systems. By this he means that many people take part and many interests and purposes are served. Many events occur at a given moment and a consequence of their simultaneous occurrence is that participants have little time to reflect. Decisions have to be immediate.

This potentially complex information environment is inhabited by teachers and pupils who are considered, in Doyle's model, to have limited capacity to deal effectively with the abundance of information. They cannot attend to many things at once. These limitations are such that selections must be made from available sources of information. Strategies must be developed to optimise these selections in order to increase the manageability of classroom life. To this end Doyle suggests that it is necessary to make many actions routine in order to focus attention on monitoring the environment. This process of automation may be compared with that of learning to drive a car. Initially basic controls demand almost all of the driver's attention. Once the basics are made automatic, attention is available for the road. When reading the road becomes routinised or automated, attention is available for erudite conversation with the passengers.

In Doyle's model learning is a covert, intellectual activity which proceeds in the socially complex, potentially rich environment described earlier. In respect of learning, the crucial features of the environment which link teachers to learners are the tasks which teachers provide for pupils.

The pupils' immediate problem with regard to these tasks is to gain an understanding of what features of their task response the teacher will reward. In Doyle's terms the pupils must develop "interpretive competence," i.e., they must learn to discern what the teacher wants. This is not always easy because both tasks and rewards may be complexly and ambiguously defined by teachers. The following example observed in this study illustrates this.

The teacher talked to her class of 6-year-old children for 45 minutes about the countries of origin of the produce commonly found in fruit shops. This monologue was illustrated using a small map of the world and extensive reference was made to many foreign countries. She finished by asking the children to "write me an exciting story about the fruit we eat." The children had to decide what she meant by this! They were helped in part by the fact that they had heard this same instruction before in respect of other tasks. In fact the children wrote very little. They took great pains to copy the date from the board although the teacher did not ask them to do this. It was presumably taken for granted as part of the task specification. They formed their letters with great care and used rubbers copiously to correct any slips of presentation. Whilst this went on the teacher moved about the class commending "neat work" and "tidy work" and chiding children for "dirty fingers" and "messy work." No further mention was made of "exciting" content or of "stories." It seemed that the children knew perfectly well what the teacher meant when she asked for an "exciting story about fruit" even though in this case the teacher's overt task definition, her instructions, stood in sharp contrast to the rewards she actually deployed.

Once children have discerned what teachers want there is some evidence that they offer resistance to curriculum change (Davis & McNight, 1976). They reported that children showed a marked lack of interest and an increase in disruptive behaviour when new demands were made on them. This was particularly so when they found it difficult to discern the manner in which to fulfil the demands (as is the case in problem-solving approaches to learning, for example). Doyle (1980) suggests that pupils learn how to respond to one form of task specification—an achievement which brings predictability to their classroom lives—and resist having to discover a new specification and how to fulfil it.

This view of the classroom provides a cautionary note about the dangers of over-simple analysis and interpretation of classroom learning. Implicit in it is the message that before attempts are made to alter the quality of learning experiences provided in the classroom, researchers should endeavour to understand the nature of current provision and identify the forces which sustain and or inhibit learning.

In order to account for classroom learning it seems clear that the processes of task allocation and task working must be monitored in classrooms. It also seems necessary to identify the intellectual demands made by teachers on children and the manner in which children meet, avoid or adapt these demands.

The research reported here attempts to address some of these problems. The study has been influenced by Doyle's theory of the potential complexity of classroom life, and was designed in recognition of the view that learning proceeds in a complex social situation and that the notion of quality must refer, at least, to the context as well as the content of learning experiences.

2 Research Design

The focus of the study is on the nature and content of classroom tasks and the mediating factors which influence their choice, delivery, performance and diagnosis. In the study itself these were considered holistically but for the purposes of clear description the whole has been broken down into four sub-studies. The matching study which considered the entire task process in classrooms in aspects of number and language work led into two separate strands: the first was the transfer study in which a sample of the same children were followed through into their next class or school. The second was the utilisation of the data from the matching study to develop an experimental in-service course for teachers in an attempt to explore problems in the improvement of the matching process. Finally the grouping study investigated the effect on task performance of working in classroom groups.

Figure 2.1 is a simplified representation of these studies.

The research approaches for the matching, transfer and in-service studies are described below. The design features of the grouping study are presented in Chapter 8.

THE MATCHING STUDY

This study was specifically concerned with the task process in all aspects of language and number work in classes of 6- to 7-year-old children. These activities in their various forms comprise a majority of curriculum tasks at this age level in Britain (Bassey, 1977; Bennett et al., 1980).

The first requirement was for a conceptualisation and specification of the task process which would allow for exhaustive description and analysis. Models of task processes are rare. However note was taken of those proposed by Blumenfeld (1980) and Fisher et al. (1980) together with the theories and perspectives outlined in Chapter 1. From these it became

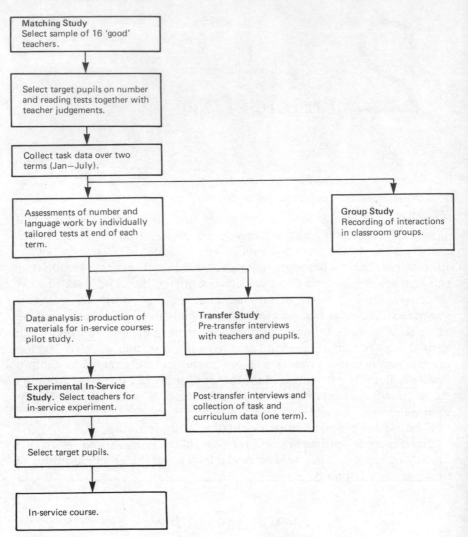

FIG. 2.1.   Simplified research design.

clear that for each assigned task it would be necessary to know:

1. The teacher's intention in assigning the task.
2. How that intention was manifested in the particular task set.
3. The teacher's task instructions, i.e., how it was presented and specified.
4. The pupil's perceptions of (3).

5. The materials available for the task.
6. The pupil's task performance, including interactions with the teacher or other pupils.
7. An assessment of short term learning outcomes, i.e., immediately following the task.
8. An assessment of longer term learning outcomes, i.e., at the end of each term, in order to evaluate development and retention of learning over series of curriculum tasks.

The transformation of those specifications into a research design incorporating appropriate data gathering techniques is shown in Fig. 2.2.

The design contains four elements for each task description. A pre-task interview with the teacher was followed by observation of the task presentation and subsequent pupil performance. A clinical or diagnostic interview was then held with the target pupil prior to discussing the same task performance with the teacher. Each of these elements is discussed below and is followed by an example of a completed task description.

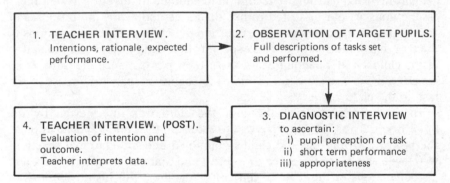

FIG. 2.2.   Research design: matching study.

Pre-Task Teacher Interviews

The teacher was interviewed before the school day commenced in order to ascertain the tasks and activities that had been planned for six target children (a high, average and low achieving boy and girl). The teacher was questioned about the purpose and rationale for each task and how it fitted in to the broader pattern of work for each child. Expected outcomes, in terms of both quality and quantity of work, were also predicted by the teacher together with any anticipated problems each child might encounter.

Observation of Target Pupils

Following this interview two of the target children were observed each day for 2 days every 3 weeks. Fine details of the task presented and the target child's actual performance were required. This was achieved by recording in continuous fieldnote form the teacher's exact presentation together with details of the task presented, materials employed, the child's actual response and any support system used, whether material or human. This continued until the task was completed. On completion, the child's actual performance, or a facsimile was retained.

Diagnostic Intervention

Inferences concerning appropriateness of task to the child could have been made on the basis of the fieldnotes above, but this was rejected as insufficient. Such a strategy would necessarily involve acceptance of certain assumptions, for example, that the child had understood the task specification and associated operations and that the child's performance actually involved learning. The argument adopted in this study is that these assumptions should be tested rather than accepted. Thus the purposes of the diagnostic interview were to ascertain the child's affective reactions to the task, his definition of the task specification and to obtain an indication of the child's understanding via a short term performance measure, from which to make decisions concerning the cognitive appropriateness of the task to the child.

Thus on completion of the task the child was interviewed by the fieldworker. The first objective was to ascertain the child's specification of the task. Following this the child's emotional and motivational reactions were acquired, i.e., his degree of interest and familiarity with the task and his perceptions of the level of difficulty, together with his attributions of success or failure.

In previous research, performance has been assumed to equate with learning. This assumption is suspect since the performance could simply be a reflection of previous learning. A short term performance measure was thus devised to assess task specific learning outcomes in order to guide judgements concerning appropriateness.

During the fieldnote recording of the child's task response, the fieldworker generated hypotheses about the child's competence. These hypotheses were transformed into small test items which were put to the child. For example, if the child had been provided with a work card on number of the type $15 - 9 = \underline{\quad}$, and was perceived to be having difficulty, the fieldworker would create easier items in order to establish his or her level of competence in the specific task area, in this case subtraction. If on the other hand the child showed no difficulty, items would be generated at a more difficult level for the same purpose. Once levels of competence were ascertained a judgement concerning appropriateness could be made. This is a simplified example. Further examples are provided at the end of this section and throughout the text.

Other indices of appropriateness were also ascertained: specifically, appropriateness of the task to the teacher's intention; of procedure and of task management. The appropriateness of intention to the task set can be assessed by relating the teacher's intentions to the child's performance and learning, a process considered under "post-task interview with teacher" in the next section.

Appropriateness of procedure and task management concerned the appropriateness of the materials made available for the task set, whether the child had the skill and competence to utilise them and whether the management of the classroom ran smoothly. Examples here would be whether the skill to use scissors or a ruler were evident when they were necessary for the completion of the task or whether the child spent much of his time wandering round the classroom in search of materials.

Finally, the completed work, or a facsimile, was acquired by the fieldworker together with a record of the items in the short term performance measure, and the child's responses to them.

It will be clear from this that the role of the diagnostic interview and the competence of the fieldworkers in carrying it out were crucial.

The diagnostic interview is a task oriented, flexible interview between a pupil and interviewer wherein the interviewer is expected to follow and pursue the pupil's thinking, asking questions until the pupil's reasons for response are understandable to the interviewer. The method of interviewing cannot be divorced from the particular task since it involves progressive hypothesis testing on the part of the interviewer. Familiarity with the tasks and the variety of possible responses is the only way that the interviewer can have the flexibility to conduct a good interview.

In order to meet these criteria fieldworkers were employed who had long and varied experience in teaching this age level. They included ex-College of Education lecturing staff, headteachers and advisers who had decided on early retirement, and teachers who had left teaching temporarily either to take a further degree course or had recently moved into the area. On appointment they were provided with an intensive training course on interview and observation techniques.

Post-Task Teacher Interview

The purpose of this interview was to gain the teacher's reaction to the target child's work on the tasks observed. To aid this, the child's response to the task was set before the teacher as were the fieldworker records. The teacher was invited to comment on the quality of the work and on the appropriateness of the task. Discussion included the teacher's views on the fieldworker's interpretation and of her future intentions for the child in the light of the work produced. This same procedure continued the following day focussing on different target children.

The observation in each classroom was timetabled for 2 days every 3 weeks during the first term. In the first observation phase of the second term a 4-day sequence was incorporated to gain an extended observation of task sequences. The remaining observation phases were as in the first term.

An actual example of a task description follows. The example chosen is that of Helen, a detailed analysis of which is provided in Chapter 5. Helen's responses are in italics.

PRE-TASK INTERVIEW WITH TEACHER

Target: Helen, an average ability girl.

Teacher Intention: Money, familiarisation with half-pence in simple shopping exercises.

Reasons: Children have been working with money for some time but $\frac{1}{2}$p only introduced on Monday in accordance with the sequences of the highly-detailed maths scheme.

Perceived Problems: Helen lacks effort and determination. She ought to be doing better work than she produces.

TASK DESCRIPTION (FIELDNOTES)

Task History: For the past three days children have been working on simple shopping sums some of which involve $\frac{1}{2}$p.

Teacher's Task Instructions: Class work on getting change from 10p using $\frac{1}{2}$p, and converting $\frac{1}{2}$p to pence. Teacher gave out work cards and said "Do the top card first."

Task Record:
  9.25   1.4.81. Money (written in book by teacher).
          I have 9p.
          I buy a box of crayons for
          I have   change.
  9.30   Helen can't find cost of a box of crayons. She is looking at wrong list (which are colour coded).
  9.40   Teacher asks what she is looking for and it is established that Helen has not only misread crayons and got chocolate instead but is looking at wrong colour of list.
  9.42   Teacher moves correct list in front of Helen but she still can't find

cost and has to search through the picture cards to eventually find the cost of crayons.

9.44   Counts out plastic money without success (not enough $\frac{1}{2}$p). She tries again with cardboard money counting out 9p in $\frac{1}{2}$ps and puts them on her desk. Returns to cardboard coins and counts out another $11 \times \frac{1}{2}$p. Puts in answer of 5p by counting all the $\frac{1}{2}$ps?

9.49   *I have 19p*
        I buy a car for
        I buy a rocket for
        I spend
        I have   p change.
        She again has to look at picture cards for prices.

9.53   Still hasn't found the cost of a rocket. Tries the list.

9.55   She counts out $\frac{1}{2}$p again and says to the world in general, "*I've lost count now*."

9.57   She has 19p in $\frac{1}{2}$p.

9.59   Gets a 10p puts it on the desk then goes and collects more coins but changes her mind and returns to desk. Counts out 17p in $\frac{1}{2}$ps.

10.02   Counts all the $\frac{1}{2}$p again and puts $18\frac{1}{2}$p in answer.

10.03   Returns $\frac{1}{2}$p coins to box.

10.04   Teacher checks her work and asks her what "change" means.

EXPLORATORY INTERVIEW

Fieldworker's Comments: Helen had difficulty finding the cost of the articles from the various lists and cards available.

She made no attempt to use 10p, 5p, 2p and 1p coins and tried to count all the amounts out in $\frac{1}{2}$p.

The Child's Specification of the Task: Did the child fulfil the teacher's immediate and overt task demand? Was help elicited and/or received?
Fieldworker: "Did you know what to do?"
    Helen: "*Yes*."
Fieldworker: "Did you get any help?"
    Helen: "*No*."
Fieldworker: "Didn't Mrs W. help you a little?"
    Helen: "*A bit*."
Fieldworker: "What could you do if you didn't know what to do and Mrs W. was somewhere else?"
    Helen: "*Ask teacher. Kindly*."
Fieldworker: "Do you mean politely?"
    Helen: "*Yes*."

The Child's View of What the Teacher Wants:
Fieldworker: "What will Mrs W. say about today's work?"
    No Response from Helen.
Fieldworker: "Do you think it's good work?"
    Helen: "*No*."

Fieldworker: "What makes you say that?"
    Helen: *"I've got it wrong."*
Fieldworker: "What is wrong with it?"
    Helen: *"Don't know."*
Fieldworker: "Have you done better work?"
    Helen: *"Sometimes."*
Fieldworker: "Where?"
Helen shows the fieldworker a previous page with all sums right.

Summary of Child's Image of the Task Requirements: Helen seems to fully understand the drill laid down by teacher, i.e., the individual work cards, where the apparatus is kept etc. but only makes sporadic efforts to follow it properly.

The Child's Affective Response: Impressions from observation (Cross out which word is less appropriate in each pair).
Was the child   ~~bored~~/interested
                 ~~challenged~~/defeated
                 cheerful/~~upset~~
                 ~~attentive~~/distracted

The Child's Expressed Pleasure and Level of Interest:
Fieldworker: "Do you like doing sums from cards?"
    Helen: *"Yes."*
Fieldworker: "Do you like it as much as doing the writing yesterday?"
    Helen nods.
Fieldworker: "What do you like doing best?"
    Helen: *"Writing poems."*
Fieldworker: "What else do you like?"
    Helen: *"I like doing games but I don't like singing."*
Fieldworker: "What don't you like doing?"
    Helen: *"Reading books."*

Degree of Perceived Familiarity with the Task:
Fieldworker: "Is this new work?"
    Helen: *"Yes."*
Fieldworker: "Is there other work like this in your book?"
    Helen: *"Just a bit."*
Fieldworker: "Do you like doing new work?"
    Helen: *"Don't mind."*

Perceived Difficulty of Task and Attribution of Success and Failure:
Fieldworker: "Did you find the work today easy or hard?"
    Helen: *"Hard."*
Fieldworker: "What was hard about it?"
    Helen: *"You have to add things up in money."*
Fieldworker: "Is it working with money which is hard or the adding up?"
    Helen: *"Adding up."*

Summary and Interpretive Comments on the Child's Affective Response: The only time Helen showed any animation was during her reference to poetry when she showed me her book of poems.

SHORT TERM PERFORMANCE MEASURE

Record of Short Term Performance Measure:
Fieldworker: "What do you have to do to find the prices?"
    Helen: *"Look for the cards."*
  The fieldworker then asked Helen to do the first problem again.
I have 9p
I buy a box of crayons for 6½p
I have ____p change.
She collected a pile of ½p coins but gave up.
Fieldworker: "What is missing from your second sum?"
    Helen: *"It should be 7p."*
Problems with a less complicated format were then presented.

Fieldworker: "I have 9p. If I spend 5p how much would I have left?"
    Helen: *"4p."*
Fieldworker: "I buy a car for 10p and a kite for 15p. How much do I
        spend?"
    Helen: *"25p."*
  She got out a 10p coin and 15 × 1p coins to do this sum.
Fieldworker: "I have 20p. I buy a doll (the card says 10p). How much have I
        left?"
    Helen: *"10p."*
Fieldworker: "I have 13p. I buy tomatoes for 3p and carrots for 5p."
    Helen: *"I spend 8p.*
        I have 2p change."
Fieldworker: "I have 5p. I spend 2½p. How much do I have left?"
    Helen: *"2p."*
Fieldworker: "I buy a box of crayons for 6½p and a pencil for 1½p. How much
        do I spend?"
    Helen: *"8p."*

Appropriateness of Means to Objectives: Even simple sums involving half-pence seem beyond her present competence. Helen would appear to need more practice in handling the units of currency and converting from one to the other. More simple and separate addition and subtraction of money including half pence would seem necessary before more complicated shopping cards.

Post-task Interview with Teacher
Fieldworker: "What do you think of Helen's work?"
    Teacher: "She could have done better. It's neat but she hasn't
        understood—she hasn't been listening or thinking. It's her big

Fieldworker:
Teacher:
Fieldworker:
Teacher:
Fieldworker:
Teacher:

problem. She doesn't think anything applies to her (in class discussion) till she has to do something for herself. Once she has got it though it stays fixed. There has been too much excitement today and this would put her off."

Fieldworker: "Has she done any informal work, handling money, shopping?"

Teacher: "Oh yes, this has been done in the past and we started work on ½p last Friday."

Fieldworker: "What about her use of all the ½p pieces when she wanted 15p for example?"

Teacher: "A tenpence piece is tenpence but with 15p it isn't one coin so she is unsure."

Fieldworker: "Have they done any work counting out values of money, e.g., 15p in the smallest number of coins or all the possible combinations?"

Teacher: "Others in the class did this when we were talking at the beginning of the lesson. Helen has more ability than she uses. She doesn't concentrate. She will have to do this again."

Long Term Assessment

In addition to the short term assessment at the conclusion of each task a longer term assessment was necessary. This was undertaken at the end of each term.

Standardised tests are typically used in studies on teaching as outcome measures. Their use has however been legitimately criticised (Berliner, 1976; Dunkin, 1976). Although such tests allow a comparison across classes it is inevitable that their validity varies to the extent that the items in the test match the content of the curriculum in any class.

The focus in this study was comparison within, rather than across, classes and as such a criterion referenced approach was more valid. In order to maximise curriculum validity a tailored testing programme was instituted in which an individual test in mathematics and language was developed for each target pupil based entirely on the work that child had covered during the term. Thus, since 96 children were involved in the study, 96 tests in each curriculum area were devised every term. The actual procedure adopted is detailed in Chapters 5 and 6.

Sampling

The number of participating teachers was, as ever, determined by such constraints as the demands imposed by the research approaches chosen, time, finance and personnel. In the light of these 16 teachers were selected to participate. The factors determining the choice were that: (1) they had to be volunteers. This was a collaborative study in which a great deal of time was to be spent in their classroom. Cooperation was also necessary for time taken in pre- and post-task interviewing and for the continuous collection of children's work. In addition, time out of school was necessary for briefing and evaluation meetings with project staff. For these reasons all accepting teachers were fully appraised of these demands prior to their final acceptance; (2) the schools should, as a group, represent different socioeconomic intakes; (3) that half should be infant schools and half infant departments of primary schools to allow the continuity study across transfer and (4) all teachers chosen should be judged as better than average by local authority advisers.

Within each class six target children were selected to represent achievement and sex differences. Thus a high, average and low achieving boy and girl were selected on the basis of their scores on two standardised tests supported by teacher judgement.

The Group Mathematics Test (Young, 1970) designed "to test the mathematical understanding of children up to the age of 8.6," and the Primary Reading Test (France, 1979) "to provide an overall assessment of children's ability to apply their reading skills to the understanding of words and simple sentences in the early stages of reading" were chosen for this purpose following a review of existing instruments. The children in each class were assigned to three categories, high, average and low on the basis of their scores. The target children were then selected randomly from each category. The teacher was consulted and if reservations were expressed, e.g., the child selected was a poor attender, easily disturbed or likely to leave, the child was replaced by further random selection.

These same children participated in all the studies reported here with the exception of the in-service experiment where independent samples of teachers and children were drawn.

TRANSFER STUDY

The study focused on 6- to 7-year-old children in their third and fourth years of schooling. This provided the opportunity to examine continuity of learning experiences across a significant break point in British schools—the transfer from infants to juniors. In some areas this requires the child to move to a separate school whereas in others the child simply moves to another classroom on the same corridor.

The same data gathering procedures were used when children were followed through to their new class or school. The timing and length of observations were modified however. It was felt important that the fieldworkers be present from the first day of term and thus agreement was gained for each class to be observed throughout the whole of the first week of term. During this period task descriptions were gathered as normal but, in addition, fieldworkers provided more general descriptions of classroom organisation and management, plus curriculum and diagnostic procedures together with notes on how pupils appeared to be settling in. These were used to supplement the interviews carried out with teachers and pupils before transfer took place and after 1 week in the new class or school.

Further 2-day periods of observation were carried out in each class after approximately one and two months. As is indicated in Fig. 2.1 the transfer study continued throughout the first term in the junior class.

IN-SERVICE STUDY

Analysis of data from the matching study raised further questions about the provision of tasks and permitted the identification of certain processes which might have been implicated in poor matching and which might have been open to amelioration. To explore these questions and processes further, a second group of experienced teachers was recruited to an in-service course. The course made use of transcripts of materials gathered in the matching phase. Participants were required to analyse and comment on these and to suggest means by which learning experiences could be improved. Discussions were tape recorded. Participants also carried out practical work in their own classrooms. They made their own records of these events and brought the records for discussion in subsequent course sessions. Further details of this phase of the research are given in Chapter 9.

3 Task Demand

The concept of quality of learning experience is a complex notion made up of many facets. Qualitative differences in learning experiences may refer to the content of material learned, the organisation and ambience of the social setting, the structure and sequence of the curriculum materials or to the types of intellectual demands made on children. The child who learns German and the child who learns French receive qualitatively different learning experiences. This is not to say that learning German is superior or inferior to learning French: it is merely different. And just as curriculum content can differ, so can the social organisation of the learning experience. Children may be seated in rows or in groups for example and each of these organisations presents different opportunities and problems for the learner.

However the main interest in this chapter is not with qualitative differences in the curriculum content or the social organisation of learning experiences, but with differences in the intellectual demands teachers place on children. As extreme examples of qualitatively different intellectual demands the reader will be familiar with learning experiences which demand that the child discovers for himself some information, rule or principle. This may be contrasted with tasks which demand the practice of, for example, number bonds. The demand for discovery and the demand for practice are qualitatively different.

There are ageless debates in education arguing the superiority of one or other of these demands. These debates are unlikely to be resolved since they rest on the view that one learning process is inherently superior to another. In the view adopted here, learning is a broad term which covers a number of different processes each of which has a distinct and important role to play in the acquisition of knowledge and skill. One type of learning process (and therefore one type of task demand) is not inherently superior to any other: it is merely qualitatively different. One aim of this study was therefore to discover the degree to which different learning processes were demanded in classrooms. In researching the different types of intellectual demands made by teachers on children, a particular view of learning was adopted from which a category system for classifying observations was

21

devised. Before describing the results it is necessary to make clear this view of the processes of learning and the manner in which it influenced the analysis.

A THEORY OF COMPLEX LEARNING

In a survey of the vast literature on children's thinking and learning, very little work was found which attempted to explain how pupils learned large bodies of complex material over long periods of time. The only attempt to develop a theory of complex learning has been made by an American psychologist Donald Norman (1978). The theory and the way in which it has been used to identify the intellectual demands teachers made on children are described here.

In Norman's view all learning is organised into schemes. New learning experiences interact with what the learner already knows. Meaningful learning proceeds by the integration of new information with relevant and available schemes.

Norman suggests that three different processes are involved in the acquisition and organisation of new experience. He calls these processes, accretion, restructuring and tuning. Accretion is the direct acquisition of pieces of knowledge. It might involve, for instance, the acquisition of facts or examples.

Restructuring is characterised by new insights. No addition of knowledge is needed. Existing knowledge is re-organised. A pattern is seen: a new way of looking at old information is adopted. It must be emphasised that restructuring is not a superior process to accretion. Patterns cannot be seen in facts unless the facts have been acquired. The two processes are complementary. Once a new pattern has been seen or a new principle recognised, the new structure guides the acquisition of further facts or examples.

The third learning process identified by Norman is called tuning. It is a process in which skills and/or the uses of new knowledge are made increasingly automatic. Readers who have learned to drive a car will be very familiar with this process. It is very easy to acquire the procedure of changing gear but in the early stages the process is far from automatic: it is very preoccupying. As experience gradually makes the process more fluent, attention is freed from gear changing to be available for other processes and thoughts. No new insight or facts are involved in the process of tuning. It is a process in which redundant steps in procedure are eliminated or short cuts are found. Tuning involves an increase in the efficiency in the use of existing routines.

The three processes of accretion, restructuring and tuning occur

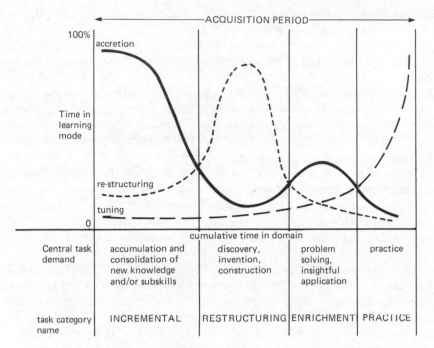

FIG. 3.1.   Task categories in relation to the growth of knowledge modules.

together in the course of learning. However, at any particular point in the pupil's experience in any one subject domain, one of the learning processes will predominate. Norman's view of how these processes interact or predominate is shown in the Fig. 3.1.

In the early stages of experience with a new idea or concept, the predominant process is accretion. That is to say, a series of discrete facts or examples are accumulated. Most of the learner's time is spent in this manner. However, once a body of discrete facts is accumulated there is an increasing likelihood that the pattern in the facts, or the concept which links them, will be perceived or invented. This is a period when restructuring predominates. Following the period of the reorganisation of existing knowledge a new period of accretion occurs. In this time new facts and skills associated with the freshly discovered structure are acquired. These skills are more likely to be relevant to the deployment of the new structure. In other words, having acquired a new concept, the learner acquires the knowledge of when to use it. These skills are often called strategic skills. Finally, the whole process of using the new structure, concept or skill is operated until it becomes automatic. The process which Norman calls tuning predominates in this phase of learning experience.

During this period the learner increases his fluency and accuracy in the use of his recently acquired concepts or skill.

As a concrete example one could imagine a young child learning to recognise letters and their associated sounds. Prior to any formal experience in this respect the child will probably have seen particular instances of a specific letter, "a" for example. Unless the letter is part of his name, this experience will probably have been ignored as largely meaningless. Under formal guidance (whether from his parents or teacher) he is taught that specific instances of "a" have a particular name and make a particular sound. Since these instances will be in different contexts the child is likely, in the early phases of his experience, to acquire these as specific facts or examples of sight–name–sound correspondences. He learns "cat" says cat and "bat" says bat but does not link the "a" sound. After some unspecified number of instances (a number which will differ from child to child) the pattern is seen, the child perceives the common role of the letter "a."

If he has been learning to write "a" during this period, the sequence of his movements begins to have coherence: he grasps the pattern and is freed from discrete steps. He is then in a position to practise recognising, using and reproducing the letter "a." In this period of tuning he is freed from the teacher's supports and becomes fluent and accurate at writing the letter "a" appropriately.

Norman's model of learning is not prescriptive: it does not tell us what to do to foster learning. It is one psychologist's attempt to describe the various processes which he considers to contribute towards the general process of learning. In this study the model provoked the following question: which learning processes do teachers demand of children?

In order to help answer this question a category system was devised from Norman's model and used to classify the tasks observed in classrooms. The model implies four different types of task, each of which makes a different demand on the learner.

Incremental Tasks. These involve the process of accretion in the acquisition of new facts, skills, rules or procedures. If the key feature of a task is to focus on new material, even if the task involves much old material, then it is judged to be an incremental task. For example, multiplication problems involve a lot of adding up but if a particular task demands the use of the new feature of multiplication and is set to introduce this, then it is judged to be an incremental task. Typically, incremental tasks require imitation or the step by step reproduction of new procedures.

Restructuring Tasks. These have the pupil working predominantly with familiar materials but he is required to discover, invent or construct a new way of looking at problems. The task might, for example, be directed to lead him to invent multiplication as a short cut to repeated addition or to discover a spelling rule. The pupil may be given hints, tips or cues to provoke such inventions.

Enrichment Tasks.   These relate to the period of accretion after the period of restructuring. They demand the use of familiar knowledge, concepts and skills in unfamiliar contexts. They extend the range of application of concepts and skills and in this way add incrementally to the knowledge domain. However, what is being added is not new knowledge as such, but ways of applying that knowledge. This type of acquisition may be called a strategic skill. For example, children very often know how to multiply but do not know when to multiply when they see a problem. Sometimes they do not see, for instance, that the problem "if a metre of ribbon costs 20p, what do 5 metres cost?" demands multiplication. They need to learn when to evoke skills and knowledge, and enrichment tasks was the name assigned to the type of work given by teachers which demanded this type of response. Typically such tasks take the form of problem solving in mathematics or comprehension in language.

Practice Tasks.   These relate to the process of tuning. They demand the repetitive and rapid application of familiar knowledge and skills to familiar settings and problems. The pupil is familiar with both the content and context of the problem: the demand is not to acquire a fact or a skill but to speed up and make automatic processes already in the pupil's repertoire. For example, a child who was totally familiar with the process of subtraction might be asked to do as many "take away" calculations as he could in 3 minutes.

A fifth type of task demand was added to the category system. This category, the revision task, did not emanate from Norman's theory of acquisition. Rather, it arose from the recognition that classroom learning cannot always focus on acquisition: sometimes tasks are directed at minimising the loss of learning.

Revision Tasks.   These demand attention to materials or skills which have been set aside for some time. Material is evoked which was once familiar. The teacher's purpose may be to minimise loss from memory or to evoke the material as a foundation for learning new and related material. From the point of view of the task category system however, the critical feature is not the teacher's purpose but the nature of the task demand with respect to the learner.

The different types of task demand are outlined in Table 3.1.

It cannot be emphasised too strongly that the category system is not

TABLE 3.1
Types of Task Demand

Task Demand	Chief Characteristics
Incremental	Introduces new ideas, procedures or skills, demands recognitions, discriminations.
Restructuring	Demands a child invents or discovers an idea for himself.
Enrichment	Demands application of familiar skills to new problems.
Practice	Demands the tuning of new skills on familiar problems.
Revision	Demands the use of skills which have not been practised for some time.

prescriptive. A task demanding invention is neither superior nor inferior to a practice or a revision task. It simply makes qualitatively different demands. There may be good practice tasks just as there may be unfortunate or inadequate restructuring tasks and vice versa. From the view of learning adopted here, all types of task demand have potential value in fostering the pupil's learning.

Using the Category System of Task Demand

The classification of task demand was devised to answer only one question, "with respect to a particular learner's organisation of knowledge, what type of learning demand is being made on him by this task?"

To identify the type of task demand being made it is necessary to have information about both the task and the learner to whom it is presented. Any particular task is likely to fit into several different demand categories depending on the learners to whom it is assigned. For example, a task which demanded the sharing of sweets between dolls might make an incremental demand on a very young child (demanding that he gains experience of various outcomes), a restructuring demand on a 6-year-old (who might be expected by his teacher to discover the process of division) and a revision demand on an 8-year-old (who would be re-visiting an old routine).

In determining the type of task demand on the child it was necessary to inspect the task content and instructions, and to ascertain the child's level of familiarity with the task procedures and materials.

The process of judging the type of task demand is illustrated in the following examples.

An Example of an Incremental Task. Alison had much practical experience in coin recognition. Recently she had successfully completed exercises involving the addition of money up to 10p.

The task observed required the child to work through workcards of the type "8p spend 3p leaves __" and involved the introduction of the concept of "change." There was no documented evidence that Alison had done this before. This together with the fact that the child said she had never done such work before suggested that it was an incremental task.

Practice Task.   Having been read the story of David and Goliath and having seen it acted out the children were asked to recount it. The actual lesson was described as "practice in reportage" and was introduced by the teacher questioning the class on the story and reminding them of the sequence of events.

When asked about the work the target child, Kirsty, indicated that not only was she very familiar with the story of David and Goliath but that she was frequently asked to retell stories in this manner. Since Kirsty was familiar with the content and processes demanded in this task it was categorised as making a practice demand.

Enrichment Task.   Enrichment tasks are those which involve the skills of problem solving or comprehension.

In the example below, Nigel and Stephen were given the following workcard on the topic of space.

Space Project Card:
1. Imagine you are an astronaut going to Mars.
    Why are you going?
    How do you feel about the trip?
    What do you expect to find on Mars?
    What will you do when you get to Mars?
2. If you were on a planet with low gravity, could you jump higher or not as high?
3. Do you think you might like to live on Mars? If yes, why? If not, why not?

The children were asked to work together and, by discussion, answer the problems posed. They were both very familiar with the topic of space and yet the task involved their sifting through, and applying their knowledge in a problem solving context and thus the task was classified as enriching in its demand.

Restructuring Task.   A restructuring task is one in which a child is required to discover, invent or construct a new way of looking at material. In the following example the teacher required that, by using a 100 square,

Raymond would come to appreciate the relationship between the multiples of two and three.

The teacher gave Raymond a 100 square and told him to circle all the multiples of two. This he did extremely quickly. When asked to mark the multiples of three however he became very puzzled when he reached the number "6": it had already been circled! After much thought he asked the teacher for assistance and together they counted and marked the multiples of three. After a couple of minutes Raymond announced, "Oh, I see" and quickly completed the pattern. Thus it can be seen that while Raymond had no real idea of the relationship between the multiples of two and three at the start of the lesson he made the connection during the course of the task. In other words he restructured his already existing knowledge of the number multiples.

INTENDED AND ACTUAL TASK DEMANDS

The above examples show how tasks as actually presented to children were categorised according to the system developed from Norman's model of learning. However, the actual task demand was not always what the teacher intended. Teachers assign tasks to children with particular purposes in mind. These intended demands are not always converted into action. The extent of this discrepancy between intended and actual demand and the processes by which it comes about are discussed in later sections.

In the following section an analysis is made of the demands actually experienced by the target children. Whatever the intentions of the teacher, it is the actual demands which determine part of the quality of the child's learning experience.

Frequency of Actual Task Demands

In the matching study detailed data were collected on 417 tasks. Using the category system described above, the demand made by each task was identified. The frequency of different demands actually experienced by the target children is shown in Table 3.2.

Overall, practice predominated. Tasks demanding practice accounted for 60% of all tasks presented. It is impossible to say whether this is too much or too little practice. There can be no criteria for judging this question using data which have been pooled from a group of children. The optimal quantity of practice must depend on the needs of individual children.

It is interesting however, to contrast the incidence of practice with the incidence of the introduction of new work. Incremental tasks made up 25%

TABLE 3.2
Frequency of Task Demands for Number and Language Tasks

Task Demand	Number	Language	Total
Incremental (i.e., introducing new ideas, procedures or skills)	72	32	104
Restructuring (i.e., demanding that a child invents or discovers an idea for himself)	2	0	2
Enrichment (demanding the use of old skills on new problems)	14	10	24
Practice	93	156	249
Revision	21	3	24
Other	10	4	14
Total	212	205	417

of the total number of tasks observed. Thus, on average, there were 2.4 practice tasks for every incremental task. Taken at face value, this evidence might suggest that since one quarter of the tasks presented focus on new work, a brisk progress through the curriculum was maintained and that this was consolidated using a ratio of more than two practice tasks per incremental task. However, as noted above, judgements about the value of this ratio can only be made in the light of its effect on the learning needs of individual children.

Noteworthy was the very low incidence of enrichment and restructuring tasks. Twenty-eight such tasks (approximately 7%) were seen in two terms. Of these, only two were restructuring tasks (approximately half of one per cent). Clearly, tasks demanding discovery or invention were very rarely presented.

Approximately 6% of the tasks in the sample were revision tasks. In interpreting this figure it is worth remembering that the observations were carried out in the Spring and Summer terms of the school year. In the latter part of this period it might be expected, especially with high attainers, that revision might have become prevalent as the syllabus was completed. This does not seem to have been the case. Progress and consolidation predominated.

The 14 tasks labelled "other" refer to tasks whose demands were complex, multiple or not identifiable.

Number and Language Compared

The distribution of the types of demand was very different in the two broad areas of the curriculum observed. In number, 43% of tasks involved practice whilst in language it was 76%.

Another way of looking at this is to note that in number, 1.3 practice tasks were observed for every incremental task. On average this might be taken to indicate a brisk momentum through the maths scheme. In the absence of other evidence this must not necessarily be assumed to be a successful momentum. In contrast, there were almost five practice tasks observed for every incremental task in the language curriculum.

The differences almost certainly arise out of differences in the structure of the two curricula as worked by the teachers. These differences are analysed in detail in subsequent chapters, but it is clear that at this stage in the infant curriculum, mathematics was finely structured so that the children were frequently called upon to make new steps or meet new procedures. In contrast the language curriculum observed contained few new concepts or procedures. The major variant was the content on which procedures were exercised.

Whilst the incidence of incremental and practice tasks varied across these curriculum areas, the incidence of enrichment tasks was remarkably similar. Enrichment tasks accounted for 7% of number tasks and 5% of language tasks. In interpreting these incidences it is worth remembering that enrichment tasks include problems in mathematics and comprehension in language.

There was an almost total absence of restructuring tasks. In mathematics this might be considered surprising. Restructuring tasks demand invention. Practical mathematics, at almost all stages, gives great scope for the provocation of invention. Two such tasks were observed.

For example one of the teachers was trying to stop the target child, Richard, using his fingers or bricks when adding up. She simply gave Richard a book of addition calculations and told him to do as many as he could in the time available.

Initially Richard worked very slowly counting on his fingers for every sum. However, with insistence and encouragement from the teacher he speeded up dramatically, ceased using mechanical aids and successfully completed the last page of 60 calculations in a minute. To achieve this, Richard had to abandon the practice of an old and familiar routine and discover a better procedure. It appears that he had made the transition from using practical aids to doing simple computations in his head during the course of the exercise. Thus restructuring was inferred to have occurred, under the teacher's insistent demand.

Comparisons Between Classes

The pattern of task demands observed varied widely between the sixteen classes. Table 3.3 shows this variation, for incremental and practice tasks.

Restructuring, enrichment and revision tasks have all been combined,

TABLE 3.3
Incidence of Practice and Incremental Tasks Across the Sixteen Classrooms

Demand/Class	1	2	3	4	5	6	7	8	9	10	11	12	13	14	15	16
Incremental	6	9	6	5	10	3	7	9	6	6	4	5	0	9	12	7
Practice	17	12	19	13	13	15	10	12	17	17	17	17	20	10	16	18
Other	2	1	3	6	3	5	4	5	0	5	5	4	8	5	7	1
Total	25	22	28	24	26	23	27	26	23	28	26	26	28	24	35	26

since they showed very little variation between classes. The only restructuring tasks observed were in class 6.

There was considerable variation in the ratio of incremental and practice tasks observed. In class 13, only practice and revision tasks were seen. Other classrooms manifesting a low incidence of incremental tasks were classes 6 and 11.

Variations in the ratio of incremental to practice tasks reflect an important difference in the quality of learning experiences provided for children. The lower the ratio of incremental tasks to practice tasks, the quicker is the pace through the curriculum. However, it must be emphasised that an ideal absolute ratio in these demands cannot be determined: the optimal ratio must reflect the needs of individual children. Additionally, the ideal rate of progress is related to the size of the steps in the structure of the curriculum. Some curriculum materials, especially in maths, allow very fine gradations in each step of progress. A brisk rate of meeting incremental tasks may thus be expected. Other aspects of the curriculum are less easily thought of in terms of a fine sequence of steps. In this case a rapid rate of progress through incremental tasks would not be expected. These comments merely serve to emphasise caution in the interpretation of the frequency of types of task demand and the relationship between them. Whilst these data provoke interesting questions, the answers cannot be provided without reference to the structure of the curriculum and the learning rates of particular children.

It is worth recalling that in the pre-task interview with the teacher her objectives for the task were ascertained. Whilst the teachers were not introduced to the theoretical perspective adopted by the research team their expressions bore considerable resemblance to the task demand category system used. Teachers described their objectives not only in terms of content but also in terms of enrichment or practice or revision, e.g., they used the expression "introduce" rather than "incremental." Interestingly, teachers made no real distinction in task type when planning tasks for males and females although there was a tendency to assign more enrichment tasks to boys in number but to girls in language.

Language Tasks

Table 3.4 shows the frequency with which teachers' intended demands corresponded with actual demands for language tasks. Only the predominant categories of incremental, practice, enrichment and revision tasks are shown.

Eighty-two per cent of the teachers' intended demands were actually made on the children. This average hides interesting variations. Noteworthy was the very high success in converting an intention to make children practise a skill into an actual practice task. However, children got 17% more practice tasks than intended. This appeared to be a consequence of problems in converting an intention to provide an enrichment or an incremental demand into actual enrichment or actual incremental demands. Less than half the intended enrichment tasks actually made enrichment demands. How did this come about? Two processes appeared to be at work: sometimes separately, occasionally operating together.

In some instances the task simply did not demand what the teacher intended or imagined it to demand. For example, in one instance a teacher's intention was that the task should develop the child's capacity to interpret what she read. The child, Karen, was told to read the next story in her reading book and answer the following questions:

1. Where did Suzy live?
2. How old was Suzy?
3. What was Suzy's dog called?
4. At what time did Jane come to tea?

All the questions were direct and in no case was Karen required to interpret the content of the story in order to respond. Thus whilst the

TABLE 3.4
Actual Task Demands in Relation to Teachers' Intended Task Demands for
Language Tasks

Teachers' Intended Demand	Actual Demand					
	Incremental	Enrichment	Practice	Revision	Other	Total
Incremental	28	0	11	0	0	39
Enrichment	1	10	11	1	1	24
Practice	3	0	129	1	0	133
Revision	0	0	2	1	0	3
Other	0	0	3	0	3	6
Total	32	10	156	3	4	205

teacher intended Karen to deploy or develop interpretive skills the task provided Karen only with an opportunity for copying out appropriate words already in the text: a skill which Karen's work book showed she had done many times before.

This kind of problem with task design was sometimes compounded by the actions of children who altered the demands of the given task. In one such case the teacher intended to "improve the use of adjectives and adverbs." The words in question were assumed to be already in the child's vocabulary. What the teacher intended was that the child learned how to use them appropriately in a variety of contexts. She gave the child the title "Dracula" as a stimulus from which to write a story and supplied him with a workcard showing some adverbs and adjectives. However, there was no discussion of the proposed story, nor of the workcard. The boy was simply told, "Get on with your story." The task, as far as the child was concerned, did not demand what the teacher intended. It still could have made an enrichment demand had the child spontaneously used the card or understood from previous experience that he must use the card. In fact he did not use it. He did not use any adverbs in his story, nor many adjectives, nor any of the supplied adjectives. In evaluating his work later the teacher made no comment on this. In the main this task failed to make its intended demand due to a lack of teacher direction. This was compounded by actions of the child. The actual task thereby became just another story writing exercise.

A similar discrepancy between intended and actual demand may be seen in the case of incremental tasks. Almost a quarter of tasks intended to make incremental demands in fact made practice demands.

Three processes or factors seem to account for this discrepancy. The two most common were:

1. The child was already familiar with the ideas assumed to be novel. This was observed in cases of high attainers receiving class lessons. What might possibly have been new to their classmates simply gave the high attainers more practice.
2. The task means did not match the ends. In one case the teacher wanted to improve her pupils' grasp of sentence structure. She used a picture to form a basis for class discussion and from the discussion drew attention to key features such as capital letters and full stops. Following this the target child was asked to do a missing word exercise. This task required a knowledge of the meaning of words but did not require attention to the structure of sentences in the sense used by the teacher.
3. The third process in which intended incremental tasks were converted involved conversion of the task by the child. This was less

common than the other processes and arose mainly out of a lack of attention on the part of the child. In one case there was an extensive discussion of the "ar" sound and its printed form. Examples were put on the board. However, the target child did not participate. When the class copied these words from the board he did likewise but he could not read them, he merely practised copying.

Of the 22 unintended practice tasks, 14 contained design problems in that, either in the structure of the task, or in the teacher's instructions, the intended demand was not made. Therefore, children usually received more practice than intended because of problems in the design or delivery of tasks.

Number Tasks

The relationship between intended demands and actual demands for number tasks is shown in Table 3.5.

Overall 72% of number tasks made the intended demand. This may be contrasted with a rate of 82% for language tasks.

The major sources of discrepancy in number task demands appeared to lie in difficulties with incremental and practice demands. Approximately one in six tasks intended to introduce new work made practice demands. A similar ratio of intended practice tasks actually made incremental demands. Thus whilst it appears that the target children got almost exactly the quantity of incremental tasks (72) as intended (71), a quarter of the actual experience of meeting new work was unintended or accidental.

The common problem of false diagnosis of what children had or had not grasped seems to be at the root of unintended demands on number tasks.

TABLE 3.5
Actual Task Demands in Relation to Teachers' Intended Task Demands
for Number Tasks

Teachers' Intended Demands	Actual Demand						
	Incre-mental	Restruc-turing	Enrich-ment	Practice	Revision	Other	Total
Incremental	54	0	0	12	1	4	71
Restructuring	0	1	0	1	0	1	3
Enrichment	0	0	12	3	1	1	17
Practice	14	0	1	69	1	2	87
Revision	1	0	0	3	17	0	21
Other	3	1	1	5	1	2	13
Total	72	2	14	93	21	10	212

In 11 of the 12 observed cases in which tasks were intended to be incremental but in fact made only a practice demand, the children were perfectly familiar with the concept or skill involved. Familiarity, by the child's account, arose from experiences in school in 9 instances and from experience at home in 2 instances. The remaining instance was not a case of mis-diagnosis. It arose from faulty task delivery: the instructional means did not match the ends. In this case the teacher's intention was to have the child gain experience of the concept of "10." She wanted the child to work subtraction problems involving figures up to 30. Where appropriate, she wanted him to use cubes in bundles of 10. Unfortunately she failed to mention the idea of grouping cubes to the child. On task, the child counted out all cubes individually: a process he was well used to and adept at.

In the case of the 14 practice tasks which turned out to be incremental, all instances arose from teachers' false impressions of what children had achieved. In one instance a child was given "practice in doing shopping calculations" when in fact she was unable to add. Other cases were more subtle. In one, a boy was given "practice in multiplication." He had had plenty of previous practice using the expression "lots of" but in this instance the task involved the new concept of the times sign ($\times$). He was not acquainted with this and therefore could not practise. Practice requires that a concept or skill be in the child's repertoire. The status of children's acquisitions is difficult to ascertain. In one instance for example, a child had done several days' successful work on division of the type $2\overline{)6}$ and $2\overline{)40}$. The teacher intended to give her "further practice in her newly acquired skill of division." However, she set examples of the type $2\overline{)14}$. In response the girl wrote $\frac{1}{2}2$ in the answer space. She could not practise on the presented calculations because they took her beyond her "newly acquired skill."

It is probable that the range of children's acquisition at this age may be very limited and the pattern of their acquisitions unknown. In this light, whilst misdiagnosing children's attainments necessarily diminishes the quality of the learning experiences provided for them, teachers may be considered to do very well to diagnose correctly in seven cases out of ten.

INTENDED DEMANDS, ACTUAL DEMANDS AND LEVELS OF ATTAINMENT

Language Tasks

It will be recalled that the children in each class were divided into three levels of attainment: high, average and low. Did teachers intend to make different demands on children at different levels of attainment? Table 3.6 shows the teachers' intended demands in language tasks assigned to high,

TABLE 3.6
Frequencies of Intended Demand of Language Tasks Assigned to
Children at Different Levels of Attainment

Intended Task Demand	Levels of Attainment			
	High	Middle	Low	Total
Incremental	14	13	12	39
Enrichment	12	9	3	24
Practice	48	40	45	133
Revision	1	1	1	3
Other	1	3	2	6
Total	76	66	63	205

middle and low attainers. These may be contrasted with the actual demands shown in Table 3.7.

The net changes between intended and actual demands were discussed earlier (see Table 3.4). However the net changes hide complex shifts of losses and accidental gains which had different effects on different levels of attainment.

For example, of the 14 incremental tasks intended for high attainers, 4 turned out to be practice tasks, of the 13 incremental tasks intended for middle attainers, 6 were practice whilst of the 12 incremental tasks intended for low attainers, one was a practice task. However, the middle attainers gained 3 incremental tasks which were initially intended to be practice tasks and the high and low attainers gained none and one such task respectively. Overall then, there was a tendency for teachers to underestimate high attainers' knowledge of language concepts and skills, to be very accurate with low attainers and to have mixed diagnostic problems with the middle group.

TABLE 3.7
Frequencies of Actual Task Demands of Language Tasks Assigned to
Children at Different Levels of Attainment

Actual Task Demand	Levels of Attainment			
	High	Middle	Low	Total
Incremental	10	10	12	32
Enrichment	6	3	1	10
Practice	57	51	48	156
Revision	2	1	0	3
Other	1	1	2	4
Total	76	66	63	205

The loss of intended enrichment tasks similarly affected the children at different attainment levels to different degrees and in different ways.

Of the 12 enrichment tasks intended for high attainers, only 6 actually made that demand. The other 6 made practice demands. As shown earlier, this was due to problems in task design such that the means (the task as set) did not fit the ends (the teacher's intention).

For middle attainers, only 3 out of 9 intended enrichment tasks made enrichment demands. Four were practice tasks (as a result of design problems) and 1 became an incremental task as a result of misdiagnosis of the child.

Of the 3 intended enrichment tasks for low attainers, 1 was delivered, 1 became a practice task and 1 an incremental task.

Thus lower and middle attainers suffered a slight tendency for over-estimation as well as from the general problem of task design.

These accidental shifts in demand had different consequences for children at different levels of attainment. All groups got radically fewer enrichment tasks than intended but the lower groups were affected more than the high group.

More interesting is that in the intended tasks a very similar rate of consolidation (the ratio of practice to incremental demands) was planned (3.4, 3.1, 3.8 for the high, middle and low attainers respectively). However, these were actually converted to 5.7, 5.1 and 4.0 respectively. The higher the attainment level the greater was the actual rate of consolidation.

Number Tasks

Table 3.8 shows the teachers' intended demands in number tasks assigned to high, middle and low attainers.

Table 3.8 must not be taken to imply that high attaining and low attaining children were practising similar tasks. A high attainer might have been practising division with remainders whilst a lower attainer in the same class was practising adding up number to sums less than ten.

Nevertheless, Table 3.8 reveals an important point. The intended demands were very similar across attainment levels. In particular, teachers intended very similar ratios of practice to incremental tasks for each level. If this ratio is taken to be an index of consolidation then it appears that a consistent rate of consolidation was expected. No more consolidation was planned for low attainers than for high attainers.

This is a matter of no great importance if each child was on a programme of work in which the step size and sequence was purpose-designed for his needs. If however, the children were at different points on the same programme, demanding similar consolidation rates may have caused learning

TABLE 3.8
Intended Demands for Number Tasks Assigned to Children of
Different Levels of Attainment

Intended Task Demand	Levels of Attainment			
	High	*Middle*	*Low*	*Total*
Incremental	25	22	24	71
Restructuring	0	1	2	3
Enrichment	8	6	3	17
Practice	27	30	30	87
Revision	7	4	10	21
Other	3	6	4	13
Total	70	69	73	212

problems in the form of delays for high attainers and confusions or incompetence for low attainers. These aspects of learning experience are examined further in the chapters on the curriculum.

Table 3.8 shows teachers' intended demands for number tasks which were to be assigned to children of different attainment levels. Previous analysis provokes the question, "Are these intentions converted into actual demands to the same degree across the attainment levels?"

In respect of practice and incremental tasks, Table 3.9 shows that the answer to this question is, "No."

Teachers intended to give high attainers 25 incremental tasks. Of those, 8 actually became practice tasks. However, 6 of the 27 tasks intended to demand practice, actually became incremental tasks. Thus the high attainers actually received 23 incremental tasks: a quantity made up of 17 intended and 8 accidents. Teachers had less trouble with children at other levels of attainment.

TABLE 3.9
Misdiagnosis of Progress on Number Tasks for Children of Different
Levels of Attainment

	Levels of Attainment		
	High	*Middle*	*Low*
Number of intended incremental tasks	25	22	24
Number of these which became practice tasks, i.e., tasks underestimating progress	8	2	2
Number of intended practice tasks	27	30	30
Number of these which became incremental tasks overestimating progress	6	5	3

The rates of misdiagnosis for intended practice and incremental tasks taken together are 25% for high attainers, 13% for mid-attainers and 9% for low attainers.

The misdiagnosis of the progress of high attainers is provocative. It was almost three times the rate of that of low attainers and was approximately equally composed of over- and underestimates of where the child was in respect of the number scheme. In attempting to understand this, matching tasks to a high attainer may be likened to firing at a rapidly moving target. A pattern of 75% hits and an even distribution of misses about either side of the target may be expected. The child is, of course, much more complex than a target. He brings to the task a fund of personal knowledge that would be unpredictable for any given task and which would be expensive, in terms of time, to ascertain. Lest this speculation be considered complacent however, it is clear that high attainers were as frequently overestimated on these tasks as underestimated. Occasionally teachers assumed that these children had made generalisations which they had not. In the case cited earlier, the girl, perfectly able to solve $2\overline{)6}$ and $2\overline{)40}$ could not generalise her knowledge to $2\overline{)14}$. Thus she was not necessarily good at number (in the sense of seeing relationships, patterns or implications) so much as good at following teachers' instructions. Lacking task-specific instructions she sometimes failed.

SUMMARY

The general kinds of cognitive demands made by teachers have been described. A predominance of practice tasks was evident, particularly in the language curriculum. Teachers intended very similar patterns of task demands for children at different levels of attainment. To a significant degree children did not actually face the demands teachers intended. Thirty per cent of number tasks and 20% of language tasks did not carry the teachers' intended demand. The origins of these discrepancies were shown to be partly in diagnostic errors and partly in task design problems. The discrepancies affected children at different levels of attainment to different degrees. High attainers suffered most from these problems.

4 Matching

As was observed in Chapter 1, the aim of good matching is to ". . . avoid the twin pitfalls of demanding too much and expecting too little." As HMI (1978) found, this is easier said than done in classrooms and thus two of the aims of this study were to establish the degree to which tasks were matched to children, and to ascertain how problems, if any, came about.

It has been assumed that the quality of learning experience is in some way related to the degree of matching between a task and a child. For example, if a child is assigned a task which is far too difficult for him and his neighbour is assigned one which is far too easy, the two children have qualitatively different learning experiences. However, the relationships between these distinct experiences and subsequent learning or attitudes to learning are not known. An easy task might bolster confidence or induce boredom; a difficult task could be inspirational or depressing. Little is known about the consequences of matching or mismatching as these processes operate in normal classrooms. With this in mind a further aim of the study was to ascertain children's responses to matched and mismatched tasks assigned to them in the classroom and to endeavour to relate patterns of match and mismatch to momentary experiences and to longer term learning outcomes.

ASSESSING THE DEGREE OF MATCH

Any attempt to answer the questions posed earlier requires some means for assessing the degree of match between a task and the child who receives it. The critical empirical question to be answered in each individual case is, "to what degree does this particular task make a contribution to the learning process of the particular child?"

To answer this question it is very tempting simply to consider how many errors the child makes on the task. Lots of errors would indicate the task was too hard. If the child made no errors the task might have been too easy. A few errors would seem to indicate that the task was about right. The problems with this approach are fairly obvious. Error rate on a task is not, in itself, a very clear indication that a child is or is not learning. A child could do a page of addition with only one or two mistakes and have learned nothing; he has simply performed on the basis of previous learning. In another case a child might make a whole string of errors but be provoked into thinking about how to sort out the problems. In this way he might learn a lot. Error rate, taken on its own, is thus not a very clear basis on which to judge the quality of matching. Furthermore, there are practical problems in judging error rates. In some tasks (e.g., silent reading) errors are not observable. In others (e.g., reading aloud) errors, hesitations, rescued errors, and pauses are very difficult to categorise and interpret. Error rate was therefore considered to be an important but not a sufficient basis on which to judge matching. As such it was decided not only to inspect the child's work product but also to observe his working process and to discuss the task with the child in a post task interview. In this way the child's work and his or her on-task strategy gave clues to the construction of the post task interview tailored to assess the child's capacity to cope with the work he had been given and with related tasks. Thus in deciding whether a task was matched or not, consideration was given to three sets of data

1. The product of the child's work.
2. The record of the child's strategy.
3. The record of the post task interview.

The manner in which these data were interpreted depended on the type of task demand which the child had been set. The reasons for this are made clear in the following examples.

JUDGING THE APPROPRIATENESS OF PRACTICE TASKS

It will be recalled that a practice task demands increases in fluency of performance. It is assumed that the to-be-practised skill or concept is already possessed by the child. A practice task which does not increase fluency is thus inappropriate. This inappropriateness may come about in several ways. A child could have reached maximum fluency. A child may do 30 calculations (of a specific type) in 5 minutes. If he is observed to work non-stop, uses no mechanical aids, makes no errors (or one or two errors shown in an interview to be slips of the pen) then the task cannot increase his fluency. He has reached the limit of his mechanical speed. The task is thus not making its intended contribution to his learning. Such a task would be judged to underestimate the child's attainment.

Another child might make a lot of errors on the task. The errors would attract attention, but would not be the sole basis of the decision on matching. Such a decision would rest on the post task interview. If it showed that the child lacked a concept or procedure crucial to the practice, the assigned task would be judged an overestimation: the child cannot practise what he does not know. If the interview showed the child ready and able to practise, error rates notwithstanding, the task would be judged appropriate. That is, it would be inferred, from the error rate, that practice was needed and, from the interview, that it was being provided.

JUDGING THE APPROPRIATENESS OF INCREMENTAL TASKS

These tasks introduce new work. They frequently, at this stage of schooling, involve copying, discriminating or repeating in writing, work done orally. Once again, pace and error rate attract attention in judging the appropriateness of these tasks. They inform the design of the post task interview. If the child proceeds rapidly and without error on the incremental task there is a suspicion that he already has the concept or skill assumed to be new. This can be assessed in the post task interview by giving the child tasks involving questions on the next concepts in the sequence. If these are easy to the child, and if the concepts are in his repertoire, it is assumed that the original task assigned by the teacher was underestimating the child's attainment. For example when introducing the concept of simple subtraction of tens and units, the teacher asked Darren to complete sums of the type $24 - 13 = \underline{\quad}$ with the aid of cubes. On being questioned by the fieldworker however it transpired that Darren had no difficulty in subtracting hundreds, tens and units in his head. Thus the original task was considered as underestimating Darren's attainment.

In a similar fashion, if the on-task errors and pace suggest a child is struggling, tasks involving simpler concepts in the subject hierarchy are given. If these prove too difficult the reasonable suspicion is that the child has been given a task he was not equipped to tackle, i.e., he has been overestimated. Thus when a child showed difficulty in estimating and measuring the length of a cupboard using his own feet as a measure, the fieldworker became suspicious and initiated the following conversation:

Fieldworker: "It took fourteen feet to measure that distance. Would it take fourteen dominoes?"
Susan: "Yes."

Fieldworker: "How many cubes would it take? Fourteen or more or less?"
      Susan: "Fourteen."

Eventually Susan realised that her feet were longer than a cube but clearly the original task of estimating and measuring had overestimated her attainment.

THE APPROPRIATENESS OF ENRICHMENT TASKS

Enrichment tasks demand that recently acquired skills be deployed in novel contexts with a view to developing strategic skills, i.e., those skills which are required to recognise when and how to use a concept or procedure. These tasks mainly take the form of problems in mathematics or comprehension tasks in language. Judging the appropriateness of such tasks requires attempting to answer the question "Is the child learning the intended strategic skills?" Such tasks may be inappropriate in two ways. It might be the case that the child already has the strategic skills. The intended enrichment task is then actually a practice task. On the other hand, the child might not have the requisite core skill in the first place. Without this he cannot develop the strategic skills.

Once again the child's on-task errors provoke questions in the post-task interview. However, in this case it is less the quantity than the quality of the child's error which is provocative here. Two children could be making 100% errors—one from random behaviour the other from a systematic, thoughtful effort. Each would get a distinct post task interview with a view to establishing his degree of preparedness and comprehension of the task in hand. If the post-task interview showed the first child to be deficient in either, the task would be judged an overestimate. If the second was systematically deploying procedures and assessing the sense of his answers the task would be judged appropriate, 100% error notwithstanding.

In summarising the approach on assessing the match of a task to a learner, observed error rates and strategies on task were used to suggest a hypothesis on the match. This hypothesis was tested in the post task interview. Tasks were judged to be matched if there was no compelling reason to judge them inappropriate.

Using the above method judgements were made on the match or mismatch of the 417 tasks observed. Judges interpreted error rates on performance in the light of the record of the post task interview. In the following sections analyses of matches and mismatches are set out. It is worth noting that a task was judged a match unless there was a good reason (of the sort indicated above) to judge it a mismatch. In an examination of the reliability of judgements, two judges made independent decisions. They agreed in more than 90% of cases.

MATCHING: THE GENERAL PICTURE

Table 4.1 shows the frequency of matched and mismatched tasks assigned to children at different levels of attainment in number and language.

Overall there is a remarkably consistent picture for the two areas of the curriculum. In number, 43% of tasks were matched (40% in language), 28% were too difficult (29%) and 26% too easy (26%). In both areas of the curriculum, high attainers were underestimated on 41% of tasks assigned to them and low attainers were overestimated on 44% of tasks. Middle groups got a diversified experience in number but tended to be overestimated in language.

The overall picture hides wide differences in the levels of matching observed in different classrooms. These differences are shown in the chapters on the curriculum where they are related to the width and structure of the curriculum and to longer term learning outcomes.

It will be recalled that the levels of attainment were decided with reference to each class. Because of this, and the decision to select schools serving very different socioeconomic areas, a child classified as high in one class would not necessarily be considered to be so in another. For example a child with quotients of 112 in number and 110 in language could be categorised high in one class but average in another, dependent on the range of quotients within both classes. Thus in Table 4.1, while the high attainment category contains all children who were so designated in their own class, their quotients varied widely. An interesting question therefore arises—does the rate of overestimation relate to the child's standardised quotients or to his attainment ranking within his own class? In order to assess this the children were divided into four groups—those whose quotients were in the top third of the distribution in the whole sample and who were also similarly designated in their own class; those who were in the top third of the distribution for the whole sample but were categorised of average ability in their own class; those who were in the middle of the

TABLE 4.1
Incidences of Matched and Mismatched Tasks in Number and Language
Assigned to Children of Different Levels of Attainment

	Number Attainment				Language Attainment			
	High	Middle	Low	Total	High	Middle	Low	Total
Match	29	30	32	91	33	24	24	81
Overestimate	9	18	32	59	7	24	28	59
Underestimate	29	18	8	55	31	14	8	53
Undecided	3	3	1	7	5	4	3	12
Total	70	69	73	212	76	66	63	205

TABLE 4.2
Matching and Overestimating on Number Tasks as a Function of
Within Group and Within Class Attainment

Attainment with Respect to Sample and Class	Number of Tasks Assigned	% Matched	% Overestimated
High in sample/high in class	60	40	12
High in sample/mid in class	14	21	36
Mid in sample/mid in class	37	54	16
Mid in sample/low in class	12	42	58

distribution in the whole sample and were similarly designated in their own class and those who were in the middle of the distribution for the whole sample but were categorised of low ability in their own class. Table 4.2 shows the relevant data for these groups in respect of number tasks only.

These data show that overestimation appears to be a function of within class level of attainment. Children who were high attainers in respect of the whole sample but only middle attainers in their own class received a much larger proportion of tasks which overestimated them. The lower half of Table 4.2 illustrates the same point. Children who were middle attainers with respect to both sample and class were overestimated less frequently than children with the same general attainment but who were in classes so good that they were low attainers with respect to their own class.

The effect may be tentatively explained if it is assumed that the teacher paces the tasks at a level which she judges appropriate for her class. The children's more absolute levels of proficiency may be either unknown to her or, if known, irrelevant to her decision. The effect casts some doubt on the frequently heard claim that children proceed at "their own rate." In terms of matching at least, high attainers within a given class operated mainly within their own rate. Low attainers in a class (whatever their general level of proficiency) were frequently asked to operate beyond their attainment.

Infant/Primary Comparisons in Matching

Another factor which might influence matching is the type of school the children attended. It will be recalled that of the 16 schools in the sample 8 were infant schools and 8 were primary schools. Table 4.3 shows the distribution of matching by subject and school type.

In both number and language it is clear that teachers in infant schools were more successful at matching than those in primary schools.

In number this difference is partly accounted for by the primary

TABLE 4.3
Matching as a Function of Subject and Type of School (Percentages)

| | Number | | Language | |
| | Type of School | | Type of School | |
Appropriateness	Infant	Primary	Infant	Primary
Matches	47	39	47	33
Overestimates	25	30	31	27
Underestimates	27	25	15	36
N	102	103	91	102

teachers' tendency to overestimate: the percentage overestimates being 25% in infant, and 32% in primary schools.

The comparison between infant and primary schools is even more striking in language tasks: 47% of the infant tasks being matched compared to 33% in primary schools. The discrepancy between the two types of school appears to be accounted for by the fact that in primary schools the underestimation of language tasks (N = 38) is more than twice as likely to occur as in infant schools (N = 15). Overestimation in language was approximately the same in both types of school.

Matching and Task Demand

Matching may be expected to be most difficult when new work is being introduced. In some small way the teacher is taking the child into the unknown. However careful the preparation there is an infinite number of ways to get something wrong. In contrast, practice tasks involve work considered to be familiar to the child. There is little risk of the unknown

TABLE 4.4
The Incidence of Levels of Appropriateness for Incremental and Practice Tasks

| | Task Demand | | | |
| | Number | | Language | |
Appropriateness	Incremental	Practice	Incremental	Practice
Match	47%	40%	41%	38%
Overestimate	35%	23%	31%	29%
Underestimate	14%	34%	22%	28%
N	72	93	32	156

and matching might thus be expected to be relatively more simple. However the findings are not consistent with this expectation.

In both number and language there was a higher proportion of matching on incremental tasks. Where an incremental task was a mismatch it was more likely to be an overestimate than an underestimate. This might suggest that teachers were progressing through the curriculum at a pace which carried some cost (as least in terms of the momentary consequences of overestimation). Behind the mesh of progress through the curriculum however a picture of mislocated practice tasks was revealed (see Chapter 3).

Any explanation of this differential rate of matching new and old work is bound to be speculative. It might be suspected however that either new work was prepared with greater care or familiar work was delivered with greater complacency.

THE TEACHERS' VIEW OF MATCHING

Understanding the teachers' perspective on matching is crucial to the comprehension of the general problem of the match as it is manifest in schools. Two complementary approaches were made to gain insight into the process of matching as seen by teachers. The first made use of the teachers' responses in the post task interview. In this interview teachers were asked to evaluate the child's work, to comment on whether the task had been well matched to the child or not and to identify what the next step would be for the child. In these interviews the technical terminology of the project was not used. Teachers responded to the above questions in their own terms. These were idiosyncratic. In imposing patterns on the responses across the 16 teachers it was necessary to look for expressions which could be taken as synonymous.

For example, no teacher said that a task "overestimated" a child's attainment level. However, expressions such as, "he is in trouble with this" or, "she is in difficulty" or, "he cannot cope with this" were taken to be indicative of a teacher's view that the task was too difficult.

In this way teachers were perceived to identify three levels of children's capacity to cope with an assigned task. These were:

1. The child was in difficulty.
2. The child was getting by.
3. The child was doing well.

No tasks were seen by teachers as too easy for the child, i.e., none of the teachers' expressions could be interpreted as implying that a task was

TABLE 4.5
Percentages of Number and Language Tasks at Different Levels of
Children's Responses as Judged by Their Teachers

Teachers' Judgements of Child on Task	Number	Language
In difficulty	30	22
Getting by	42	49
Doing well	14	13
Vague or not recorded	14	16

wasting a child's time or beneath his attainment level or not challenging or, simply, too easy.

Using the above levels, the distribution of teacher's judgements for number and language tasks is shown in Table 4.5.

If perception of the child in difficulty is taken to mean that the task overestimated the child's current level of attainment then the problem of overestimation is clearly visible to these teachers in their own classrooms.

In comparison with project decisions teachers saw a greater incidence of overestimation in number (28% on project criteria) and rather less in language (29% on project criteria).

In contrast to the manifestly obvious incidence of overestimation, teachers did not see a problem of underestimation. The issue simply did not arise. This finding is entirely consistent with the results of the other study of teachers' matching decisions.

In that study, 6 of the 16 teachers had volunteered to read complete data sets on which classifications of matching had been made by the research team. The teachers did not know of the criteria used in the project and were invited to use their own subjective judgement. In this way the teachers made judgements on 24 tasks. These contained 8 matched, 8 underestimated and 8 overestimated as judged on project criteria. Teachers' and project judgements are shown in Table 4.6.

Only 1 task in 24 was judged too easy by the teachers and that was 1 out of 8 so judged on the project criteria. Six underestimates were judged to be matched. Thus, even when suggested as a category of judgement, teachers did not perceive tasks as being too easy. On the basis of these analyses it is inferred that the problem of underestimation, as conceived in this project, is invisible to teachers in classrooms.

The above analyses establish the incidence of mismatching and that this varies according to the attainment level of the child and, to a lesser degree, to the type of demand being made. It does not establish that mismatching is a problem. In order to explore that possibility it is necessary to relate

TABLE 4.6
Teachers' Judgements of Matching Compared with Project
Judgements Where All Decisions Are Based on Reading Logs of Tasks

| | Project Decision | | | |
Teacher's Decision	Match	Too Hard	Too Easy	Total
Match	6	1	6	13
Too hard		4		4
Too easy			1	1
Cannot decide	2	3	1	6
Total	8	8	8	24

mismatching to the child's moment to moment experience and to his longer term learning. The former is done in the following sections of this chapter and the latter is discussed in subsequent chapters.

THE CHILD'S EXPERIENCE

What was the child's response to tasks which overestimated or underestimated him and what was his view of these experiences?

Children's responses may be illustrated by reference to their work on practice tasks. In theory practice tasks serve the valuable purpose of increasing the facility with which skills and routines are deployed: they increase fluency. They should be presented to children who already have in their repertoire the skills to be practised.

In this respect, low attainers were frequently overestimated. Their response to tasks intended to increase the fluency of "free writing" may be characterised as follows. The children typically had limited memory for the stimulus to writing. They were slow to get to the task and the preliminaries of writing the date took up much of the time available. Performance on the task was slow; less than one word per minute of allocated time was produced. They made persistent demands on the teacher's time, notably with requests for spellings. Consequently a large proportion of their time was spent standing in queues. Error rates were high even when copying words from the blackboard or from their word books. Despite this the children had every appearance of working very hard.

Approximately 50% of number tasks assigned to low attainers overestimated their attainments. Frequently, in practice tasks, the object was to increase proficiency with routine calculations using the four rules. Output was very low. On average the children took 3 minutes to complete each calculation. These were typically 4 rules with quantities less than 20.

Most of the time was spent industriously on task but much of this effort was concentrated on the production features of the task rather than on progress through the exercise. That is to say, a lot of time was spent on copying out the calculation, on going over figures and rubbing out or boxing answers.

Whilst most of the calculations were done correctly, post task interviews revealed limited understanding of the processes used. For example, in order to consolidate Frank's knowledge of the three times table, his teacher asked him to complete some simple division sums of the type $12 \div 3 =$ ____. He only made one error and yet, on being asked to recite the three times table in his post-task interview, Frank began "$3 \times 1 = 3$, $2 \times 5 = 10$, $4 \times 2 = 8$." It later transpired that he had completed the original task by copying all the answers from a wall chart illustrating multiplication and division by three.

Errors in such performances were frequently production errors. For example, children miscounted or misplaced cubes. In one instance a girl was asked to divide 48 by 3 using cubes. It took her a long time to collect sufficient cubes. She did not estimate what 48 cubes might look like but rather kept counting what she had and making persistent journeys for more. The cubes took a lot of space. Several were knocked to the floor. She then allocated them one at a time to three piles. She did not know she was not starting with 48. Miscounting the quantities in the three piles, she got three different answers; she was evidently puzzled. This was taken to imply that she expected the same answer from each pile. It is difficult to know what she might have learned from this exercise.

In another example a boy was asked to make four sets of five using Unifix cubes. He had to find out how many there were altogether and to draw his working and answer in his number book. He found it easy to fix two and even three cubes together. In trying to fix four or five however, the string of cubes frequently jack-knifed. He persisted in making the sets of cubes throughout the lesson. He did not complete the task.

In these cases the use of apparatus radically diminished the children's experience. They were totally occupied with managing the equipment rather than with the concept or process at issue: concepts which post-task interviews suggested were not in their repertoire.

The responses of children working on tasks which were too demanding may be contrasted with the behaviour of children being underestimated. "Free writing" tasks for high attainers took the same form as for low attainers. A stimulus was presented and children were typically asked to "write a story about . . . ." The responses of these children were generally rapid and concentrated. Some produced 200–300 words in less than 45 minutes. In terms of quantity there seemed little scope for improving facility and to that degree, further practice seemed unprofitable. More noteworthy was that the stories lacked organisation, structure and punctuation. Post task interviews suggested that the children were ready to learn new skills—or indeed that they already had more advanced skills which they did not deploy.

In one case, for example, a class watched a TV programme on cheese making and, after a discussion, was told to write about the programme. The teacher wanted ". . . some really good stories." Angela (a mid attainer in the class) produced the following:

> today on TV there was a programme and it was about cheese. Gouda cheese and it showed a farmers wife making it and the farmers wife had to get a big tub and then put three cutters and then get all the cheese out and then put it all in a tub.

The following exchange then took place between the fieldworker and Angela:

> Fieldworker: "Will you read your story for me?"
> Angela: No response (smiles).
> Fieldworker: "Don't you want to?"
> Angela: "No."
> Fieldworker: "Can you write me a better story about how the cheese was made, where it came from and all the other things that were on the programme?"
> Angela: "Yes."

Angela then wrote:

> On the TV it was all about cheese and there was a lady that was making some cheese and it was milk that was in the tub and then it was put into a small tub and the tub was upside down and next it was the right way up and it was like a flat biscit but it wasn't a biscit it was Gouda cheese.

> Fieldworker: "Will you read me this?"
> Angela: No response.
> Fieldworker: "Would you like me to read it?"
> Angela: "Yes."
> The fieldworker read the story and then said:
> "Angela, you don't really need 'and then, and then' if you use full stops and capital letters. Would you like to cross them all out and put capital letters and full stops?"
> Angela: "Yes."

Angela then altered the original by crossing out and re-writing. She effectively produced the following:

> On the TV it was all about cheese. There was a lady that was making some
> cheese. It was milk that was in the tub. Then it was put into a small tub. The
> tub was upside down and next it was the right way up. It was like a flat biscit
> but it wasn't a biscit it was Gouda cheese.

The fieldworker then read this corrected version and Angela agreed it sounded a lot better.

The child clearly had the knowledge and skills necessary to do a piece of work with which she was more pleased. The teacher's task had not demanded that she use these skills.

Experience on number tasks was often equally restricting. On tasks judged to underestimate children, performances were quick and accurate. In many cases the teacher found the work rushed and untidy. In most cases the production or recording routines limited the cognitive experience offered by the task.

In one instance for example, a child able to do shopping problems in his head was required to draw round coins to illustrate his answers. The demand that answers were to be illustrated took up time that could have been used in extending the child's intellectual experience.

In most cases, post task interviews showed children to be capable of calculations and problems well in advance of those practised. One child was set to work on shopping problems with a limit of 22p but in an interview did calculations adding up to £1.62 without hesitation. In another case a child was required to show quarter to and quarter past the hour on clock faces but showed in interview that he could tell the time at any setting of the clock. In instances like these, practice, rather than increasing facility actually limits its expression: production features of the task slow down the rate of cognitive response and the practised task ruled out opportunities for the child to work nearer the limits of his attainment.

In summarising the children's responses to unmatched tasks it may be said that whatever the longer term consequences of working on mismatched tasks, the momentary experiences seem unproductive and, for overestimated tasks, seem likely to produce confusions. This is especially the case in mathematics.

Children's Emotional Responses

Two views of the children's emotional responses are available through the data collected. Fieldworkers were asked whether the children appeared bored or interested, defeated or challenged, upset or cheerful and distracted or attentive. Additionally the children were asked how interesting they had found the task, how difficult it had been and to what they attributed their difficulties (if any).

From the fieldworker's point of view the children appeared almost always cheerful, challenged and interested regardless of attainment level or of the degree of appropriateness of the tasks being worked. It is worth recalling that all the fieldworkers were experienced at teaching young children. With this perspective they rated children to be cheerful on 98% of tasks presented. Surprisingly, low attainers were rated cheerful on 100% of tasks in both number and language.

Perceived levels of attention were not so high, especially on language tasks. Overall children were rated as distracted on 17% of number tasks and 25% of language tasks. For number tasks the average level of distraction hides large differences between children at different levels of attainment. High attainers were rated as distracted on 5% of number tasks whilst low attainers were perceived to be distracted on 29% of such tasks.

The level of perceived distraction on language tasks was consistently over 20% for all attainment levels and as high as 29% for low attainers.

Perceived levels of distraction were not, however, related to matching. The child was as likely to appear distracted on a matched task as on an over or underestimating task. Perceived distraction and perceptions of other facets of the child's response, gave no clue to the appropriateness or otherwise of the assigned task. It would thus appear difficult for the teacher to use these aspects of children's behaviour to aid her diagnosis of the appropriateness of tasks.

Copying or turning to friends for help, might also be thought of as indications of mismatching. Copying was found to be rare. It occurred on 4% of number tasks and, in so far as the low incidence permits a conclusion, was not related to the appropriateness of the task. Only one case of copying was observed in the 205 language tasks observed.

Turning to neighbours for help was almost as rare as copying. It occurred in 5% of number tasks and 8% of language tasks. 50% of all efforts to secure help from a neighbour were associated with overestimating tasks.

Observing children copying or turning to neighbours for help are thus yet other aspects of children's responses which are unhelpful to the teacher in identifying mismatches.

The Child's Perspective

In the post task interview each child was asked if he had found the task interesting and whether he had found it easy or difficult.

The children's expressed levels of interest were coded on to a five point

TABLE 4.7
Percentage of Tasks on Which Children Said They Were "Quite
Interested" at Least

Curriculum Content	Level of Attainment		
	High	Middle	Low
Number	86	83	79
Language	72	66	72

scale: "very interested," "quite interested," "O.K.," "not very interested,"
and "not interested."

Table 4.7 shows that children were at least "quite interested" in most
tasks.

There was very little difference between children at different attainment
levels. There was less interest in language than number. Noteworthy is that
the children expressed interest less frequently than the fieldworkers
perceived interest.

The incidence of expressed interest bore some relationship to the levels
of appropriateness of the task. This is shown in Table 4.8.

From the child's point of view a task which overestimated him in number
was much less likely to be felt to be interesting than matched or
underestimating tasks. In language, any mismatched task was less likely to
be perceived as interesting.

Children said that they were "not interested" or "not very interested" in
9% of all tasks (number and language combined). They were thus, by their
own account, at least averagely interested in more than 90% of tasks
assigned. This being said, when asked whether the task in hand was their
favourite work in school they rarely said yes. They almost always
nominated some other activity!

However, both by their own account and in the view of observers, the

TABLE 4.8
Percentage of Tasks at Different Levels of Appropriateness in Which
Children Said They Were "Quite Interested" at Least

Curriculum Content	Appropriateness		
	Match	Overestimate	Underestimate
Number	88	69	85
Language	81	64	60

TABLE 4.9
Percentage of Tasks Found Easy

Curriculum Content	Level of Attainment		
	High	Middle	Low
Number	78	60	65
Language	89	73	59

children were happy with their tasks in the great majority of cases. Whatever the consequences of mismatching it did not appear to be related to loss of interest at this stage.

The children were also asked whether the task was hard or easy. Their overall responses for the curriculum areas of number and language are shown in Table 4.9.

Not surprisingly, high attainers found more tasks easy than low attainers. However, high and middle attainers found more language tasks easy than number tasks whilst the reverse was true of the low attainers. For low attainers, tasks were more often easy than not: but often not!

Children's perceptions of ease were related to judgements of level of appropriateness. This is shown in Table 4.10.

Table 4.10 gives at least some face validity to judgements of appropriateness. Children's discrimination ran in the expected direction. In number they perceived overestimating tasks to be difficult more often than easy.

The children were asked what they attributed their ease or difficulty to. They were asked, for example, "what made this easy/hard?" or "how was this so easy/hard?" This question proved very difficult for children to answer. In 30% of cases they did not respond or they changed the subject. In the cases in which they did respond they attributed ease and difficulty to themselves in approximately 25% of cases or to the task in 25% of cases. Attributions to themselves took the form of claims to knowledge or abilities. "It is easy because I am clever," or "Because I am good" or

TABLE 4.10
Percentage of Tasks at Different Levels of Appropriateness Which
Children Declared To Be Easy

Curriculum Current	Appropriateness		
	Match	Overestimate	Underestimate
Number	69	44	84
Language	76	63	86

"Because I know how to do these" were common responses. Negative attributions to themselves ignored the dimension of ability. No child said he was a slow learner! Rather, children's responses took the form of tautologies. They claimed tasks were hard because "I can't do it" for example. Children finding the task hard "because this is a hard card" or "it is difficult" were common observations.

However, some attributions to tasks were more specific. One child noted that her writing was easy because "It was an easy story to remember" and some said that writing was difficult because the story was long or hard to remember.

Perhaps the most important conclusions to be drawn from these observations are firstly, that attributions are difficult to obtain at this age. Secondly, where responses were obtained they showed, on the part of the children, a very balanced appraisal of the relationship they had to their work. There was no hint of lack of confidence or negativism. These features, of course, could be hidden amongst the non-responses.

In summarising the observations of the effects of mismatching on children's experience, it may be said that it appeared to create no short term emotional problems for them. However, concern does appear warranted over the immediate effects of what children learn and what they understand of the content and processes of classroom learning under the conditions of mismatching.

To alleviate this concern it is necessary to understand how mismatching comes about and what sustains it. To do this it is necessary to describe and to attempt to explain the whole business of task allocation and task working as it is operated in the classroom.

ASSIGNING AND WORKING TASKS IN THE CLASSROOM

A number of processes are involved in classroom tasks. These include: (1) the process of presenting the task to the children; (2) the child's interpretation of the task; (3) the child's work on the task; (4) the child's product or work output; (5) the teacher's interpretation of the child's work and product; and (6) the selection of the next task. Taken together, these processes may be said to make up a task cycle—the move from one task to the next. It must not be thought however, that these processes occur as a sequence of discrete events following the order set out above. They are processes not events. Each process may be prolonged or curtailed. The processes might (and probably do) overlap. Some of the processes might not be evident in a particular task cycle.

For example, whilst teachers frequently present tasks to children at the beginning of a session they may add to that presentation throughout the period the children are working on the task. Teachers give reminders, supplementary instructions and general and particular help. And just as the teacher's task specification may be prolonged and segmented, so might be the child's interpretation of the task. Additionally, the teacher's interpretation of the child's work could be a momentary event occurring at the end of the session. Alternatively the teacher might monitor the child throughout the period of task presentation and of the child's work. Her evaluation could thus be over before the child completes the task and her assessment, if any, might not relate to a task product at all.

The above sets out some of the possible modes of operation of task related processes. The problem for anyone attempting to understand how these processes actually do operate to the benefit or detriment of children's learning is that a task cycle for any one child is embedded in the more general life of a classroom containing a large number of other children.

This maelstrom of activity is well illustrated in a teacher's account of her attempt to focus her attention on one child:

> The class contains children aged 4–7 years. Twenty eight children were present. Robert sits at a table with seven other children. Each of his group was working on a different number task and the four other tables were working on number games (e.g. attribute dice, number dominoes, threading beads). The children doing number were constantly asking for help or wanting work marked. The other children interrupted frequently to ask for disputes to be settled, for permission to go to the toilet, to complain of toothache, to talk about things that happened last night or were going to happen later. There was no chance to concentrate attention on Robert. There were constant interruptions from within the class and from children coming into the class with lost property, taking the numbers for school lunch, junior children to borrow infant books and so on. I started to record the number of interruptions but I soon lost count . . . I felt very tense and found myself getting impatient and sharp with the children.

Thus, whilst any particular task may be matched or not to a particular child, and whilst, for that child the particular event may be critical, any understanding of the task processes which focus only on these events may be incomplete or misleading.

The social scientist is faced with the problem of interpreting an ever moving scene from a series of snapshots. Some of the complexity of classroom teaching and learning (and its interpretation) is illustrated in the following account and analysis of a 7-year-old girl's efforts to work through a number assignment allocated by her teacher.

> The girl, Helen, is of average ability for her top infant class and she is one of 28 children being taught by a very experienced teacher of infants.
>   The teacher had placed a number of workcards in Helen's book. Helen collected her book and then the following took place:

9.25   In Helen's book the teacher had written "1.4.81. money" under
         which Helen wrote:
         I have 9p
         I buy a box of crayons for
         I have   change.
9.30   Helen looked at a price list.
9.40   The teacher asked Helen what she was looking for and concluded
         that Helen had mis-read "crayons" and had been trying to locate
         the cost of chocolate instead.
9.42   The teacher showed Helen the price list she should have been
         looking at. Helen studied it and eventually found the price of
         crayons.
9.44   She began counting out amounts in half-pence pieces but did not
         have enough of them for her purposes. She then got a box of
         cardboard money and counted out 9p in half-pence pieces. After
         laying these out on her desk Helen counted out 11p in half-pence
         pieces. She counted all the half-pence and wrote 15p in the space
         for recording the change.
9.49   Helen's next card was as follows:
         I have 19p
         I buy a car for
         I buy a rocket for
         I spend
         I have   change.
         Having read the card, Helen searched the pictures on the price list
         for the cost of the items.
9.53   She established that a car cost 10p but failed to find the cost of a
         rocket.
9.55   Eventually Helen found that a rocket cost 7p. She began counting
         half-pence pieces and then announced. "I've lost count now."
9.57   Helen had 19 pence worth of half-pence pieces on her desk.
9.59   She collected 10p and put it on her desk. She then apparently went
         in search of more coins but changed her mind and returned to her
         desk without any. She counted out 17p in half-pence pieces.
10.02   Helen counted all the half-pence pieces on her desk and wrote
         down 18½p.
10.03   She returned all the coins to their box and went to the teacher's
         desk.
10.04   The teacher marked Helen's work and asked her what "change"
         meant.
     The work in Helen's book looked like this:
         I have 9p
         I buy a box of crayons for 6½p
         I have 15p change
         I have 19p
         I buy a car for 10p
         I buy a rocket for 7p
         I spend 1½p
         I have 18½p change.

On the basis of the above record it seems that this task was very much too difficult for Helen. She appeared to be struggling with some of the reading necessary to the task. She did not appear to know when to subtract in respect of these money problems. She did not appear to know about the denomination value of coins and indulged in a strange preoccupation with halfpenny pieces. This in turn led her into performance difficulties. She failed to keep track of her counting behaviour in the face of the sheer quantity of half-pence coins. Finally she did not appear to know what the word "change" meant.

Helen appeared to be so far out of touch with this task that we are bound to ask why she was given it in the first place. Why was the teacher so late in discovering that Helen did not know what the word "change" meant? How had the teacher failed to notice all of Helen's other problems?

Before observing Helen the research worker had asked the teacher why she had allocated this task to her. The teacher had said that she wanted to familiarise Helen with half-pence in simple shopping sums. All the children had been working with money for some time. The teacher pointed out that half-pence had been introduced 2 days earlier in accordance with the very detailed school mathematics scheme.

In the light of this information the teacher's behaviour becomes much more comprehensible. That is not to say it was justifiable. However it is at least clear that the teacher was moving Helen through the maths scheme.

When Helen had completed her work for the teacher, the research worker interviewed her in an attempt to understand her problems with the task. He first established that she could read the work cards and the price lists. The following discussion then took place:

The fieldworker asked her to do this sum:
I have 9p
I buy a box of crayons for
I have   change.
Helen wrote in that the crayons cost 6½p but, having collected a pile of half-pence coins, she appeared to give up and did not complete the sum. When the fieldworker asked what was missing she said "7p." The conversation continued in the following manner:

Fieldworker: "Helen if I have 9p and I spend 5p, how much would I have left?"

Helen: "4p."

Fieldworker: "If I buy a car for 10p and a kite for 15p, how much do I spend?"

Helen: (Having got out a 10p coin and fifteen 1p coins replied) "25p."

Fieldworker: "If I have 20p and I buy a doll, how much have I left?" (The card in front of Helen showed that a doll cost 10p).

Helen: "10p."

Fieldworker: "Can you do this card for me?"
            I have 13p. I buy tomatoes for 3p and carrots for 5p.
            I spend
            I have   change.
Helen completed the card writing that she spent 8p and had 2p change.
Fieldworker: "If I have 5p and I spend 2½p, how much do I have left?"
    Helen: "2p."
Fieldworker: "Can you do this sum for me please?"
            I buy a box of crayons for 6½p and a pencil for 1½p.
            How much do I spend?
            Helen wrote "8p."

This interview forces us to re-appraise radically our initial view of Helen's limitations. It appears that she could read the pertinent materials. She did know when to add and subtract on money sums. She did know the denomination value of at least some coins. There is still some doubt about whether she understood the word "change." She could add half-pence but, it appears, could not subtract them.

The teacher's behaviour in assigning the task now becomes much more comprehensible. The task would not appear, on the basis of the above interview, to be wildly beyond Helen. Why then, did she have such problems with it? Why did she make it so much more difficult than the teacher intended by attempting to do it in half-pence only? And why did the teacher not recognise her difficulties?

We have to infer answers to these questions. Helen had worked on money over the previous 2 days. Every example had focused on half-pence and their conversion to pence. Every calculation had been done using half-pence only. On the day of the shopping problems the teacher had given Helen no specific instructions. The nature of the task was assumed. Helen knew what to do when she found the cards in her book, i.e., she assumed that they had to be worked in half-pence. The performance problems caused by handling such large quantities could have caused her to regress in the execution of familiar, simple skills. Such regression is well known (Jensen, 1974). On her own initiative Helen presumably got little but confusion out of this task.

The teacher's behaviour can be understood if it is recalled that Helen took her work to the teacher's desk. The teacher did not see Helen in action on these examples. She did not see the processes by which Helen got into her mess. She saw only the product. Given that, the teacher's insight was impressive in identifying Helen's difficulty with the word "change." Nonetheless she was of no help to the child on this task. Clearly, even if the teacher had closely monitored Helen's on-task performance and had thereby dealt with her confusion as it emerged, it is likely that she would have missed another problem somewhere in the class.

The above case serves to illustrate the potential for misinterpretation and for limited communication in the classroom. In order to adapt to this environment, pupils and teachers may be expected to render this potential complexity into simpler predictability. Pupils can avoid a life of perpetual confusion by learning what teachers want. Teachers can avoid frustration by making what they want clear to children. For children of age 6–7 years this may be seen to necessitate the simple description of concrete objectives.

These were the predominant intentions the teachers claimed to have for the tasks set. Teachers were asked to state the objective for the task to be assigned to the target child and to give the reason for holding the objective. It was possible to categorise teachers' responses as referring to either cognitive or procedural objectives. Examples of cognitive objectives are, "to improve logical thinking" or, "to stimulate the imagination." Examples of procedural objectives are, "to use full stops and capital letters" or, "to continue with the scheme" or "to show subtraction of tens and units carrying a ten." Ninety-four per cent of objectives for number tasks and 92% for language tasks were procedural. In order to establish the child's view of the task, they were asked a series of questions including, "What did you have to do?" and "What did your teacher want?" In the majority of cases, the child's view of the task was identical to that of the teacher. This was the case in 87% of both number tasks and language tasks. For example, children knew they had to "get some information from the graph," "add those sums but you mustn't add the tens first," "do ten sums" and when a fieldworker asked, "Did you do it well?" a pupil said, "I finished all the card and I wrote the date." When asked, "What did the teacher mean when she said do it well?," a pupil remarked, "Don't chatter and do good writing." Most of these remarks were exact reproductions of the teachers' instructions.

In language tasks, teachers frequently emphasised that they wanted "lots of good writing." This objective was rarely lost on the children. For example, one child said, "This is going to be the best. I might write three pages." Another said, "She wanted me to do as much writing as I could."

The children were thus anxious to complete a card of calculations or to complete a page of writing rather than to achieve some less concrete goal such as understanding a process or exciting a reader. However, the goal of completion is not absolute. In the main, what children may be expected to complete depends on the teacher's expectation for an individual child. On evaluating children's work in the post-task interview one dominant dimension of appraisal was the contrast between the child's product and what might be expected for that child. Indeed the comment most frequently expressed about children's work made just this comparison. Teachers observed that the work was, "Average for Steven," or, "It's not very special but it's good for her," or "She obviously could do better but it is good for her." Seventy-five per cent of remarks which contrasted a task product with the teacher's expectation of that child were positive or neutral. The child disappointed the teacher in 25% of cases.

The second most frequent criterion of teacher's appraisals of children's work referred in mathematics to the number of procedures and in language to quantity. Comments on procedure on number tasks rarely referred to understanding. Rather they referred to a capacity (or its absence) to reproduce a procedure. For example, "He couldn't remember to borrow tens" or, "I hope he now knows most of his bonds."

References to quantity produced in response to language tasks came to less than half the references in which teachers contrasted the child's product with his usual performance. The former included, for example, "There was very little done," and "She added more than had been discussed."

The emphasis on quantity and procedure together with a predominant tendency to judge the child by his own standards meant that children could almost always be praised. All they had to do was make the effort to produce something. This achieved, they would be rewarded. Production pleased the teacher who cheered the child.

The above account is consistent with the evidence on teachers' perceptions of under and overestimation. Teachers did not see the evidence of underestimation. They saw children following a procedure and producing work in quantity. Since these appeared to be teachers' criteria of effective work, there was no problem to be seen. The teachers did not compare the child's product with his actual level of understanding. In contrast, overestimation was highly visible to teachers. In this respect the child did not follow the teacher's procedure or, if he did, he did not produce work in quantity, he was following the procedure with difficulty.

Teachers' responses to this perception are interesting. They are also consistent with the view that procedure is more critical than understanding. In the evaluation of the child's work, teachers were asked what the next step would be. Their responses, in relationship to their perceptions of the child's performance, are shown in Table 4.11.

Teachers' plans for the next step were placed in four main categories. They appeared to plan more practice on the same procedure using very similar examples, or to move on to the next task in the scheme, or to go back in the scheme to sort out the child's trouble or to leave the issue and proceed with something rather different.

For children perceived to be in difficulty the predominant response was to plan more practice on the difficult procedure. In only one in nine cases did the teacher's plan to go back to sort out the difficulties. Indeed it was just as likely that they planned to move on in the scheme.

TABLE 4.11
Frequencies of Teacher's Planned Next Step in Respect of Their
Perceptions of Children's Performances

	Teachers' Next Step					
Teachers' View of Performance	*More of the Same*	*Move on*	*Go back*	*Something Different*	*Other*	*Total*
Child in difficulty	48	9	10	7	20	94
Getting by	60	60	4	9	24	157
Doing well	15	26	1	3	6	51

It is not that teachers were cavalier about children's lack of understanding nor that they did not perceive understanding to be important. In commenting on children's number work, references to understanding were made as frequently as comments on presentation and more frequently than comments on quantity.

Whilst noting the child's problem however, the matter of misunderstanding was not seen to be critical. Rather it appears that teachers expected to have to allow children to carry this problem, at least for a while. This was often revealed in pre-task interviews with teachers. At this stage teachers were asked what problems they might expect the target child to have on the task. This was not to imply that teachers would deliberately give children tasks on which they would inevitably fail. Rather, the question was intended to identify the risks teachers felt prepared to run with children.

Teachers predicted the possibility of cognitive problems in 45% of all maths tasks, and in 66% of maths tasks assigned to low attainers. In language tasks, teachers thought there might be a problem in 48% of all cases, and in 73% of those given to low attainers. It must be emphasised that the teachers were asked to describe only the possibility of problems. In the main, the teachers noted that the child in question "might find this difficult to follow" or, "he might confuse multiplication and division," or "perhaps she will have difficulty where the instructions change their format."

In some cases however, teachers were more definite about the likelihood of problems. In different instances teachers observed that:

"She has had endless problems. She will find it difficult to understand written instructions."
"He won't be able to do borrowing."
"He will not know what he is being asked for."
"She will get confused. The card covers a number of different sums."

"He cannot sound the words he wants to write so he will get stuck."
"He will have problems because he has not reached the reading book which
the comprehension test covers."

Notwithstanding these certain difficulties, the tasks were assigned.

To make progress through schemes of work teachers have to risk the
possibility of children misunderstanding new work. In some instances,
there was no risk in the teacher's view: misunderstanding was a certainty.
Progress through the scheme appeared to become more important than
progress on the basis of immediate understanding.

The issue however is not as stark as it might appear. Teachers were
clearly aware of the consequences of children's learning without
understanding, or of performing without success. This emerged very clearly
in the in-service phase of the project which is reported in Chapter 9.
Pertinent to the immediate discussion are the teachers' responses to
reading case studies of task logs from the matching phase of the project. In
cases of overestimation, the teachers in the in-service phase concluded that
the children were in danger of learning that they were incompetent, of
acquiring negative self concepts and of the destruction of their confidence.
Thus lack of understanding, in these teacher's eyes, became critical when it
was associated with negative emotional responses. In the experience of
class teachers in the matching phase however this was never the case. It will
be recalled that whatever the children's level of understanding of the task,
they were always cheerful and industrious. Thus lack of understanding
never reached critical proportions. The teachers contained the emotional
consequences of performing without understanding by rewarding effort
according to the personal lights of individual children.

Unfortunately, this form of managing learning does not address the
cognitive consequences of such performance. Indeed, as will be shown in
Chapter 9, teachers might not even be aware of the extent of these
consequences.

SUMMARY

More than half the observed tasks were mismatched. The nature of the
mismatch was related to children's level of attainment relative to his
classmates. High attainers were underestimated and low attainers
overestimated.

Mismatching appeared to have important immediate consequences in
terms of lost opportunities and limiting experiences for high attainers and
confusion for low attainers.

Teachers did not perceive instances of underestimation. In no instance was a task considered by a teacher to be too easy for a child. They saw, but were prepared to live with overestimation. Whilst teachers recognised the dangers of performing without understanding, they avoided the worst consequences by sustaining children's production efforts. This they did by rewarding endeavour on a scale determined by their perceptions of the individual child. In their cheerfulness and industry the children failed to signal to the teachers, the extent of their cognitive problems. Because of the way teachers managed their classrooms, they remained unaware of these problems.

5 The Number Curriculum

The match between a task and a child's attainment level is an important facet of the quality of the child's learning experience. It is not, however, the only facet. The content of a particular task represents a crucial dimension of experience. In this chapter the content of the children's mathematics experience is examined. Additionally, relationships between groups of tasks are examined. When several tasks in the same curriculum domain are viewed in series, important features of the structure and sequence of provision may be revealed.

THE TEACHERS AND THEIR APPROACH TO NUMBER

None of the 16 teachers had any special qualifications in mathematics, nor did they indicate that this area was a particular interest of theirs.

In planning their number work, six of the teachers said that they followed a commercial scheme very closely. Seven teachers had developed schemes of their own using a variety of commercial schemes as a quarry of ideas. The remaining three teachers followed school-based schemes. These were also quarried from commercial schemes but they had been designed, or at least agreed, by a group of teachers rather than by the class teacher alone.

Whatever the origins of the schemes, analysis of the tasks observed showed that teachers stayed very close to the sequence laid down in them. No opportunistic tasks were observed. When asked for their reasons for giving particular tasks, 41% of teachers said that it was routine to do so because the appropriate place in the scheme had been reached.

Thirteen of the teachers said that all the children in their respective classes worked through the scheme at their own rate. The other three teachers each adopted an idiosyncratic strategy. One said that children in the same classroom group were always given the same material at the same time. A second presented all number tasks as class lessons and arranged extra practice for those children who were quick to finish. The third teacher said that whilst she allowed all pupils to work at their own rate, all new work was taught to the whole class.

In effect, most children worked on individual mathematics assignments, each at some particular point in their respective scheme. In 4 out of 5 of the 212 tasks observed, the child worked from a textbook or workcard. Half of these tasks lasted between 20 and 40 minutes and 98% of all tasks required the child to write his responses. Almost half the tasks required practical work of some form. This almost always took the form of structuring apparatus, e.g., cubes, blocks, equalisers.

Although the children sat in groups round a set of resources such as crayons and blocks, for example, they almost always worked on their own task. Productivity varied enormously. Obviously this was in part a function of the type of task being worked. Producing a graph or measuring the classroom takes longer than a routine calculation. However, in similar periods of work on number, 1 child completed 2 calculations whilst another completed 300. This difference in productivity is extreme, but the general range of productivity was also large. Whether this was a result of or underwrites the need for the very high level of individualisation of task assignment must remain a moot point.

Although the actual tasks worked were individualised, initial task instructions were frequently given to the whole class. The pattern for task allocation was that teachers told the whole class what to do in 52% of all cases. This class instruction sometimes took the form of a general order: "Get on with your number cards." Alternatively, it took the form of a review of what each group of children was required to do. In this way children frequently got the opportunity to listen to instructions or see demonstrations of tasks which they had either completed or had not yet reached.

However, in 30% of all task allocations, not only did the child work on his own task but he got his own personal instructions. Whether the instructions were individualised or not, teachers gave supplementary instruction to individual children in 50% of all cases, and in general, instructions placed heavy emphasis on routines and recording.

CONTENT COVERED

All the number work covered by the target children was documented at the end of the Spring and Summer terms. Inspection of the curriculum in the 16 classes reveals considerable variety both between and within classes. This variety is difficult to demonstrate in a concise way. Also, summarising the variety loses important points of detail with respect to the structure and sequence of the curriculum. With these reservations in mind the maths

TABLE 5.1
Major Areas of Work in the Top Infant Maths Curriculum

Work in Four Rules	Supplementary Areas
Addition	Fractions
Subtraction	Money
Multiplication	Time
Division	Length
Sums involving more than one of the four rules	Area
	Shape
	Weight
	Capacity
	Number concepts
	Number language
	Graphs
	Games and puzzles

curriculums actually presented in the 16 classes are set out below in a variety of ways.

Table 5.1 shows the number work done in two major categories—four rules which appear at the core of every curriculum, and supplementary areas.

It shows a wide range of areas covered in these classes. However, it does not show the variety of coverage both between and within classes. This variety is illustrated in Table 5.2 and it shows the coverage of maths by target children in the different schools in the two terms of observation. The letters in each box refer to the group of target children known to have done some work in that particular area. H represents high attainers, M middle attainers, L low attainers and A all attainment levels.

Table 5.2 is a gross, minimal representation of content coverage. It docs not indicate how much work was done in a particular area nor the quality of the coverage in terms of sequence and structure. It does, however, permit some interesting initial comparisons.

There was a wide divergence between schools in the range of matters covered. Class 5 did work in 15 of the 17 areas whilst Class 13 worked in only 8.

Some areas were much more popular than others. All schools did the four rules, money and time, whereas graphs, capacity and area were not majority interests.

Not all children covered all the areas. Amongst the supplementary areas 31 of the 130 citations refer to top or top and middle group children only. Thus, presumably by working at their own rate, low attainers frequently did not get experience of these concepts even when they were in evidence on the curriculum in their classroom. This effect is most marked in School

TABLE 5.2

The Major Categories of Number Curriculum Covered by the Classes, and Attainment Levels During the Spring and Summer Terms

Area								Class								
	1	2	3	4	5	6	7	8	9	10	11	12	13	14	15	16
Addition	A	A	A	A	A	A	A	A	A	A	A	A	A	A	A	A
Subtraction	A	A	A	A	A	A	A	A	A	A	A	A	A	A	A	A
Multiplication	A	A	A	A	A	A	A	A	A	H/M	A	A	A	A	A	H
Division	H/M	H	H	H/M	A	H/M	H	A	A	A	A	A	A	A	A	H
Sums involving more than one rule																
Fractions			A	A	A	A	A	A	H	H	A	A	A	A		H
Money	H/M	A	A	M	A	A	A	H	A	A	A	A	L	A	A	A
Time	A	A	A	A	A	H/M	H	A	A	A	A	A		A	A	A
Length	H	A	A	A	A	A	A	A	A	A	A	A		A	A	A
Area		H				H					A					
Shape	M	L	A	A	A	A	A		H/M	M/L	H	A		A		A
Weight	M/L	M/L	H	A	H	A	A		M	H	A	A		M/L		A
Capacity		A	A		A	A	A				M					A
Number concepts		A	H/M	H	A	A	A	H	A	H/M			H	A		A
Number language			A	A	H	H/M	M/L	H/L L	A					A	A	H
Graphs	H/M	H/M			A	H/M								A	A	
Games and puzzles	H/M	H/M									A					

6, in which the top children worked in 13 areas whilst the lower attainers worked in only 8.

Whilst Table 5.2 permits useful comparisons, it says little about the structure of the maths curriculum at the level of detail at which the children worked. In order to produce a finer grain picture of this structure, a list was made, for each area, of all the types of task which children were given throughout the sixteen classes in the sample. The entries in each row represent similar contents and layout across classes. In subsequent discussion these are referred to as procedures. These procedures were arranged within each area in a notional order of increasing difficulty. It must be emphasised that the hierarchies developed were not based on a detailed analysis of the psychological processes involved in each step nor on any psychometric scale of difficulty evinced by the pupils.

Space does not permit an exhaustive account of all the work done, but Table 5.3, showing the steps worked on in the area of subtraction, is presented for illustrative purposes. Complete tables for all the areas of the number curriculum are given in Appendix A.

The letter(s) in each box refers to attainment levels described earlier and indicate which target children worked on that procedure in the Spring term.

Whilst all classes did some work on subtraction in the Spring term, Table 5.3 shows considerable variety in the attention paid to this topic. Of the 15 steps seen to be presented across the 16 classes, 6 classes worked on 8 steps whilst School 11 worked on only 2. This class, together with others whose coverage was slight, might, of course, have done extensive earlier work in the previous term.

More interesting than the range of cover was the nature of the quality of cover. Some children made huge moves through their experience on subtraction. In Class 1, for example, the two low attainers moved from horizontal subtraction of units straight to the vertical subtraction of tens and units with carrying. In Class 10 the two high-attaining target children moved from very basic counting-back tasks to the subtraction of tens and units with carrying in two steps. In the same class the experience for the mid-attainers is more provocative since they made the same move whilst omitting the step of subtraction without carrying.

This apparently patchwork coverage may be contrasted with that in Class 6 in which progress, whilst less ambitious in range, was certainly more finely sequenced.

Reference to Table 5.2 shows that in all of the classes under observation children from all attainment levels covered at least some aspect of subtraction during the course of the two terms.

This was not so for division, where in seven of the classes work in this area was restricted to high and mid-attainers. Table 5.4 shows the work covered in division by each attainment group.

TABLE 5.3
Procedures Worked on in Subtraction by the Target Children in Each Class in the Spring Term

Subtraction										Class						
	1	2	3	4	5	6	7	8	9	10	11	12	13	14	15	16
Counting back, less than		L		A		H/M				A						A
Problems involving units (with picture aids)										M/L						
Horizontal subtraction (units only)	A															
Vertical subtraction (units only)									L	M						
Horizontal subtraction (maximum number 20)	H	M/L	A	M/L		A	A	M	A	L	A	A	A	A	A	
Vertical subtraction (maximum number 20)			H/M			A		A		M		H/M	M	A	H/L	H
Missing number sums, e.g. 6 – ___ = 2 (horizontal layout)	M	H		H		A	A							A		M
Missing number sums (vertical layout)			H					H							H	
Subtraction of multiples of 10 (horizontal layout)																
Subtraction of tens and units (no carrying) horizontal layout	H/M	M	H	H	H	H				H	A	A	H/L			H/M
Subtraction of tens and units (no carrying) vertical layout			H		H	H/M	H/L			H			H	H/M		
Subtraction of tens and units (carrying) horizontal layout								A	M	H/M		A				
Subtraction of tens and units (carrying) vertical layout					H	H/M	H		M	M		A	A	H	H	
Problems involving units (no picture aids)	A			M/L						H		M/L				
Problems involving T and U				M/L	H						A				H/M	H/M

It will be observed that one-third of the procedures were worked by high attainers only. In nine of the classes low attainers tackled some aspects of division and in several cases this was of an advanced nature. For example, in Schools 8, 12, 14 and 15 low attainers were given problems to solve. These usually required only the manipulation of units—"John and Jane share 8 sweets. How many sweets each?" The only low attainers who were given problems involving tens and units were in Class 12.

Some topics were obviously more prevalent than others. Eleven of the sixteen classes covered horizontal division of tens and units with no carrying or remainder, and twelve did problems of various types. In Class 11 children did vertical division of tens and units with carrying but no remainder, but no class tackled these in a horizontal format. Further, none of the children in the study had reached the stage of doing calculations involving the division of tens and units with both carrying and remainders.

As with subtraction, children in some of the classes made apparently large moves between procedures while others followed a far more graded sequence. The children in Class 8 covered the division of tens and units in a variety of formats before proceeding to simple problem calculations. The children in Class 12, on the other hand, jumped from doing calculations of the type $15 \div 3 = \underline{\quad?\quad}$ to problems of an advanced nature, for example, "There are 20 children in the hall. They stand in 4 teams. How many in each team?"

Table 5.4 shows that some teachers put a great deal more emphasis on division than others. Classes 5 and 15, for example, worked on 7 different procedures in division whilst Classes 1, 3 and 11 worked on only 1. This differential coverage was not due to differential ability levels between these classes. It is likely that the differences relate to differences in schemes. In this respect it is interesting to note that Classes 5 and 15 both operated school-based schemes whilst Classes 1, 3 and 11 did not.

It was noted earlier that all the children worked on the four rules but that there was a tendency for the high attainers in a class to cover several of the supplementary topics while the less able children had a less varied curriculum (see Tables 5.1 and 5.2). A further example of this differentiation is given in Table 5.5, which shows the procedures met in the curriculum area of money. Top attainers are featured in 81% of the entries in the table but low attainers only appear in 51%. Two entries refer to mid-attainers only but, with the exception of Class 2, it was more common for them to cover the same work as high or low attainers. It is perhaps noteworthy that mid-attainers only featured in 59% of the entries, suggesting that their width of coverage was more similar to that of low, as opposed to high, attainers.

As with subtraction and division, some children received a finely sequenced curriculum on money while others made large moves between

TABLE 5.4

Steps Worked in Division by the Target Children in Each Class in the Spring and Summer Terms

Division	1	2	3	4	5	6	7	8	9	10	11	12	13	14	15	16
Sharing												H/M				H
Repeated subtraction										H		H/M				
Problems involving division of units (with picture aid)			H		H				H	H						
Division of units (vertical layout) no remainders				H			H									
Division of units as table practice (horizontal layout)					M				H/M			A	A			
Missing number division sums, e.g. ? ÷ 3 = 3								L								
Division of units (vertical layout) with remainders										M/L					M/L	
Grouping, e.g. Group 8 in 3's = 2 groups of 3 + 2				H/M			H									

Division of tens and units: horizontal layout, no carrying, no remainder	H	H/M	A	H/M	A	A	H/M	H/L	H/M	H
Division of tens and units: vertical layout, no carrying, no remainder	H/M	H/M	A	H/M	A	A	H/L	H/M		
Division of tens and units: horizontal layout, no carrying, with remainder		H	H	H/M	H	H/M			M/L	
Division of tens and units: vertical layout, no carrying, with remainder		H	H/M	H/M	A	A	M/L	A		
Division of tens and units: horizontal layout, with carrying, no remainder		H/M	H/M							
Division of tens and units: vertical layout, with carrying, no remainder					A			H/L		
Problem involving division of units (no picture aid)	H	H/M	H/M	A	H	A	H/M	A	L	
Problems involving division of tens and units	H	H	M	H	A		A		H/M	

TABLE 5.5

Procedures Worked in Money by the Target Children in Each Class in the Spring and Summer Terms

								Class								
Money	1	2	3	4	5	6	7	8	9	10	11	12	13	14	15	16
Coin recognition	H/L		A				A		L	L						
Composition of coins		H/L			A	H	A	M/L		A	A	H/M			A	
Converting pence to two pence and vice versa					H			H								
Converting pence to half-pence and vice versa								H				H/M			H	
Addition and subtraction of pence	M/L		A	A	M/L		A			M		H/M				
Addition and subtraction of sums involving half-pences	H					H		H	H/M			H/M		M/L	H	
Simple bills	M	M		A	H/L	H	H		H/M	A	A		A			A
Simple bills with change				M/L	M/L	H	H/L		A	H	A	A	H/M	H		A
Shopping: problem sums, no fractions		H		A		H/M						H/M				
Bills involving multiples of a given item(s), e.g., 3 buns at 2p per bun	H		H	A	H/M	H		H/L	H	M/L		H/M		L		A
Bills involving fractional multiples of an item(s), e.g. 1½ kg of sugar at 20p per kg			H		H/M					H						

procedures. Such contrasts may be observed in Class 12, where the high and mid-attainers covered four steps before encountering simple bills. The low attainers, on the other hand, had no such preparation.

Again, some classes covered more procedures than others. Classes 11 and 13, for example, only considered two topics while classes 5, 10 and 12 did seven.

Examination of work on other topics shows similar contrasts between and within classes, and yet no class appears to be systematic across all topics. Thus one class, for example, might have a finely sequenced curriculum in the topic of addition but not in subtraction, while another class might have exactly the opposite.

To summarise, there was a wide variety in curriculum coverage both within and between classes and in terms of both content and structure.

CASE STUDIES IN CURRICULUM COVERAGE

The detailed way in which provision varied for different children may be illustrated by reference to records of the work covered by particular target children. This is done in the following sections.

Matthew and Ian

Matthew and Ian were two low-attaining children in different classes. They were of similar levels of attainment as indicated by performance on a standardised number test: Matthew scored 90 and Ian scored 95. They were both considered to be low attainers by their respective teachers. The children were of similar social backgrounds and both attended similar primary schools. Their number curricula for the Spring term are shown in Table 5.6.

It is apparent that, apart from brief references to money and length, most of Matthew's work focused on addition and subtraction in various guises. Additionally, he revisited procedures in a form of cyclical curriculum. Thus, in the three months he met horizontal addition three times, money recognition twice and addition of tens and units three times. There was little evident progress in his experience in these elements of work.

In contrast, Ian's curriculum had a broader range. A wider variety of topics was covered. Additionally, Ian's work seemed to progress during the term. He moved from basic number ideas and names through small-scale addition onto number bonds up to 18. Ian did not reach as far in the hierarchy of four rules work as Matthew, who had progressed as far as adding tens and units. Ian had, however, a much more diversified experience of shape, capacity and measurement.

TABLE 5.6
The Mathematics Curricula of Two Low-Attaining Children for the
Spring Term

Matthew's Curriculum	Ian's Curriculum
January	
1. Horizontal addition of three units, e.g. 6 + 1 + 2 = ____	1. Odd and even numbers, i.e., colouring the odd numbers in a 100 square
2. Addition and subtraction in written form, e.g. seven − one =	2. Time: 5 minutes to and 5 minutes past the hour
3. Money: recognition of 1p, 2p, 5p and 10p	3. Odd and even numbers, e.g. 21 → odd 10 → even
4. Vertical addition of tens and units (no carrying figure), e.g. $\begin{array}{cc} T & U \\ 2 & 3 \\ +7 & 4 \\ \hline \end{array}$	4. Shape: properties of squares, circles, triangles and rectangles
5. Mental arithmetic: number bonds up to ten	5. More than and less than, e.g. 4 ____ 10
February	
6. Horizontal addition of units, e.g. 2 + 6 =	6. Time: different ways of recording time, e.g. 10.05 → 5 minutes past 10
7. Vertical addition of tens and units (as item 4)	7. Shape: properties of octagons, pentagons, ellipses and hexagons
8. Horizontal addition and subtraction of units, e.g. 5 − 3 → ____	8. Addition: counting on, e.g. count on 6: 4 $\overset{+6}{\to}$ ____
9. Mental arithmetic: counting in twos	9. Capacity: concepts of "full", "½ full" and "¼ full"
	10. Horizontal addition of three numbers up to twenty, e.g. 10 + 3 + 6 = ____
March	
10. Horizontal addition and subtraction of units (as item 8)	11. Capacity: practical recording activities involving the nature of a litre in different containers
11. Mental arithmetic: length: spans, "longer and shorter than a metre"	12. Money: addition and subtraction of half pences, e.g. 7p + ½p =
12. Money: recognition of 1p, 2p, 5p and 10p	13. Composition of tens and units, e.g. 22 = ____ tens and ____ units
13. Vertical addition of tens and units	14. Number bonds: ways of making 8, 13 and 18
	15. Money: horizontal addition of three coins, e.g. 10p + 2p + ½p = ____
	16. Measurement: practical recording activities involving measurement of lines in centimetres

Interestingly, Matthew scored 100% on an end-of-term test of his number work—a score which might suggest he could have coped with a more challenging curriculum. Ian was not so proficient. He had problems in dealing with questions on the properties of shapes, the notions of odd and even and number bonds with quantities over 10.

It seems from these two examples at least that the number experience provided for a child has less to do with his level of attainment or proficiency than with the scheme which happens to operate in the school he attends.

Lillian and Maria

These two high-attaining girls scored 136 and 138 respectively on a standardised number test. As with Ian and Matthew, they were similar in most major respects. The only important difference in this context was that they attended different schools. Their Spring term curricula are shown in Table 5.7.

Both children did a lot of work on addition and subtraction. However, Lillian met these in the forms of both horizontal and vertical layout while

TABLE 5.7
The Mathematics Curricula of Two High-Attaining Children in the Spring Term

Lillian's Curriculum	*Maria's Curriculum*
January	
1. Vertical addition of tens and units (no carrying figure), e.g. $\begin{array}{r} T\ U \\ 2\ 0 \\ +1\ 7 \\ \hline \end{array}$	1. Horizontal multiplication of tens and units by two and three, e.g. $42 \times 2 =$ ___
2. "More than" and "less than", e.g. $15 > 10$	2. Horizontal division of tens and units by two and three, e.g. $39 \div 3 =$ ___
3. Vertical subtraction of tens and units (no decomposition), e.g. $\begin{array}{r} T\ U \\ 2\ 6 \\ -1\ 1 \\ \hline \end{array}$	3. Linear measure, e.g. The red line is ___ cms. $\vdash\!\!\overset{\text{red}}{\rule{4cm}{0pt}}\!\!\dashv$
4. Time: $\frac{1}{4}$ to and $\frac{1}{4}$ past the hour. Minutes to and past the hour.	4. Time: minutes past the hour, i.e. 5, 10, 20 and 25 minutes past.
5. Composition of 5 pence, e.g. $2p + 1p +$ ___ $= 5p$	
6. Place value, e.g. 13 is ___ tens and ___ units.	

TABLE 5.7
(*Continued*)

Lillian's Curriculum	Maria's Curriculum
February	
7. Horizontal addition and subtraction of units, e.g. $9 - 4 =$ ___; $1 + 5 =$ ___	5. Horizontal addition of tens and units (with a carrying figure), e.g. $63 + 28 =$ ___
8. Vertical addition of tens and units (with a carrying figure) e.g. $\begin{array}{cc} T & U \\ 1 & 7 \\ +1 & 3 \\ \hline \end{array}$	6. Horizontal subtraction of tens and units (with decomposition), e.g. $68 - 29 =$ ___
9. Money: bills (including multiple items), e.g. a kite at 16p = 3 marbles at 2p each = ___ total ___	7. Fractions e.g. (i) $\frac{1}{2}$ of 4 is ___ (ii) "There are 12 birds. $\frac{1}{2}$ fly away. How many are left?" ___
	8. Time: minutes to the hour, i.e. 5, 10, 20 and 25 minutes to.
March	
10. Horizontal addition of units, e.g. $8 + 7 =$ ___	9. Horizontal multiplication of tens and units by two and three (with a carrying figure), e.g. $38 \times 2 =$ ___
11. Vertical subtraction of tens and units (with decomposition), e.g. $\begin{array}{cc} T & U \\ 4 & 6 \\ -2 & 7 \\ \hline \end{array}$	10. Horizontal division of tens and units by two and three (with a carrying figure but no remainders), e.g. $51 - 3 =$ ___
12. Time: revision of item 4	11. Perimeters, e.g. The perimeter of the square is ___cms.
13. Money: bills (including change), e.g. 3 buns at 1p each = ___ 1 cake at 24p = ___ total ___ change from 50p ___	12. Horizontal addition and subtraction of tens and units (with a carrying figure)
14. Money: introduction of half pences, e.g. $5p - 3\frac{1}{2}p =$ ___	13. Partners of eleven and twelve, e.g. $1 +$ ___ 11 $6 +$ ___
15. Number sequences: consecutive numbers, e.g. 37, 38, ___, ___, ___, 42,	14. Time: earlier and later, e.g. $\frac{1}{2}$ hour later than 2 o'clock is ___
16. Horizontal subtraction (numbers less than twenty), e.g. $18 - 5 =$ ___	
17. Linear measurement, e.g. This line is ___ cms.	

Children in both schools did mental arithmetic in the basic rules from time to time.

Maria experienced only the horizontal format. Although both girls often worked on the same concepts. Maria met much more difficult examples. In horizontal addition, for instance, Lillian worked on calculations of the form 8 + 7, while Maria worked with 63 + 28.

Maria's curriculum extended way beyond Lillian's in other respects also, since she did work on both multiplication and division.

Another difference in the provision of these children's number experience lies in the degree to which the introduction of particular ideas was staggered. For example, in learning about clock time, Lillian spent 8 days in January covering all the basic aspects of minutes to and past the hour. These ideas were revised 2 months later. In contrast, Maria spent two sessions in January on minutes past the hour, two sessions in February on minutes to the hour and two sessions in March on the notions of "earlier" and "later than." Thus, although the syllabuses of both children covered similar aspects of time, the actual experiences of learning the time were rather different.

As in the case of Matthew and Ian, the differences in provision for Lillian and Maria seem to rest on decisions made at the school level. Despite this difference in provision both girls performed well in their end-of-term tests, Lillian scoring 96% and Maria 93%.

Christopher and John

The above examples show between-school differences in curriculums. Similar differences may be found within any particular class. Christopher was a high attainer and John a low attainer in the same infant classroom. Christopher scored 136 on the standardised test of number; John scored 102.

Table 5.8 shows the curriculum experienced by these two children. Both children had a relatively narrow curriculum in comparison with that offered in other schools in the project.

Even on this narrow front there is very little overlap between the experiences of the two boys. One topic, time, was studied in common. This was taught as a class lesson. That apart, the result of individualised teaching led to almost total differentiation of the curriculum.

Additionally, the two boys had very different routines for their progress in number work. John worked on a procedure for 5 or 6 days and then returned to it a week or two later. Christopher, on the other hand, began new work every 3 or 4 days and, with the exception of vertical division, never revised anything.

What the boys had in common was a strong emphasis on routine calculations involving some or all of the four rules.

TABLE 5.8
Number Curricula for High and Low-Attaining Boys in the Same Class

Christopher (a high attainer)	*John* (a low attainer)
Week beginning	
April 27th	
1. Vertical multiplication of tens and units by two (no carrying figure), e.g. $\begin{array}{cc} T & U \\ 1 & 4 \\ \times & 2 \\ \hline \end{array}$	1. Vertical addition of tens and units (with a carrying figure), e.g. $\begin{array}{cc} T & U \\ 1 & 4 \\ +2 & 7 \\ \hline \end{array}$
May 4th	
2. Vertical subtraction of tens and units (with decomposition), e.g. $\begin{array}{cc} T & U \\ 5 & 2 \\ -1 & 9 \\ \hline \end{array}$	
3. Time: o'clock, minutes past and to the hour	2. Time: o'clock, minutes past and to the hour
May 11th	
4. Horizontal multiplication by two, three and four, e.g. $9 \times 2 \times$ ____	3. Vertical subtraction of tens and units (with decomposition), e.g. $\begin{array}{cc} T & U \\ 3 & 1 \\ -1 & 6 \\ \hline \end{array}$
5. Vertical multiplication of tens and units by two (with a carrying figure), e.g. $\begin{array}{cc} T & U \\ 1 & 6 \\ \times & 6 \\ \hline \end{array}$	4. Horizontal multiplication by two, three, and four e.g. $7 \times 3 =$ _____
May 18th	
6. Vertical division of tens and units (no carrying figure), e.g. $4\overline{)48}$	
Half term ———————————	
June 8th	
7. Vertical division of tens and units (as item 6)	5. Vertical subtraction of tens and units (with decomposition) (as item 3)
June 15th	
8. Vertical addition of hundreds, tens and units (with a carrying figure), e.g. $\begin{array}{ccc} H & T & U \\ 2 & 6 & 9 \\ +1 & 2 & 4 \\ \hline \end{array}$	6. Horizontal multiplication by two, three and four (as item 4)

TABLE 5.8
(*Continued*)

Christopher (a high attainer)	*John* (a low attainer)

June 22nd

9. Vertical subtraction of hundreds,
   tens and units (with decomposition),
   e.g. $H\ T\ U$
   $$\begin{array}{r} 1\ 3\ 8 \\ -\ \ \ 2\ 9 \\ \hline \end{array}$$

10. Money: bills with change, e.g. How
    much change from £1 when I buy:
    4 oranges at 5p each =
    1 banana at 3½p =
    1 kg. apples at 60p = _____
    _____

DIFFERENTIATION IN THE CURRICULUM: A QUANTITATIVE ASSESSMENT

The total number of different maths procedures observed in the 16 classes throughout the two terms was 133. As has been illustrated, different classes and children at different levels of attainment covered very different samples of these procedures. Table 5.9 shows these differences.

It is worth recalling that the notion of a procedure refers to many qualitatively different processes (see Tables 5.3, 5.4 and 5.5 for examples). Additionally, considering individual procedures met is probably less important for the child's construction of mathematics than considering the families or structured sequences in which he met them. For these reasons Table 5.9 pools many "unlikes." Its useful purpose, however, is to give some indication of the quantitative scale of differences in materials covered between and within classes.

TABLE 5.9
The Average Number of Procedures Covered by Target Children at
Different Levels of Attainment in Two Terms

Attain-ment Level	Class																
	1	2	3	4	5	6	7	8	9	10	11	12	13	14	15	16	*Mean*
High	27	22	35	38	51	38	42	29	30	33	30	40	22	26	32	44	35
Mid	23	18	25	34	42	35	28	21	29	22	29	42	21	25	28	39	29
Low	12	17	28	29	32	12	28	26	24	20	27	23	19	18	30	36	24

Some classes, in these terms, covered less than half the procedures studied by other classes. Within-class variations are striking. In Class 6, for example, the high attainers covered more than three times the procedures of the low attainers. On average, high attainers worked on 35 procedures, mid-attainers on 29 and low attainers on 24. There is no clear reason why Class 6 should be radically different from this pattern. The attainment range (as assessed by the standardised test) was normal. The differences most likely have their origins in teachers' decisions on individualisation.

Another way of looking at the differentiation of the curriculum within classes is to examine the number of procedures covered in common by children at all levels of attainment as a proportion of procedures met uniquely by the children at different levels. The lower this proportion, the greater would be the degree of curriculum differentiation. Suppose, for example, that in a particular class the top attainers covered 25 procedures, the mid-attainers 20 and the low attainers 15. Suppose also that five of these procedures were covered by all levels. Then the index of differentiation expressed as a percentage (common procedures divided by unique procedures) would, in this case, be: $5 \div (20 + 15 + 10)$, i.e., 11%. If however, the number of common procedures had been 10, then the index of differentiation would have been 33%, i.e., $10 \div (15 + 10 + 5)$.

The indices must be interpreted with caution since the same index could be derived in a number of different ways. For example, an index of 33% could also reflect the curriculums in a class where fifteen procedures were covered by all attainment levels and each of the attainment levels covered fifteen unique procedures (i.e., index $= 15 \div (15 + 15 + 15)$. Nevertheless such an index provides a useful indication of the overlap of curriculums for different attainment levels.

Table 5.10 shows the differentiation index for the 16 classes. Classes 2 and 10 had highly differentiated curriculums as shown by their low differentiation indexes. Children at different levels of attainment not only covered different numbers of procedures, they covered largely different procedures. In contrast, the index for Classes 11 and 16 shows that in the 2 terms many of the procedures covered were met by all attainment groups. Interestingly, if the classes are ranked in order of the degree of differentiation, six of the eight most differentiated curricula were in infant

TABLE 5.10
Curriculum Differentiation Index for the Project Classes

Class	1	2	3	4	5	6	7	8	9	10	11	12	13	14	15	16
Differentiation Index (%)	39	10	27	28	31	18	43	42	48	11	65	25	48	46	19	58

schools as opposed to primary schools. Perhaps the infant school philosophy of individualisation lives most strongly in schools uniquely devoted to infants.

The case studies illustrated not only an interesting diversity of experience but also a strong degree of uniformity of concern amongst teachers to provide a core of work with routine calculations using the four rules of number (see Table 5.2). That being said, the diversity shown provokes a number of issues.

First, it must be said that diversity per se is neither a "good" nor a "bad" thing. However, the consequences of this differential provision are largely unkown. Whilst all the children cited here may be said to have "done the basics," it is clear that this has a potentially bewildering variety of meanings. The children were all happy and confident with their experiences. This is not at issue. What is at issue is what position these experiences put the children in with respect to subsequent mathematics learning. Secondly, it raises questions about what might have been for particular pupils. If Ian and Maria could cope with wide-ranging mathematics curriculums, what might Matthew and Lillian have achieved in the same situation? Is this differential provision justifiable?

The diversity appeared to come about from two sources. In part it arose from the schemes which schools or teachers opted to use. Secondly, it arose from decisions class teachers made on the individualisation of instruction. Thus, children were very much at the mercy of the class teacher. The major implication from this might be that arrangements be made to reduce the isolation of class teachers and to provide opportunities for them to compare case studies of work done in their class with that done by children in similar classes elsewhere. In this way perhaps teachers would have to make explicit some of the assumptions underlying their decisions and be alerted to possibilities and problems.

PERFORMANCE ON THE CURRICULUM

Each target child was tested at the end of each term on his performance in number.

In the face of the wide diversity of curriculum experience illustrated above it would have been inappropriate to assess terminal performance using a common test. Such an instrument would have been selectively invalid for all pupils since it would have been valid only insofar as the items on the test matched the individual's curriculum experience.

As an alternative to standardised testing, individual number tests were designed for each of the target children. The aim of this individually tailored testing programme was to ascertain how much and what particular aspects of their number work had been retained by the children.

The procedure required two days per class, the first day in acquiring a test specification and the second for test administration. The test specification was created by collecting and inspecting all the completed written work of each target child supplemented by conversations with the teacher to ascertain the type of oral work completed which had not been represented in the written work. On completion of the test specifications they were discussed with the class teacher to ensure validity.

Test specifications were represented as in the following example:

Test Specification—Paul (a mid-attainer in the top infant class of a primary school)

Type of task	Date(s) when tasks done
1. Area: perimeters, e.g., measuring the perimeters of surfaces using paces	28/4/81, 6/5/81, 13/5/81, 20/5/81.
2. Multiplication: horizontal multiplication of tens and units by two, three, four and five (no carrying figure), e.g., 32 × 3 =	29/4/81, 1/5/81, 5/5/81, 12/6/81, 22/6/81, 23/6/81.
3. Addition: horizontal addition of tens and units (with a carrying figure), e.g., 35 + 19 =	6/5/81, 8/5/81, 11/5/81, 12/5/81, 20/5/81, 21/5/81, 22/5/81, 13/6/81, 15/6/81, 18/6/81, 19/6/81.
4. Time: 5 minutes past and to the hour	7/5/81, 14/5/81, 21/5/81, 10/6/81, 14/6/81, 24/6/81.
5. Subtraction: horizontal subtraction of tens and units (with a carrying figure)	8/6/81, 9/6/81, 11/6/81, 12/6/81, 15/6/81, 16/6/81, 17/6/81.
6. Simple graphs	3/6/81, 10/6/81.
7. Measurement: practical measuring of lines in centimetres	17/6/81, 24/6/81.
8. Division: horizontal division of tens and units by two, three, four and five (no carrying figure), e.g., 39 ÷ 3 =	24/6/81, 25/6/81, 6/7/81, 7/7/81, 8/7/81.
9. Money: composition of coins, e.g., 4 ½p coins = ___ p.	1/7/81, 6/7/81, 8/7/81.

TEST CONSTRUCTION

On the basis of the specification questions were developed for each child. Originally it was decided that the number of questions of each type of task should be representative of the number of days spent on each particular topic; however, it was found that this tended to result in rather unwieldy tests which took considerable time to complete. Furthermore, it soon became apparent that if a child had grasped a particular concept he usually demonstrated this when tackling the first question on a given topic, making subsequent questions redundant. It was decided, therefore, that the tests should comprise one question per type of task covered in the syllabus. It would be unrealistic to presume that this was always a satisfactory method to adopt, however, as it is relatively easy to make an arithmetic error and in many cases a child's response would not reflect whether he had merely made a slip in his calculations or there was a fundamental flaw in his understanding. Thus, in cases where a child made an incorrect response, a back-up question was used which required the same conceptual understanding as the original and which provided the child with a further opportunity to demonstrate his ability to tackle a given type of calculation.

To ensure the maximum possible curriculum validity the tests consisted of items which the child had already successfully completed during the course of the term.

Finally, taking all the above points into consideration, a mathematics tests was written for each of the target children. The format of each depended largely on the format of the original work and the aim of a particular question. A specification such as that shown earlier resulted in the following test.

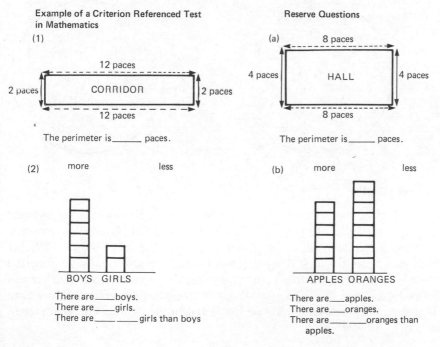

Example of a Criterion Referenced Test in Mathematics

(1)

12 paces

2 paces   CORRIDOR   2 paces

12 paces

The perimeter is_____ paces.

(2)   more   less

BOYS GIRLS

There are____boys.
There are____girls.
There are____ ____ girls than boys

Reserve Questions

(a)   8 paces

4 paces   HALL   4 paces

8 paces

The perimeter is_____ paces.

(b)   more   less

APPLES ORANGES

There are____apples.
There are____oranges.
There are____ ____oranges than apples.

(3)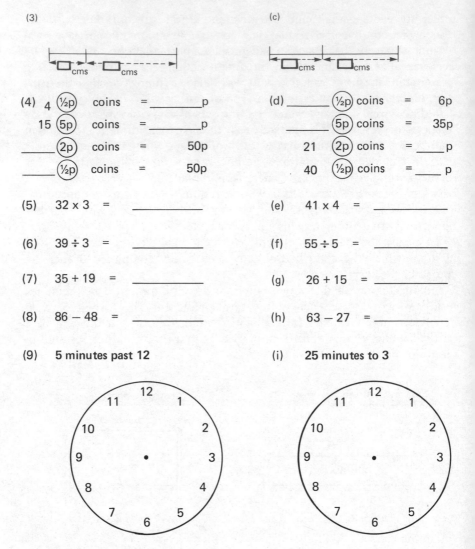

(c)

(4) 4 (½p) coins = _____p

15 (5p) coins = _____p

_____ (2p) coins = 50p

_____ (½p) coins = 50p

(d) _____ (½p) coins = 6p

_____ (5p) coins = 35p

21 (2p) coins = ____p

40 (½p) coins = ____p

(5) 32 x 3 = _____

(e) 41 x 4 = _____

(6) 39 ÷ 3 = _____

(f) 55 ÷ 5 = _____

(7) 35 + 19 = _____

(g) 26 + 15 = _____

(8) 86 − 48 = _____

(h) 63 − 27 = _____

(9) **5 minutes past 12**

(i) **25 minutes to 3**

Administration of the Tests

With the cooperation of the teachers the tests were individually administered by the Research Officer or a trained fieldworker in a morning session. Each test lasted approximately 20 minutes, the time being dependent on the test length and the child's ability. In scoring the children's responses to the tests, one point was awarded for each correct procedure. Thus, if a child got "42–10" wrong but correctly answered the supplementary question "37–10" he would score one point. In cases of ambiguity (for example, on children's reversals in writing numbers or on the correct use of units, e.g. cm) the item was referred to the class teacher.

It must be emphasised that the tests were not intended to assess whether children understood number. The post-task interviews had focused on that issue. Rather, the intention was to ascertain whether he could reproduce the routines he had been taught.

Test Performance

The results of the tests are shown in Table 5.11. The numbers in each box represent the number of procedures correctly produced as a percentage of the number of procedures tested.

In general the scores were very high. On average the high attainers, scored in excess of 90%. Taken at face value this is an achievement of which to be proud. It is worth asking however, whether the higher attainers were being challenged or whether the high scores were a consequence of cautious aspiration.

Low attainers scored 75% on average. Again, this is open to contradictory interpretations. Any secondary school would be proud of this as an achievement for its low attainers. At the infant stage however it means that a large fraction of the foundations of mathematics was very insecure amongst these children. They met problems very early.

Five classes (numbers 2, 4, 6, 10 and 15) obtained an overall average score in excess of 90%. It is noteworthy that the first four of these were in infant schools. Thus, not only did the infant schools present a more differentiated curriculum than primary schools, they were also more successful at what they attempted.

Performance and Differentiation

The general relationship between differentiation and overall success is shown in Table 5.12.

Each class is shown in its appropriate category. Four of the six lowest attaining classes had relatively undifferentiated curricula whilst four of the highest six attaining classes had highly differentiated curricula.

Performance and Attainment Level

Not only was there a wide variation between schools—one scoring an average of 94% and another of 56%—but, in some schools, there was also a considerable difference in the scores between each attainment level. In six schools for example the top attainers scores were more than 20% higher than those of the low attainers. The average scores for children at different levels of attainment are shown in Table 5.13.

TABLE 5.11

Average Percentage Scores on Individually Tailored Tests of Two Terms Number Work

Average Scores	Class																Average
	1	2	3	4	5	6	7	8	9	10	11	12	13	14	15	16	
High attainers	96	95	75	94	93	100	91	91	84	94	98	89	100	83	95	94	92
Mid attainers	81	97	44	85	78	86	81	91	71	95	76	87	91	82	92	64	81
Low attainers	81	80	49	90	60	95	86	66	64	90	73	74	75	66	89	64	75
All six target children	86	91	56	90	77	94	86	83	73	93	82	83	89	77	92	74	83

TABLE 5.12
Relative Curriculum Differentiation and Success on Tailored Terminal
Tests

		Relative differentiation	
		Higher	Lower
Relative success	Higher	2, 4, 6, 10, 15	1, 7, 13.
	Lower	3, 5, 12.	8, 9, 11, 14, 16.

TABLE 5.13
Range of Cover and Degree of Success in the Number Curriculum by
Children at Different Levels of Attainment

Level of Attainment	Average Number of Procedures Covered	Average % Success On Tests
High	35	92
Mid	29	81
Low	24	75

Had the children been given standard norm referenced tests one might predict such a difference between attainment groups. As, however each test was designed specifically to assess the procedures that the child being tested had covered during the course of the term, the results are provocative.

Even though low attainers covered only two-thirds as much work as the high attainers, this degree of differentiation did not enable them to perform at the levels of success achieved by the higher attainers, nor did it remove the incidence of both over and underestimation.

The teachers claimed that children moved "at their own rate" through the number scheme. This raises questions about what "rate" referred to. The rate seemed too fast for some children's assimilative capacities and too slow for others. Rate thus seemed to refer to "rate of performance" rather than "rate of understanding" or "rate of assimilation."

Matching and Curriculum Outcomes

As discussed in Chapter 4 some teachers were considerably better at matching individual number tasks than others. The criterion used to determine whether a task was matched or not was whether the work was appropriate to the child's level of understanding. If it were not then the task was deemed an underestimation if it was not advancing the child's

TABLE 5.14
The Distribution of Schools by Level of Matching and Test Scores

	End of Term Tests	
	Higher Success	Lower Success
Higher level of matching	4, 6, 10, 13	5, 12, 14
Lower level of matching	1, 2, 7, 15	3, 8, 9, 11, 16

conceptual understanding or an overestimation if it was beyond the child's level of comprehension.

In contrast, the end of term tests assessed not levels of understanding but the children's ability to recall and perform procedures acquired during the course of the term. Are the two related? Did the children in classes where there was a higher level of matching—and hence understanding—perform better on procedural recall and performance than those who were frequently mismatched?

Table 5.14 suggests that there was a slight tendency for higher test scores to be associated with higher levels of matching. Somewhat surprising however, the tendency is only slight.

Children performed well in four classes in which there was a relatively low level of matching: concurrent measures showing that children were being either over or underestimated were not consistent with terminal assessments of the ability to reproduce procedures encountered.

A less ambiguous measure of comprehension is provided by the incidence of overestimation found in each class. It might be expected that a high incidence of overestimation (i.e., a high incidence of incomprehensible number tasks), would result in poor performance on end of term tests. This, in fact, was not the case. Classes with high levels of overestimation were as likely to do better than average on terminal tests as classes with lower than average levels of overestimation. Additionally, classes in which there was a higher rate of overestimation and yet in which higher than average performance was observed, did not necessarily cover a narrower curriculum. Thus, whilst it was shown that the concurrent consequences of mismatching were unacceptable in terms of the child's comprehension, in the longer term, mismatching appears to have little impact on children's capacities to reproduce number procedures.

Performance and Width of Curriculum

Do children held to a narrower curriculum retain more of their procedural skills than those who cover a wider curriculum? Does laying a narrow foundation mean laying a firm foundation of mathematics procedures at this stage? Analysis of the data shows that the width of curriculum cover appeared to make little difference to the high attainers' success on the tests. Four high attaining groups scored well with a wide curriculum coverage and six did relatively well with a narrower curriculum.

However, both mid and low attainers tended to perform better with a narrow curriculum. For example six out of nine mid attainers with a narrow curriculum scored above average on their tests but only three out of seven of those with a wide curriculum coverage had the same success. A similar trend held for low attainers.

Such considerations might partially explain why some children performed better than others but they do not account for the exceptions. For example, despite a wide curriculum for the class all the target children in class 4 performed well on their tests. On the other hand, with the exception of the mid attainers, children in class 14, which had a narrow curriculum, did rather worse than average.

PROVIDING QUALITY MATHS EXPERIENCES

In the terms adopted here, providing a quality mathematics experience on a day to day basis entails minimising the amount of mismatching between task demands and children's attainments. It might be expected that one of the outcomes of this experience would be the successful performance on terminal tests. It was shown earlier that this expectation is not sustained by the data. Several classes had better than average terminal performances with worse than average matching records (classes 1, 2, 7, and 15 for example). These classes however, had a relatively narrow curriculum coverage.

With the additional criterion of a wide curriculum in mind, two teachers (classes 4 and 6) appear to have been particularly successful in providing mathematics experience. Children at all levels of attainment in class 4 not only performed better than average, they covered a wider than average curriculum. The children in class 6 also performed better than average at all levels of attainment and had a wider than average curriculum for the high and mid attainers but the narrowest of all curricula for the lower attainers.

Clases 4 and 6 had several features in common. They both had bigger than average class sizes and they had greater than average spans of ability. These features thus cannot be used to explain away their relatively successful performances.

Whilst school 6 had a predominantly middle class catchment area, school 4 recruited a predominance of working class children. Thus, for class 4, at least, the success cannot be attributed to special home background influences.

If special advantage does not account for the success of class 4, what does? Whilst it is not possible to give a definitive answer to this question it is possible to explore some potential factors and perhaps exclude others. Already excluded, for example, is the notion that special advantage is necessary to capitalise on a sound mathematics curriculum.

In terms of the notion of tasks, the scheme in operation becomes a serious candidate as a potentially powerful factor in the provision of number experience. In particular, the structure and sequence of the scheme might be considered to be important.

In asking whether one scheme more than another is likely to sustain steady progress in children's mathematical understanding, it is necessary to consider whether topics are covered in finely graded steps and whether tasks are met in a close-order sequence in a hierarchy. But children do not meet schemes in classrooms. They meet only the tasks which teachers give them. Unfortunately there is no easy way of contrasting the sequences and structures of groups of tasks actually assigned to and worked by children in the classroom. It proves necessary to make subjective judgements on records of such tasks. It will be recalled that records of the procedures worked in the classes are shown in appendix A and that an examination of those in subtraction, division and money was made in Tables 5.3, 5.4 and 5.5. There it was concluded that no classes scheme-in-practice appeared to be consistently superior to that of other classes.

To underline this point reference may be made to Table 5.15 and 5.16 showing parts of the work experienced in the early stages of the addition of tens and units and clock time respectively. 1 and 2 refer to the high-attaining boy and girl respectively; 3 and 4 the mid-attaining boy and girl, and 5 and 6 the low-attaining boy and girl. These tables permit selective contrasts between classes 4 and 6 on the one hand and classes 3 and 5 on the other. These latter schools both had a wide curriculum cover and higher than average differentiation. Class 5 had the best matching record. In these respects classes 3 and 5 were similar to 4 and 6. The major difference however was that children in classes 3 and 5 were less able than average at reproducing their work at the end of term.

Examination of Table 5.15 shows no obvious inferiority in the structure of the work presented in classes 3 and 5. All the children in class 5 were given a detailed diet of work on tens and units. In contrast, apart from the high attaining girl, the highly successful children in class 4 did not appear to follow a detailed programme in this aspect of the curriculum. The mid and low attaining girls, for example, apparently jumped from the composition of tens and units to horizontal addition with carrying.

Similar contrasts can be made in the work on clock time. Classes 3 and 4

TABLE 5.15
Introductions to the Addition of Tens and Units as Covered by
Classes 3, 4, 5 and 6

Procedure	Class			
	3	4	5	6
Composition/decomposition of tens and units, e.g. 16 = ___tens and ___ units		1, 2, 3, 4, 5, 6	1	1, 2, 3, 4
Vertical addition of tens and units (no carrying figure)	1, 2, 3	2, 3	1, 2, 3, 4, 5, 6	1, 2, 3, 4
Horizontal addition of tens and units (no carrying figure)	1, 2, 3, 4, 5, 6	1, 2	1, 2, 3, 4, 6	1, 2, 3, 4
Vertical addition of tens and units (with a carrying figure)	1, 2	1, 2	1, 2, 3, 4, 5, 6	2, 3, 4
Horizontal addition of tens and units (with a carrying figure)	1, 2	4, 6	1, 2, 3, 4, 5, 6	

followed a very similar pattern with only the more able children doing the relatively advanced work. Children in class 3 however, fared far less well on terminal tests. All the children in class 5 covered (with the exception of "half past") the same topics as those in class 4. Again however, they were less successful at reproducing these procedures later.

TABLE 5.16
Work on Clock Time as Done by Classes 3, 4, 5 and 6

Procedure	Class			
	3	4	5	6
O'clock	1, 2, 3, 4, 5, 6	1, 2, 3, 4, 5, 6	1, 2, 3, 4, 5, 6	2
Preparing work for telling the time, e.g., colouring the quarter sections of clockface				
Half past	1, 2, 3, 4, 5, 6	1, 2, 3, 4, 5, 6	1	1, 3, 4
Quarter past	1, 2, 3, 4, 5, 6	1, 2, 3, 4, 5, 6	1, 2, 3, 4, 5, 6	1, 3, 4
Quarter to	1, 2, 3, 4, 5, 6	1, 2, 3, 4, 5, 6	1, 2, 3, 4, 5, 6	1, 3, 4
The 5 minute intervals past the hour	1, 2, 3, 4	1, 2, 3	1	
The 5 minute intervals to the hour	1, 2	1, 2, 3	1, 2, 3, 4, 5, 6	

These particular contrasts emphasise what a general examination revealed: no consistent differences in the structure of maths schemes-in-action were apparent. All the classes had a somewhat patchy record in respect of the structure of the number experience. Differences in relative success did not appear to be strongly related to differences in structure. It is perhaps important to stress that what is not being argued here is that detailed sequence is irrelevant. Rather, it appears to be the case that at the level of structure achieved in practice, differences between schools appeared slight and/or inconsistent. Differences in structure on the scale observed, did not appear to account for differences in relative success. There was, however, a striking difference in the way learning was managed in the two better classes. Each, in a different way contrasted with relatively less successful classes.

Class 6, it was revealed, had a middle class intake. The teacher adopted a "play safe" philosophy—especially with the low attainment groups. Her high level of differentiation was produced almost entirely by drastically narrowing the curriculum for the low attainers. The curriculum for these low attainers was the narrowest observed. She did not contemplate moving on with this group until she was sure they had grasped the process in hand. Not a single overestimating task was observed in her class. One third of her number tasks were underestimates.

In contrast, the teacher in class 4 had a relatively high level of overestimation and adopted a policy which might be described as persistently pushing forward whilst persistently looking back. In general, but particularly with lower attainers, tasks carried a revision rider. Thus a child would be given two cards, the first showing new work (on time, say) and the second some work on addition. What was remarkable about this was the persistence with which it was done. The revision policy was matched in its insistence by the urge to push on. The children each worked on their individual cards. Class instruction was minimal. But whatever the content of the card the teachers urged them to "choose cards you have not done before and work quickly." This urgency was matched with a great deal of individual attention—especially for the low attainers.

SUMMARY

Work on the four rules of number was heavily emphasised in all classes. A wide variety of supplementary material was covered in the 16 classes but the choice between classes varied considerably. The content of the curriculum as experienced by the children varied within each class—sometimes extensively so. Between-class and within-class curriculum provision did not seem to relate to any discernible characteristics of the children: rather it seemed to emanate from teachers' decisions on content and pace made in the design of their schemes.

Diversity was also evident in the structure of the experience provided for maths work. Structure (in terms of the relationships between families of procedures in the same content area) was very patchy.

High attainers evinced a very high degree of success in terms of the reproduction of procedures they had studied. Their near maximum scores on end of term tests, seen in conjunction with their high levels of underestimation, suggest a lack of challenge in their experience.

Even on measure of reproduction, low attainers had significant gaps in their competence. They covered a narrower curriculum and did it less well than high attainers. Whatever the degree of curriculum differentiation operating, it was clearly not profitting high or low attainers.

A large amount of pencil and paper work on routine calculations was seen. Whilst the tasks frequently had concrete support materials which demanded some form of manipulative work, the tasks lacked real-world practical relevance. Even the most successful class in which a wide curriculum, brisk pacing, and attention to progress and consolidation were evident, was marked by the lack of attention to genuine practical relevance in the maths experience provided.

6 The Language Curriculum

OVERVIEW

The aim in this chapter is to give some indication of the kinds of experiences provided for the children with the intention of improving their capacities in the use of language.

Detailed records were made of all the target children's work in language throughout two terms. Additionally observations were made of 205 tasks assigned to the target children. The majority of these tasks was centrally aimed at the development of writing skills. Thus, 54 of the tasks demanded topic writing, 39 creative writing, 10 news writing and 8 copy writing. The major distinction between topic writing and creative writing was that in the former, consequent upon observing a demonstration or listening to an account of some process or event (either from the teacher or the television), the child had to reproduce as much of the facts of the matter as he could. Creative writing tasks demanded that the child indulged in fiction. News writing, presumably, occupied a midway position on the fact/fiction dimension. Comprehension tasks were observed in 30 instances and 34 tasks focused on phonics or spelling. The bulk of the remainder of the tasks emphasised the enhancement of reading skills.

Whilst it may be considered that there is no easy distinction between the development of reading and writing skills, such a distinction was clearly and emphatically made in the teachers' expressions of intention. Writing tasks were to enhance writing skills whilst comprehension and phonics tasks were to enhance reading skills. Where, in these latter tasks, writing was involved, it served merely a recording purpose: there was no evidence of an integrated language curriculum in operation in any of the classrooms studied.

It is notable that of the 205 tasks only four focused on reading alone. This is not to say that little attention was paid to reading. Reading was an important activity which permeated the curriculum but during the observation period, reading tasks per se were rarely set to the target children in class. Reading was an activity which both teachers and children took up in and around other curriculum activities.

In terms of general provision the language curriculum differs from the mathematics curriculum in a number of important ways. In mathematics, the majority of tasks were individualised; children worked on their own number card at their particular point in the scheme. In language however, three quarters of the tasks were given as class lessons. In 80% of these cases the tasks were presented verbally by the teacher in a relatively extended task preamble which was frequently supported by pictures (50% of cases), work cards or books (32%) or television (14%).

Another distinctive feature of the language curriculum was that the majority of tasks did not come from sequenced and structured schemes. It will be recalled that more than three quarters of language tasks demanded that the children practised their skills. In the provision for practice, teachers generated their own ideas, in particular to stimulate writing. The effect of this was that 55% of tasks observed had their origins in the teacher's repertoire of stimulating ideas.

A further contrast arises from the nature of the task preambles in maths and language. Language tasks frequently had extended preambles involving the discussion and elaboration of the stimulus, the revision of key vocabulary and the reiteration of the teacher's rules for writing (referring to neatness, grammar, use of word books, spacing for example). In comparison, preambles to maths tasks were typically very short frequently taking the form of an exhortation to "get on with your cards."

One feature that language and number tasks had in common was the general nature of the teacher's intention for the task. Both in teacher interviews and in communicating the priorities of the tasks to children, the teachers stressed procedural rather than cognitive aims. The emphasis was thus on how the piece of work was to be produced and presented rather than on attempts to identify or discuss the general and deeper cognitive processes and objectives potentially involved in the tasks. With children of this age it might be considered that the teachers had little alternative to making matters concrete and such an argument is appealing. However, it is worth asking what price is paid for this in terms of the children's understanding of the nature of language demands in school and in the development of their taste for these.

What is suggested in this brief overview is that the provision of language experience at this stage was dominated by the provision of writing practice conducted as lessons which began with some stimulating activity planned from the teacher's repertoire of ideas. Like all summaries however, it belies the variety of form and content of the provision. The following sections describe these in some detail for the different aspects of the language curriculum.

TEACHING CHILDREN TO WRITE

Perhaps the most enduring problem faced by teachers in the management of learning is the large range of performance and response to experience exhibited by the learners in any one class. In respect of children's writing at this stage, the diversity of response is illustrated in the following examples. Ian was asked to recall the story told in that morning's assembly. In 42 minutes he wrote:

> Good meyd all thees lovlly things for us to see adn the badey leads wud liiek to now Jesus is the son of coo Cood.

In contrast, Peter was asked to recall the main events of a television programme shown to the class. He wrote:

> On television today we saw a very interesting programme about France and a town called Bauge. On Wednesday it is very quiet but on Thursday it is very noisy and it is very crowded. Because on Thursday it is Market Day. The people in France speak French. Also in the town there was a shop that sold sweets and bread. The bread in France is very long. They also showed us a church were weddings are held also there was a man who spoke French but also he could speak English and told us all about it. After a while he went home.

Peter produced this in a 21 minute burst of concentrated work. In contrast Ian's work had been fragmented by chatting and by diversions he searched out amongst his classmates. For these two children, the experience of writing was radically different.

In the face of this diversity, the teaching of writing might mean different things for different pupils. This was reflected to some degree in the teachers' aims when providing writing tasks. In some instances the aim was simply to increase children's motivation to write something. In others increasing vocabulary or increasing the imaginative content of writing was the central intention. For children who appeared to have a facility for writing the aim sometimes expressed was to write to some purpose—for example, to "report observation" or "develop awareness." Notwithstanding these sensitivities, the predominant aim expressed in more than 70% of tasks intended to promote writing was to "practise writing" and to use some aspects of grammer, especially capital letters and full stops as sentence markers.

In pursuit of this common and restricted set of aims the teachers used a wide range of stimulus events. Whilst the aims across classes were generally consistent, the specific content of writing experience was decidedly not so. Children were sometimes encouraged to write their own stories, to complete stories started by the teacher, to respond imaginatively to stimulus discussion dreams, dragons, travel, snowdrops and holidays and to report on a range of television and radio programmes, visits, or on teachers' demonstrations of, for example, the action of volcanoes, floating and sinking and cookery.

Despite the diversity of expressed aims and manifest contents more than 70% of the 113 tasks aimed at the development of writing skills conformed to a single pattern. In this routine the teacher arranged the presentation of some stimulus event. There followed a revision of the salient features of the event, as identified by the teachers. This was achieved by question and answer sessions during which key words were put on the board. The teacher then asked the children to write their own account of the events and emphasised neatness and one or two points of grammar in the production of the children's scripts. Interchanges between the teacher and class during the process of writing were dominated by requests on the part of the children for spellings. The routine was completed by the teachers' evaluations of the children's work. These evaluations focused on neatness, quantity and other concrete aspects of the product. This pattern proceeded regardless of the teachers expressed aims.

The child's role as a writer was in these ways closely constrained. Even in cases of the imaginative and opportunistic choices of stimulating events or features, lively discussions were followed by routinised writing demands. For example, one teacher had planned to use the story of "Fred the Dragon" as stimulus but discovered that the children were fascinated by a spider in the classroom. She initiated a discussion on spiders, produced a spider story and some appropriate pictures. When the issue of writing arose however, the teacher had the children copy sentences from the blackboard as a preliminary to writing their own material on spiders. The target child took 15 minutes to copy the 33 words and a further 41 minutes to write 39 words of his own. The teacher was not happy with this and suggested that his poor home life resulted in his lack of concentration.

As has been noted, the predominant aims for writing tasks referred to developments in the use of simple grammar and to the increase in quantity of children's writing. However, even where greater aspirations were considered, the management of the writing events, conforming as they predominantly did to the archetypal pattern described above, failed to convert aspiration into practice. Many discrepancies between aspiration and practice were noteworthy in this respect. In one case, for example, in an endeavour to motivate a very low attaining child to write, a teacher dictated sentences to him, one at a time. The sentences related to a picture of a dog she had put on the blackboard. In another instance the teacher was of the opinion that the target child, "will do very little writing on his own. He gets totally lost. I'm lucky if I get one sentence. He won't even verbalise what he wants to write." To motivate his writing the teacher had him, in common with the rest of his class, listen to a Bible story and then copy part of the story from the blackboard. On completion of this the target child was asked to write about ways he could make friends with people he did not like.

There were exceptions to the pattern described above. These exceptions showed teachers more realistically responding to the attainments and interests of individual children and endeavouring to steer closer to their aims.

In one instance for example, the target child showed little interest in the teacher's stimulus event (intended to motivate the child to write something) in part because she could think of little other than her mother's new baby. The teacher capitalised on this and invited the girl to write about the little sister. In half an hour the girl wrote a long string of coherent script. Whilst she omitted all spacing and grammer the product was totally intelligible and started as follows: "mymumisinhospital . . .". The teacher was well pleased with this show of enthusiasm and industry.

A second instance of a teacher's attempt to respond to the writing problems of individual children took place when the headteacher took a class to cover for a teacher's absence. His general aim for the lesson was to stimulate a piece of creative writing. The lesson started with a discussion of what one might do if someone fell into the canal. Various responses were acted out. The headteacher put key words on the blackboard and then said to the class "I want you to write a story about someone falling into the canal. Tell me exactly what you did. Try to keep it in sequence. Try not to say 'and then', 'and then'. Try to make your story really exciting."

It quickly became apparent to the headteacher (who, it must be emphasised, was not familiar with the work of the children in the class) that Alan could not respond well to this task. Alan's initial attempts were minimal. The headteacher therefore asked Alan to draw a picture of what happened first and then to say what the picture showed. He then wrote down Alan's sentence in a jumbled word order and asked him to "sort these words to build your sentence." In this fashion Alan produced two pictures and two sentences in one hour. In evaluating the work the headteacher was less worried by features of the product than by identifying Alan's special needs as a writer. Thus the headteacher in this instance endeavoured to retain his general aim (creativity and sequenced account) whilst tailoring the task for a particular child.

Such attempts at sensitive tailoring were unfortunately extremely rare. Rather, the occasionally provocative thoughts and aspirations teachers had in regard to children's writing stood in stark contrast to the undifferentiated pedagogic tools for achieving their aims. For example, it was impossible to distinguish between tasks aimed at developing imaginative writing and tasks aimed at writing reports. Similar stimuli were provided, similar instructions with heavy emphasis on presentation were given and similar evaluations followed. Neither sets of evaluations referred to imagination or observation and recall: both referred to presentation, quantity and grammar.

The routine described above was not only undisturbed by different aims, it was insensitive in the face of different levels of attainment. Day-to-day observation and end of term records both confirm that in this aspect of language teaching all ability levels met the same kinds of experience and demand. The approach was undiscriminating in providing support for the less competent pupils and uninformed in the development of the more competent.

Despite, or perhaps because of, the almost total predictability of the daily writing event the children were very frequently interested and industrious. They were clear about what would please their teachers. They recognised and were able to rate neatness as an important criterion and strove to finish another page to fulfil their quantity quota. Only in two cases were reservations articulated. When asked if the teacher would like his work one child said, "Don't know, she never seems to tell me." And when asked whether she enjoyed her writing, one high attainer burst forth with, "No! I'm fed up of doing the same thing every day—writing, writing, writing. All you do is write down words."

PROGRESS IN WRITING

In order to chart the progress of this important skill in the children in this study it was necessary to conduct a complementary study concerned with identifying the extent and nature of the development of writing in response to task demands similar to those met in infant classrooms.

As noted earlier the teachers all tended to introduce a stimulus, used to generate interest, accompanied by an oral preamble and discussion followed by a writing requirement. It was decided therefore to use a tape-slide sequence as the common stimulus based on interesting and topical stories which were not familiar to the children in the 16 classrooms. This was first administered in the schools in January 1981 and again in June of the same year. Thus in choosing the stories it was also necessary to keep in mind that the exercise was to be repeated. After consultations with independent teacher groups and pilot testing it was decided that different stories would be preferable for the January and June testings. This in turn led to issues relating to comparability of stories.

Two stories were selected. One related to a cartoon character Zap who makes a boat/car which can fly and he flies off into the sky. The other story was of a family of mice who are frightened by a cat and sail away to find an island. After a night on the island a shadowy figure appears on the beach. The text of both stories can be found in Appendix B.

Essentially both stories were similar, each comprising:

1. Approximately 340 words (340 Zap, 337 Island).
2. An essential knowledge base familiar to children.
3. Basic ideas likely to have been met before in some form or other.
4. An introduction grounded in the children's experience.
5. A sequential story containing 28 ideas.
6. An open ended finale.
7. A musical accompaniment before and after the story.
8. Twelve colour slides.

Administration

The procedure was administered by the class teachers with the assistance of a member of the research team. In order to assure uniformity across classrooms however the teachers were given precise instructions as to how to conduct the test. For example before the tape-slide sequence for the story of Zap they were asked to introduce it thus: "Today I have a story on tape. We are going to listen to the story and look at the pictures which go with the story, then you are going to do some writing. The story is called 'Zap and his flying machine.' "

And after the story teachers were asked to read the following: "I hope that you enjoyed the story about Zap and his flying machine. Write about what happened in the story and also about what kind of adventures Zap had. Can you write the story about Zap and his flying machine and about what might have happened to Zap afterwards?" The children were then given 25 minutes to write their stories.

As the research team was anxious to ascertain the children's level of writing development it was decided that they should perform the task completely unaided. Thus, contrary to common practice, they were given no help whatsoever in, for example, the formulation of ideas and spellings.

Assessment of Children's Writing

In order to look within and across performance some form of assessment was needed which would allow for discrimination in developmental terms as well as the documentation of status. The following sources of information were explored and used to generate categories for assessment.

1. The elicited views and observed practice of two able teachers and their respective headteachers, one in a formal situation, the other in an informal situation.
2. Analysis and evaluation of 6–7 year old children's scripts by a group of experienced practising teachers during 8 workshop sessions.
3. Categories extracted by 2 independent assessors from a batch of 6–7 year scripts.
4. Evaluation, using a first crude analysis of scripts by 5–8 year old children, in response to pilot sessions with 2 tape slide story stimuli.
5. Previous research studies.

All the categories generated and used in analysis will be discussed in detail elsewhere (Wilkinson, in preparation). However for the purposes of this analysis five main categories were considered. All the stories were scored independently by three experienced infant teachers. They focused on the following aspects of the children's work.

1. The length of the story.
2. The use of ideas. The number of different ideas was counted: each being classified as given or imaginative. For example "Zap thought he would make a flying machine" was in the original stimulus and was considered given whereas "Then suddenly two mighter big eyes apeared" was an extension of the story and was classed as imaginative.
3. The number of connectives used to link words, phrases or sentences. These included "who," "then" and "because" but, due to its almost universal usage, omitted "and."
4. The organisation of the story. Scripts were awarded a mark of 1 to 9 depending on the quality of their structure and organisation. Thus "mos hpe" scored a low mark but the story beginning "Zap saw a pere of godles. he was going to make a veickle First he thougt of what he was going to make . . ." did considerably better.

   Although no objective criteria could be given for scoring a story's organisation the judges agreed on the same mark in 83% of instances.
5. An overall assessment of the story focusing on its quality and content. A 5 point scale was used: 5 being awarded to stories which showed a sense of audience, read well and were, for the most part, correctly written. In contrast, stories with minimal content, little communication and no sense of audience were given 1. The markers agreed in 89% of cases.

The Quality of Children's Responses

As might be expected, the quality of the work produced varied considerably. Whilst this variance may be entirely expected it is important to appreciate fully its extent and the implications it has for the teacher in properly responding to the range of children in her class.

The examples below illustrate the scope of these performance differences. Mark's work is typical of a low performer on this task. In his 25 minutes in January he wrote:

One day, misd soq.

Other examples of low level performance are:

Onoes there was a boy c

and

supsmsnpn tucheoferthenases and oferthecarsandthepippei.

In contrast Gillian wrote:

Zap was a happy little fellow and he had'ent a care in the world. He made a machine that flied floated and it had wheels. Zap called his machine Zapobeel and got in it and began to fly in it his adventure was just beginning. He flew up up up in the air untill he met the sun hello shiny sun hello but the sun did not anser him oh well suit your self but I am off for an adventure and he flew on. He met Mrs black bird and he said hello Mrs black bird went tweet tweet tweet then he flew higher than the clouds and when he looked down he saw a lake now it is time for the boat bit of my machine thought Zap and he flew down so fast that Mrs black birds feathers came off every single one and she was left flying in her pink skin she nearly fell on the ground. Any way Zap was sailing in the lake.

Whilst Mark and Gillian represent aspects of the outer ranges of the January performances, more typical work is exemplified below.

Once a puon a Time There lived a green man He was dreming and dreming and dreming abaut to make a flaying masen that can Flay a He was dreming and dreming and dreming untill he thought about it. He got a big red can and cut a circle out and two balck Wheels and put them on untill He finished it He said it is a good one I like it and he flad.

The above scripts differ in many respects. One obvious difference is the sheer quantity of work produced. On average, the children produced 67 words but 15% of the children produced less than 25 words whilst a further 15% produced more than 110. The number of ideas contained in the scripts showed similar divergence. One-sixth of the children produced more than 18 ideas, one sixth produced less than 4 whilst, on average, they raised 11 different ideas in their stories.

TABLE 6.1
Aspects of Children's Stories Showing Statistically Significant
Increases in Scores Between January and June

	Upper 15% Scored More Than		Lower 15% Scored Less Than		Average Score	
	Jan	June	Jan	June	Jan	June
Number of Words	110	171	25	62	67	117
Number of Ideas	18	28	4	10	11	19
Number of Connectives	5	8	0	1	2	4
Organisation of Story (score out of 9)	7	7	2	4	4	6
Quality (score out of 5)	4	5	1	2	3	3

From January to June the children made considerable progress in these and other respects. These changes are shown in Table 6.1.

In June, the children wrote statistically significantly more words, used significantly more ideas, deployed more connectives (excluding "and" and including, for example, "but," "then," "so," "because," "when") and scored significantly higher on impressionistic assessments of the quality and organisation of their stories. More specifically, there was a 70% increase in the number of words and ideas in the scripts and the use of connectives (other than "and") was doubled.

The following examples represent June performances at the lower and higher levels. Each has been chosen as typical of its performance level.

Mark (cited earlier) produced another relatively low performance albeit one which is clearly better than his January product.

He wrote:

One day a famly of moise went sailing to see thay the famly of maise fad an iland and the tamly of maise shpr the father of the maise thay fad an dag.

Gillian continued to produce higher quality work as shown in the following example.

Once there lived a family of mice and the Father mouse was called Bouncer and the Mother mouse was called Timely. The children were called Tim Tom Mary and Alice. All the mice were scared of the ginger cat that lived down the road. One day the mice decided to borrow a boat and sail away to an island to that they would be free of the ginger cat. So the next day they borrowed a boat and sailed away to find a peaseful island. Two days later Bouncer called land ho for in front of them there was an island. They got off the boat and Timely tied it to a tree. The next day at dawn all the mice found a large foot-print in the sand and Bouncer said lets do one of my Granddad's tricks dig a hole and cover it with straw and honey and the beast will smell the honey and fall into the trap. So that is what they did but the next morning they found the trap empty and then a big shadow apeared it was the ginger cat but Bouncer stuck a sharp stick into him and he was dead.

The improvement of both these children is evident. Mark had produced a little more. Obviously he still had gross limitations in writing but by June he produced sufficient in quantity to demand the deployment of properties of organisation. It remains difficult however, to follow quite what it is that he was communicating.

In contrast Gillian's product had improved considerably in structure and organisation. In January her performance was something of a stream of consciousness. In June she deployed a string of constructions to communicate a sequence of events and cause-effects.

Between School Differences

The above descriptions are intended to give some flavour of the work produced by the children and of their progress made in the 6 months of schooling. However, it does not show the differences between the work produced in the learning environments designed by the individual class teachers.

In their teaching of writing, all the teachers laid great emphasis on the quantity of the children's products. This emphasis was made plain to the children and, as was shown earlier, clearly perceived by them. How successful were the teachers in achieving this aspiration?

Table 6.2 shows the quantity of words produced in each class and the improvements made in this respect. As usual, there are some striking differences. Children in class 11 produced, on average, six times as much as children in class 3. In interpreting this contrast however, it must be noted that class 3 contained immigrant children only. Classes 10 and 11 may be more properly compared since both had very similar catchment areas, class sizes and levels of attainment on standardised tests. Class 11 children produced almost three times the number of words of children in class 10.

Differential progress is also evident. In comparing progress it is necessary to contrast classes with similar January productions. For example, children in classes 2, 10 and 12 all produced approximately 40 words each in January. These classes made generally similar rates of progress and each made better than average progress.

Children in classes 4, 5, 7 and 14 produced 50–60 words each in January. However, class 14 made twice the progress of classes 5 and 7. The

TABLE 6.2
Mean Number of Words Produced per Class in January and June

| | January | | June | | |
| | *Mean number* | *Standard* | *Mean number* | *Standard* | % |
Class	*of Words*	*Deviation*	*of Words*	*Deviation*	*Increase*
1	61	25	102	49	67
2	42	31	106	43	153
3	17	16	62	50	265
4	51	47	105	53	106
5	56	19	90	37	61
6	88	42	125	64	48
7	57	35	103	92	63
8	99	25	182	73	84
9	31	27	41	30	32
10	38	20	91	38	139
11	104	31	129	30	24
12	44	36	94	24	114
13	78	50	109	57	40
14	55	35	127	35	131
15	85	70	158	46	86
16	72	59	124	26	72
Overall Mean		61		109	75

achievement of class 14 is the more striking when it is recognised that its intake was largely lower working class immigrant whilst classes 5 and 7 recruited predominantly upper working and lower middle class children.

Similar variations in the increase in rates of production may be seen amongst the classes which had a relatively high January output. Children in classes 6, 8, 11, 13 and 15 produced in excess of 75 words each. However, from this January level, class 15 made double the rate of increase of class 6 and class 8 made almost four times the rate of increase of class 11. Since these pairs of classes had very similar catchment areas, class sizes, standardised scores on reading tests and average class ages, the differences in the degree to which teachers met their aspirations for greater quantities of writing are very provocative.

As well as urging increased quantities of writing, teachers laid great emphasis on certain aspects of grammar. They especially impressed upon children the need to use capital letters and full stops as sentence markers. In nine of the classes tasks were given which specifically focused on punctuation (see Appendix B for details) however these features were also stressed as part of the pre-task instructions in more than a third of the writing tasks observed. As with the teachers' communication of the importance of quantity, the children were very clear that teachers would be impressed by the use of capital letters and full stops.

In the testing task, these aspects of production were not specified. Table 6.3 shows the degree to which children used these features of grammar when they had not been reminded to do so.

In calculating the percentage of correct usage, the number of times the child appropriately used a capital to start a sentence was divided by the number of times that the child should have done so in his or her script. This, of course, demanded some judgement of the sentence structure of the child's script. In these judgements, normal English conventions were used.

Clearly, the incidence of correct usage of both capital letters and full stops was low. With respect to capital letters, correct usage even appeared to deteriorate. This however may be an artifact of the way in which the percentages were calculated. A child could have had the same level of competence in the use of these markers in January as in June but, because he wrote more in June his percent use was lower.

An alternative way of looking for progress can be expedited by identifying, for January and June, the numbers of children who showed no evidence of the proper use of full stops and capitals in sentences. These

TABLE 6.3
Correct Usage of Aspects of Simple Grammar

Class	Use of Capital Letter to Start a Sentence		Use of Full Stop at the End of a Sentence	
	% Correct January	% Correct June	% Correct January	% Correct June
1	32	34	34	48
2	31	14	28	11
3	81	34	20	25
4	53	49	32	46
5	42	31	30	30
6	34	52	60	47
7	23	42	17	29
8	31	37	25	25
9	42	19	4	0
10	48	22	16	18
11	32	32	8	19
12	30	18	9	16
13	44	53	25	54
14	29	19	0	13
15	17	34	16	20
16	57	20	20	6
Overall	37	30	23	28

children were identified as those who in January did not use any full stops or capitals in their scripts. However, some children started their script with a capital and/or ended it with a full stop but used no others—however much they wrote. This was also taken to be indicative of an absence of competence with these features. Table 6.4 shows the number of target children in each class evincing no competence with full stops and capital letters.

It must be emphasised that Table 6.4 shows target children who showed no evidence of competence. It cannot be assumed that the other target children were therefore fully competent. Indeed the great majority of the rest of the sample showed only minimal competence in the use of full stops and capitals.

The data in Table 6.4 refer only to the circumstances of the writing test. Thus, when not reminded and when left to their own devices, 46 out of the 96 target children showed no evidence at all of using whatever knowledge they had regarding capital letters at the start of sentences. Seventy-three per cent showed a similar incapacity with full stops. After 6 months persistent emphasis these skills had been activated, to a minimal degree at least, for approximately 12 children.

With such small numbers at issue, between class comparisons seem

TABLE 6.4
The Number of Target Children in Each Class Who Were Apparently
Incompetent in the Use of Capital Letters and Full Stops

Class	Capitals		Full Stops	
	January	June	January	June
1	4	0	3	1
2	2	3	5	4
3	1	3	5	4
4	2	2	4	0
5	3	4	4	4
6	3	1	3	1
7	4	0	4	5
8	2	1	3	3
9	4	5	6	6
10	4	3	6	4
11	2	1	5	3
12	3	2	5	5
13	2	2	4	2
14	4	1	6	4
15	4	0	4	1
16	2	2	3	5
Total	46	30	70	57

somewhat tenuous. It is worth noting however, that the teacher in class 15 appeared to be generally successful at introducing these skills into children's repertoires.

Additionally, whilst all the teachers emphasised these aspects of grammar, some emphasised them more than others. For example teachers in nine of the classes (i.e., 1, 3, 4, 5, 6, 7, 8, 9, and 13) gave lessons specifically on punctuation (see appendix B for details). Especially busy in this respect were the teachers in classes 5 and 9. It is noteworthy that class 5 apparently deteriorated in the use of capitals and in class 9 none of the children mastered full stops. Whether these teachers were causing or responding to these problems is not known.

More interesting than between school comparisons however, is the overall impression that the children were very resistant to their teachers' exhortations. In respect of full stops more than half the children failed to deploy them spontaneously at the end of their infant schooling. In view of the very small return on such persistent and determined effort (and recalling that children not recorded in Table 6.4 were only minimally competent) it is worth asking whether it is appropriate to teach these constructions at this stage. Of course it could be argued that even more effort and ingenuity might be spent on teaching full stops and capital letters. But since the lack of these grammatical features does not appear to inhibit the children from making both qualitative and quantitative progress in their written work it seems that efforts towards initial punctuation skills might be premature, ineffective or possibly even detract from the quality of the experiences provided for learning to write at this stage.

Children's Inventiveness

In addition to their emphasis on quantity and punctuation, most teachers were anxious to develop the imaginative and inventive content of children's writing. Approximately 20% of the writing tasks observed were intended to develop creative writing. However most of these tasks took the form of the archetypal writing task described earlier. The teacher provided a stimulus event and conducted a class discussion during which useful words were put on the board. The stimulus took a wide variety of forms including, for example, dreams, dragons, travel and tadpoles. In all schools the children were used to completing a story which the teacher had started. Teachers frequently exhorted children to make stories "really exciting." They also emphasised punctuation, neatness, spacing and quantity.

It will be recalled that in the test-task the children were given a story and asked to write about it and about what might have happened next. In assessing their response to this in respect of their imaginative input no attempt was made to assess the quality of children's inventions. This was

TABLE 6.5
The Average Number Per Child of Given and Invented Ideas in the
Test Scripts in January and June

	January		June	
Class	Ideas Given	Ideas Invented	Ideas Given	Ideas Invented
1	8	4	13	4
2	5	2	10	4
3	3	1	7	3
4	6	1	15	2
5	8	2	13	2
6	6	8	17	2
7	8	2	14	4
8	9	6	23	8
9	3	2	6	2
10	4	6	12	5
11	4	15	5	16
12	3	5	12	3
13	6	6	13	3
14	3	3	13	2
15	9	5	22	4
16	6	5	10	8
Average	5.7	4.6	12.8	4.5

felt to be too difficult. Instead it was decided simply to count the number of facts, events or ideas which the child worked into the story which had not been provided in the stimulus. Table 6.5 shows the number of ideas given and the number of invented ideas produced by each child in the two testing sessions.

Between January and June all children made progress in the number of given ideas they reproduced, but the rate of production of inventions was almost static. In no class was there any impressive advance in the production of novel elements in the children's stories. This stands in contrast to the children's reproduction of ideas given in the story. This, the children managed to double.

Within the general pattern two classes appear especially interesting. Children in class 11 showed a remarkably high level of inventive production in both January and June. Their rate of inventiveness was four times the sample average. Of course, in compensation for this, their work on reproducing aspects of the given story was relatively curtailed, especially in June. It appears that the energies of these children were directed at elaborating the story they had heard. In accounting for this quite massive effort in invention and elaboration it is worth noting that the teacher in class 11 did not spend an unusual amount of time on creative writing: classes 12 and 13 spent more and 16 spent as much. The teacher of class 11 spent rather more time on topic writing in which the emphasis of her instructions was on the description of her stimulus event. However, she always gave the children the option to be inventive. Thus, for example, after demonstrating the action of a volcano, the class discussion focused on what had happened. The teacher's instructions were, "Now write about the volcano. Write what we did and what we saw. If you want to, you can write me a poem about the volcano or you can write about what it would be like to live near a volcano." The last two sentences of her instruction appeared almost to be throw away lines. Yet they appeared in kind in her instructions for every writing task. However, in only one out of the eleven writing tasks observed did the child exercise the option to be inventive. In all other cases children chose to reproduce the teacher's discussion. Perhaps the major difference between the set class tasks and the testing task was that there was no teacher-directed discussion between the story and the children's writing and no key words were put on the board. Whilst these activities are obviously intended to help the children and to reduce excursions for spellings, it may be that they also constrain the child's view of what he is to do.

In contrast to the inventiveness of class 11, children in class 6 showed a gross reduction in inventiveness over the two terms. The teacher in this class did no creative writing and very little topic writing. Most of her writing tasks took the form of comprehension exercises. She was avowedly anti-pathetic to "unstructured" writing exercises and felt children at this stage of their writing development were ill served by appeals to be creative. She felt that "they are not ready for it." The children in this class all came from upper middle class homes. What is interesting is that after one term with this teacher they produced inventions at twice the average rate. After three terms this fell to half the average rate. Teachers, it seems, may have made a difference. These differences may have emanated from teachers' expectations but these mentalisms did not, in themselves, impinge on children. Rather, they operated through the tasks teachers set.

TEACHING LANGUAGE COMPREHENSION

Work aimed at the development of language comprehension was assigned in all classes to children at all levels of attainment. This took a variety of forms. As stimuli for comprehension work children were given pictures, simple sentences, short written passages or whole stories in written or oral form. As response, a variety of demands were made ranging from colouring a picture according to a set of written instructions to writing interpretations of stories or pictured events. The range and variety of this work is shown in the examples below:

a. *Colouring*

Colour this picture.

The grass is green
The sky is blue
The roof is red
The door is yellow

b. *Selection of the appropriate option*

Tick __√__ the sentences that are true.
Tailors make coats ____
Buns squirt oil ____
Pins prick ____

c. *Selection of a missing word from a list*

Wellingtons   sandals   leather

My shoes are made of _____
In summer I wear _____
When it rains I wear _____

d. *Sentence completion*

"Yesterday Margaret and Jim went for a picnic. After a long walk they went into a wood. There they had their tea. They had sandwiches and lemonade. After tea the children sat in the sun. Then they climbed trees. When they went home they were tired but happy."

1. This story is about Margaret and _____
2. They went for a _____

e. *Sentence (key words provided)*

The children are given a story to read and then asked to answer questions using key words in their responses.

e.g. 1. hospital
     2. patients

f. *Sentences (no clues available)*

Using the story given in example (d) the following questions might be used:

1. Who went for a walk?
2. What did they eat?

g. *Sentence demanding interpretation*

The children might be presented with a picture of a family running and be asked,

"Where do you think the family is running?"
"Why?"
"Are they happy or sad?"

Whilst the questions in example (f) demand that the stimulus be interpreted, the questions in this section require skills of interpretation and context-appropriate invention.

From the work observed it is clear that the notion of language comprehension, as used by teachers at this stage, refers to a variety of skills including listening, reading and understanding the meaning of words, events and contexts.

Setting Comprehension Tasks

Comprehension tasks usually took the form of work cards. They were much more likely than other language tasks to be assigned to individuals or pairs of pupils. All twelve of the comprehension tasks observed which were set to whole classes involved missing word exercises of the type shown in example (c) above. Such exercises lend themselves readily to blackboard presentation.

Whilst all schools did some comprehension work, some did very little. Additionally the variety of the form in which children met comprehension tasks varied considerably between classes. For example, classes 8, 14 and 15 used only one form of comprehension exercise. In these classes, children had to complete sentences by choosing a word from a given list. These were the classes in which comprehension exercises were predominantly given as class lessons. In contrast, classes 6, 7 and 9 worked across most of the categories of stimulus and response shown in the examples above. Since classes 3, 14 and 15 did not differ in important respects pertinent to children's learning, these differential experiences in the name of comprehension were presumably due to decisions made by class teachers about what constitutes comprehension and about what their children could cope with.

Very little differentiation was seen in the provision of work for children at different attainment levels. Even though much of the work was assigned to individuals using work cards, when their turn came, low attainers were assigned the same work as high attainers. This practice not infrequently led to problems for low attainers. For example, in assigning to a low attainer a comprehension task to test children's understanding of the content of their reading scheme, one teacher observed that, "Ruth will have problems because she has not reached this book in the scheme yet." The teacher predicted that extra help would be needed—and it was. In comprehension exercises low attainers frequently needed, and received, a lot of individual attention from their teacher.

Structuring Comprehension Tasks

As noted above, some teachers presented only one form of comprehension exercise to their children. In other classes, comprehension exercises took a variety of forms. In these cases it is possible to arrange the types of comprehension tasks into a simple to complex hierarchy which permits the examination of possible sequences in the work provided. The distinctions between simple and complex in respect of stimulus and response are, of course somewhat arbitrary. Simple responses refer to those demanding direct observation or searching down a list and the answer to be recorded with a tick or a word. Complex responses refer to those demanding whole sentence responses often after interpretive work on a stimulus. Simple stimuli refer to sentences with a single word missing or to undimensional pictures for example. Complex stimuli take the form of pictures with lots of irrelevant features or to prolonged passages of text. Table 6.6 shows which classes provided various types of comprehension tasks.

Excluded from Table 6.6 are classes 1, 2, 8, 13, 14, 15 and 16 who used only one simple format for comprehension tasks.

If these distinctions are accepted as a useful means of thinking about sequencing comprehension work then it may be seen that such tasks can range from the wholly simple, through the intermediate to the wholly complex. In this respect Table 6.6 shows that classes 3, 6, 7 and 9 had work in each of these categories. Classes 4, 5, 10, 11 and 12 moved from the

TABLE 6.6
Different Approaches to Comprehension Used by Classes Doing More
Than Simple Work

| | Response Demand | |
Stimulus	Simple	Complex
Simple	3, 4, 5, 6, 7, 9, 10, 11, 12	3, 7, 9
Complex	6	3, 4, 5, 6, 7, 9, 10, 11, 12

simple directly to the wholly complex. Thus comprehension work was better structured, in these terms, in some classes than others.

Performance on Comprehension Tasks

On a day-to-day basis, comprehension tasks provided little challenge to high attainers. Finding the correct answers was exceedingly straight forward and the vast majority of the time on these tasks was spent recording responses, a procedure which was little more than further writing practice. In contrast to this, low attainers needed a lot of help from their teachers, not only in reading and interpreting the task instructions but also, in several instances, in having the correct answers pointed out to them.

Performance on comprehension tasks was also assessed in terminal tests. As with all other aspects of these tests each child was given items constructed on the basis of his work in the term. Those who had been given only simple comprehension tasks received only simple items on their tests. The content of the test items was chosen so that it was familiar to the children but not identical to the content of class exercises.

Most children performed very well on simple comprehension items and in several schools 100% success was achieved at all levels of attainment.

Performance was only slightly less impressive with more complex items. The only exceptions to this level of success were found in classes 3 and 5. Children at all levels of attainment performed badly on items demanding interpretation. Whilst both these schools recruited from populations of low socioeconomic status, and class 3 had a wholly immigrant intake, they must be contrasted with class 9 which conformed almost exactly to the recruitment of class 3. In class 9 the children had no difficulty with comprehension items of all levels of complexity.

In summarising this section it is perhaps worth emphasising that in comprehension, as in other aspects of the curriculum diversity of provision and performance between classes seemed to be a predominant feature. Diversity of lesson content seems entirely a good thing in that it permits sensitive responses to be made to the interests of particular individuals. The diversity of provision of demand and structure is less easy to justify. Many classes perform successfully on that which others choose not to attempt.

Phonic Work

As an adjunct to the teaching of reading, all schools did some work in phonics. Of the 205 language tasks observed rather more were aimed at developing phonic skills than developing comprehension.

Predictably there was a wide variation between classes in the attention

TABLE 6.7

Coverage of the Phonic Work Done by 16 Classes in the Spring and Summer Terms (After Hughes, 1972)

	1	2	3	4	5	6	7	8	9	10	11	12	13	14	15	16
Initial single consonants (i) t, b, n, r, m, s, d, c (as in cat), p, g (hard as in goat).	M/L	H/L														
Short vowels		H/M						L		A			A	A	M/L	A
Initial single consonants (ii) f, l, y, v, h, w, j, k, z	M/L	L		A	A	L		L	A							
The alphabet (or a segment of it)			A	A	A		A		A							
Double consonants (e.g. dd, bb, including ck)	H															
Initial consonant digraphs (e.g. ch, sh, wh)	A	L	A			L		H	H			A		A	M/L	H
Initial consonant blends (e.g. st, cl, gl)	H	H/M	A			A			H			M/L			M/L	H/M
Final blends (e.g. "at", "ill")	M/L	L	A	A	M	A	A	H/L	H/L	A	A	A		A	H/L	A
Vowel diagraphs (e.g. ai, ay, oi, oy, ow, ew)	A	A	A		M	A	A	H	H	A	A	A		A		
The final and silent "e" (e.g. as in (i) kettle (ii) cake)					M	L	A		A	A	A	A				
Modification of vowels by "r" (e.g. "ar" as in "car")	H					A	A		A	A	A	A		A	H/L	A
Silent Letters (e.g. b, g, gh, l)					A							A				A
Syllables (e.g. "-ing", "-ed", "ly")			A		A										H/L	H

H = High attainer   M = Middle attainer   L = Low attainer   A = All attainment levels.

paid to phonics and in the particular content chosen. Details of this work are shown in Table 6.7. On average the classes covered five topics: class 1 covered eight topics and class 11 and 13 each covered one topic. Work on single letter sounds was carried out in fifteen classes and this work accounted for 36% of all phonic teaching. 45% of phonic teaching was devoted to digraphs and double letter sound blends.

In terms of task allocation to different attainment levels, seven classes (namely 3, 4, 7, 10, 11, 13 and 14) did all their phonic work as class lessons. Since the range of reading attainments was normal in these classes this procedure seems somewhat undiscriminating. In contrast teachers in classes 8 and 15 always assigned phonic work to specific attainment groups, the latter focusing almost entirely on the lower attainment groups.

Tasks Used to Consolidate Phonic Skills

Much phonic work took the form of class lessons conducted orally. However, many forms of task demanding a written response were used to supplement and consolidate the oral work. The various forms which these tasks took are shown in Table 6.8.

What is remarkable about many of these tasks is that they do not need phonic skills for their accomplishment. In particular, the first eight tasks in the list can be done by letter recognition. Of course this is not to say that children do not use phonic approaches to these activities, only that they need not.

Whatever thought processes children used to work these tasks they found them very easy. Phonics tasks were rarely found to overestimate children; indeed 47% of them were judged to underestimate children's attainments.

Terminal tests of phonics skills revealed an intriguingly different picture. As in all the terminal tests, target children were assigned tasks isomorphic with those they had met during the term. The form of the items was identical: the content was different but familiar. The overall results of the tests are shown in Table 6.9.

High attainers clearly performed very well on terminal tests of phonics. Unfortunately the low attainers frequently evinced problems. There was a large gap between their facility shown on class tasks during the term and that demonstrated on test items at the end of term. The problem was not unique to learning phonics. Low attainers appeared slow to acquire skills and quick to lose them. For the teacher trying to individualise instruction this presents a considerable added burden. Even where low attainers acquire skills there appears to be a case for overlearning to protect against loss. This entails providing more practice for low attainers and the consequent risk of narrowing their curriculum and inducing

TABLE 6.8
Tasks Used to Consolidate Phonics

Task	Used by Class
1. Putting a given letter at the beginning, middle or end of a series of words (situation of letter indicated)	2, 3, 9
2. Replacing the first letter of a three letter word by an alternative given letter e.g. "t" in "ten" by "m"	13
3. Identifying from a list which words start with a given letter(s)	1, 3, 8, 12
4. Identifying from a list which words finish with a given letter(s)	1
5. Identifying from a list which words contain a given letter(s)	1, 5, 7, 12, 15
6. Given a list of two word families identifying which words belong to which family, e.g., sort, cat, fat, chain, at, drain	10
7. Sorting words into three or more different word families	10, 15
8. Underlining given phonic combinations as they appear in words in a sentence	5
9. Completing words given their central letter(s) and possible solutions, e.g., given, -og, choose k, a, d	2, 8
10. Given several words which belong to the same family identifying which word completes a given sentence	14
11. Matching letter(s) to incompleted words, e.g., given fa-, choose from e, a, t, s	1, 14, 16
12. Selecting which of two or three phonic combinations completes words in a passage	5, 6, 10, 11, 14
13. Producing words which belong to the same family as a given example	8, 11
14. Selecting which of a series of letters and/or phonic combinations start the name of an illustrated object	3, 9
15. Thinking of words which start with a given (written) sound	3, 4, 6, 7, 12, 15
16. Thinking of words which finish with a given (written) sound	15
17. Thinking of words which contain a given (written) sound	2, 5, 6, 12, 16

boredom. The former is difficult to avoid. The latter risk could be reduced if teachers had a greater variety of ways in which to present familiar knowledge and skills. One art of teaching, it has been said, is that of "disguised repetition." This art does not seem prevalent in the classes observed. Examination of Table 6.7 shows that whilst across the classes 17 different ways of working with phonics were observed, very few were seen in any one classroom.

TABLE 6.9
Average Success on Phonics Tests in Terms of Attainment Level

Level of Attainment	Number of Items Tested	Percentage Correct
High	81	96
Average	84	85
Low	87	76

Provision for Reading

The teaching of reading at this stage was observed to comprise three major activities—phonics tasks, comprehension tasks and reading to teacher. The first two categories were discussed earlier.

Reading to teacher was seen in every class and almost always under similar circumstances. The teacher worked on a rota basis to have children out to read. Frequently, whilst the child read the teacher attended to a queue of pupils seeking assistance with their set work. Whether this is satisfactory or not (either to the reader or to the pupil seeking assistance) depends on the degree to which an experienced professional can constructively monitor two processes at once.

With respect to the monitoring of reading, the quality of the pupil's experience must, to some important degree, depend on whether or not he can read his set book. The more he has difficulty, the less meaningful can be his experience with or without the teacher.

With this in mind an attempt was made to assess the appropriateness of the set book to the child's reading attainment, particular emphasis being placed on identifying children in difficulty.

Criterion referenced reading tests were conducted with each of the target children. By making use of an individual's past, present and subsequent reading books, these tests were designed to provide a means of examining a child's reading performance and progress upon assigned school readers. Prior to testing, a copy of a child's current reading book, the book that he had just completed and the book that he was expected to go onto, were obtained. The page that the child was currently reading was also ascertained.

Having established a rapport with the child the tester asked him to begin reading the page prior to the teacher's assigned reading page. If this page was error free the child was told to continue reading until six errors had been made: an error being defined as any mispronunciation (including imprecise word endings, e.g., "doll" for "dolls") additions, omissions, substitutions, failures to attempt a word and jumping of lines. Any self-corrections made by a child, regardless of the number of previous attempts, were regarded as acceptable. All error types were noted on a "Reading Record."

In some cases it soon became apparent that a child had not been assigned to a book appropriate to his reading ability. If it was found that he could not successfully read, i.e., be error free, on the page prior to his current page assignment then the tester checked the child on previous pages, and, if necessary, the previous book until the child completed a page without making any errors. The child would then commence the test at that page. It seemed inappropriate to define exactly how many pages the tester should turn back as (1) the pages varied so much in length; and (2) the variation in the mismatch of books between children was so great that, given that the test could not last longer than approximately 15 minutes and that the tester was an experienced teacher, it was quicker and more efficient to decide the appropriate page interval between spot checks in practice than in theory.

In other cases it was apparent that a child could read his current assignment fluently without making any mistakes. In such instances the tester checked subsequent pages and, if appropriate, the next book, until the child made an error. The test was started from the page of the first error and proceeded until six errors had been made.

During the course of the test the research worker also noted the expressiveness of the child's reading and classified it as "very good" (i.e., varied, interesting and appropriate for the context), "Good" (i.e. average) or "poor" (i.e. monotonic and dull).

When the child had finished he was asked four simple questions about the test to ascertain his understanding and retention of the passage. Although these questions were context specific, three of them were direct and the fourth was open-ended. On the basis of his responses the child's comprehension was then classified as "very good," "good," or "poor."

The tests were carried out at the end of the Spring and Summer terms.

Table 6.10 shows the number of target children per class who were tested on the previous or next reader on the basis of the criteria described above.

Thus, in the Spring term, 20% of children could read pages beyond their assigned page in their current reader entirely without error whilst 18% of children could not read their assigned page nor selected previous pages without error.

The criterion is obviously very stringent. Even so, comparatively few children failed this test (19% in the Spring term and 10% in the Summer term). Of the 18 children who failed the test in the Spring term, 8 coped very well with the previous book, i.e., they read it with good expression and good or very good comprehension. A further 6 had at least a good comprehension of the previous book but could read it only haltingly. Two could not cope at all with the previous book and must be judged to have been badly overestimated. Of the 9 children who failed to impress on their assigned book in the Summer test, 3 could not cope with the previous book whilst the remaining 6 showed sufficient comprehension and expression to suggest that they read it meaningfully.

Thus despite the odd and potentially distracting circumstances under which teachers heard children read, less than one child in six could be judged to be overestimated on their reading books by the very stringent criterion of error free reading. Less than 3% could be safely judged as overestimated in that these children could not cope with the book previous to their assigned book. All these children were low attainers.

TABLE 6.10
Readers on Which Target Children Were Tested in the Spring and
Summer Terms

| | Spring | | Summer | |
| | Tested on | | Tested on | |
Class	Previous Reader	Next Reader	Previous Reader	Next Reader
1	2	3	0	0
2	2	1	1	0
3	1	1	0	1
4	0	1	0	3
5	2	2	0	2
6	1	3	0	0
7	1	1	1	2
8	2	1	1	1
9	0	0	2	0
10	0	0	0	1
11	1	0	0	3
12	2	0	2	1
13	1	1	0	3
14	0	3	0	2
15	0	1	0	2
16	3	1	2	0
Total	18	19	9	21

There were 19 cases in the Spring test and 21 in the Summer of pupils who could read their assigned book without error. Of these 40 cases, 39 could read the next book with at least good expression and comprehension. Thus 22% of all children coped easily with their assigned book and the subsequent one. It would not be sensible to assume that these children were not profitting from the teacher-assigned book. It could have been that the reading practice was useful or that the content was sufficiently novel as to be interesting or informative.

Setting aside these cases it is clear that the great majority of the children were reading assigned books at about their level of attainment. Of these cases 8% were judged to read their assigned book with very good expression, 23% with poor expression and the remaining 69% with good expression. Comprehension was judged very good in 64%, and good in 26%, of cases. This represents further evidence to suggest that the majority of children were on assigned books which met their attainment levels and which they read with some facility and considerable comprehension.

Additional Language Work: Spring and Summer Terms

In addition to work in comprehension and phonics, 13 of the teachers reported that they covered other topics in their language curriculum besides creative, copy and topic writing. These are shown in Table 6.11.

The various topics in Table 6.11 will be described below although it should be stressed that it probably does not provide a complete picture of the additional language work covered in the classes: it merely represents the work gathered from discussions with the teachers, records of work and the children's exercise books. It is quite possible that minor aspects of oral work and incidental teaching have been omitted.

In addition it should be recognised that the topics are not necessarily mutually exclusive—for example there are frequently word puzzles in workbooks.

Before considering the topics in detail it is interesting to note that, of the nineteen entries in Table 6.11, twelve involved all attainment levels, the rest—with the exception of class 8—being confined to the more able members of the class.

TABLE 6.11
Additional Language Work Done by the Target Children in Sample
Schools

	Topic		
Class	Word Puzzles	Workbooks/SRA	Other
1	—	—	—
2	H/M	—	A
3	—	H	—
4	—	H/M	—
5	A	A	—
6	H/M	A	—
7	—	H	A
8	—	—	H/L
9	—	A	A
10	—	—	—
11	—	—	A
12	—	—	—
13	A	—	A
14	—	—	—
15	H/M	—	A
16	—	A	—

H = High attainer   M = Middle attainer   L = Low attainer   A = All attainment levels.

Word Puzzles

Five schools did what might loosely be called word puzzles. In three cases only the more able children (i.e., high and mid attainers) were given such exercises. The tasks were to encourage spelling and word recognition. The following are typical examples.

> How many words can you find in "sensational"? "understand"?
>
> Draw a ring round one little word you can see in each big word.
>   away   near   window   began.
>
> Make two small words from each big word.
>   cannot = ___ ___
>
> Put these words the right way round (em = me).
>   eh   uoy   yeht   meht.

It appears that such exercises are relatively easy for able children but more problematic for the less able who are probably less fluent readers and seem generally less aware of word forms.

Workbooks and SRA

Six of the teachers in the sample mentioned that they used commercial workbooks. A variety of these were used the most common being "Read, Write and Remember" (Blackie). The workbooks provided a variety of practice exercises in phonics, comprehension, punctuation and creative writing. Such work was generally confined to the more able members of the class The teacher in class 5 specifically said that her pupils did their workbooks when she was too busy to attend them. She—as the teacher in class 9—used graded workbooks and the work was assigned according to ability. Thus in class 9 the less able children did simple colouring exercises while the more able had to write stories to match picture sequences.

Other Topics

At the end of the Spring term only two teachers reported covering other language topics, namely visual discrimination exercises (class 2) and poetry (class 11). By the end of the Summer term however five other teachers mentioned that they had done work which has not been discussed above. These topics have been outlined in Table 6.12 and have been grouped in terms of those which would primarily promote (1) reading and spelling (2) a more expressive and accurate use of language and (3) other skills.

TABLE 6.12
Other Language Topics Covered by the Target Children

Topic	Class
1. *Reading and spelling*	
Visual discrimination	2
Spelling exercises (graded according to ability)	7
Homonyms: . . . their/there . . .	11
to/two, four/for, piece/peace	9
2. *Language development*	
Poetry	11
Opposites	2, 15
Comparatives	15
Present participles	8, 9, 15
Past participles	8
Use of indefinite article	13
3. *Other topics*	
Days of the week and months of the year	9
Codes (e.g., "look at this code. What does it say?" 1 13 1 14 4 1)	2

SUMMARY

It has been shown that the predominant feature of the top infant language curriculum was, in one guise or another, writing practice. Very large differences in children's competence notwithstanding, most tasks were set to the whole class.

In the main, tasks had their origins in the teachers' imagination. In any one class, whilst the content of tasks varied, the intellectual procedures for working them were very limited. The large range of ideas for language work seen in the whole sample was not evident in any particular classroom. Each teacher stuck to her own narrow routines. In most classes there was a lack of sequence, structure and development in the work observed.

Teachers placed great emphasis on the development of quantity of production and on simple punctuation. Requests for spellings constituted the predominant teacher/pupil exchanges in language lessons.

Significant progress was observed in the quantity of writing produced by the children and in the quality of organisation of their passages. Earnest teaching seemed to have very little impact on either the use of punctuation or the development of imagination.

There were large differences between classes in terms of what was attempted and what was obtained. These differences do not seem attributable to differences of catchment area or intake. Rather, they appear to arise from decisions made by individual class teachers or from the design of school schemes.

7 Transfer from Infants to Juniors

The preceding chapters have set out in some detail the nature and differences in curriculum experiences in top infant classrooms. Here the focus changes to consider the continuity of those experiences when children transfer either to the junior department of their primary school or to a separate junior school. Although there have been a number of research studies on transfer at the age of eleven, none has investigated this at the age of seven. Thus we have no knowledge of the impact of this change on children, or their learning experiences, at this age.

The process of transferring to a new class or school is first considered from the perspective of both teachers and pupils who were interviewed before and after transfer. A description of the first week in their new class is then provided before considering task demand and matching in the first term of the junior year.

THE PROCESS OF TRANSFER

Teachers' Perspectives

Both the infant and junior teachers were questioned about the arrangements for transfer within and between schools. Table 7.1 presents an overview of these arrangements from which differing patterns are apparent.

All the children transferring to junior schools visited late in the Summer term but the type of visit varied. In one, the infants were shown round by a junior pupil prior to reading to their prospective teacher for the Schonell reading test. In the remaining junior schools the visit was of a more general nature designed to introduce them to the school, the headteacher and their new class. This was usually conducted by the new teacher.

In two of the primary schools visits to the new class were also arranged even though the new class was only along the corridor. But it was still strange to some children. As one junior teacher remarked, in response to

TABLE 7.1
Arrangements for Transfer

	Infant/Junior				Primary			
Visits Prior to Transfer	A	B	C	D	E	F	G	H
Junior teacher visits infant class			✔	✔			✔	
Children visit junior class	✔	✔	✔	✔		✔	✔	
Informal meetings between infant and junior teachers					✔	✔		✔
Junior head visits infant school			✔	✔	Not Relevant			
Records								
Mathematics								
i. teachers' comments			✔	✔	✔	✔	✔	✔
ii. samples of materials/childrens work			✔	✔		✔		
Language/Writing								
i. teachers' comments				✔	✔	✔	✔	✔
ii. sample of materials				✔		✔		
Reading								
i. teachers' comments			✔	✔	✔	✔	✔	✔
ii. actual reading book used			✔	✔		✔		
Standardised test data	✔							
Use made of records by junior teacher								
None				✔			✔	
None in early stages	✔							
Consulted for information only			✔					✔
Consulted and used for curriculum planning				✔		✔	✔	
First day of new school year								
children meet in infant class/school prior to moving to new class/school	✔	✔			✔			
Children go direct to junior class/school			✔	✔		✔	✔	✔
Class composition								
Same children as in infant class							✔	✔

the prospect of tears, "you would think they had come from Mars instead of down the corridor."

In three schools these visits were supported by the junior teacher visiting the infant class. This was usually of half-a-day duration during which time the junior teacher either worked as a supplementary or spent the time talking to the children and examining their work. In two infant schools the junior headteachers paid occasional visits and this involved taking infant assembly in one school.

These visits of teachers and headteachers appeared to be the only formal contacts arranged although in primary schools informal contact was easy and frequent.

There are marked contrasts in the nature and type of records passed on from infant to junior schools. In one school these consisted entirely of standardised test data including a Burt and Carver reading test, a non-standardised number test and the LEA language test. The infant teacher commented that the infant records used to be sent over but this was stopped since they seemed to serve no purpose. Thus the junior teacher had no knowledge of the children's progress or stage in reading, language or number. Nor did she want it. In another school no records were passed over, other than the official LEA record. However, the extensive records produced by the infant teacher were used by the two headteachers to allocate children to classes in the junior school.

In marked contrast the infant teacher in one school sent the actual reading, writing and number books to the junior school together with a written note about each child. This same system was used in one of the primary infant classes and a slight modification of it in another. Here the infant teacher provided notes on each child and gave advice on the maths scheme to be followed in the junior class. In addition the children's reading books were passed on with the intention that they simply opened the page they were on the previous July.

Infant teachers appeared to be very assiduous in preparing records but the use made of them would sometimes not seem to justify the effort. Two of the four junior school teachers did not use the records. One declared that she did not want ready made problems passed on and the other did not consult them in the early stages "in order to be fair to the children." The same thinking characterised that of one of the primary junior teachers, "I don't want anybody else's view of a child." Two of the remaining teachers consulted them simply to ascertain any medical or remedial problems leaving only a quarter of the teachers making any overt use of the records/material in planning the curriculum. This was usually in reading.

In only two instances did the composition of the class remain the same after transfer. Both of these were in one form entry primary schools. In the other two primary schools the class was split as a response to unequal year group sizes. In one, a junior class was constituted from the infant class with a small number of the children transferring into a mixed age class of first and second year juniors. In the other, the new junior class was larger than the top infant. To balance work load the ten youngest children in the junior class spent every morning back in the top infant class doing language and number work, and every afternoon in the junior class.

In three of the four junior schools the headteacher decided the re-grouping of children in consultation with the infant head. In the other, four infant classes were used to form three junior classes. This was achieved by random allocation except that the only four white children in the year group were placed together.

Finally there were contrasts in the manner of transfer on the first day of term. In half of the infant–junior transfers the children first reported to the infant school prior to walking to the junior school with the junior teacher. This system was also used in one of the primary schools. The children returned to their infant class for a pep talk by the infant teacher where she exhorted them to "try hard" and do their best. Following this the children were taken through the "big" archway into the "juniors"! As the teacher admitted, it was, "quite a performance."

Pupil Perspectives

Before Transfer.   The target children were interviewed towards the end of the Summer term in their infant class and again at the end of the first week in the junior class. The first interview was designed to assess their knowledge of the teacher and the class they were to transfer to, and their feelings regarding the move. The second interview focused on their reactions to the first week, noting in particular perceived changes in social, curriculum and work organisation.

The children who were to transfer to another class in the same primary school were of course more aware of their future teacher. Whether this awareness was valuable or not was a moot point. Where their perceptions, or the feedback from friends or siblings, was good, e.g. "they think she is very nice and intelligent," then no anxiety was recorded. The opposite was true of teachers not so favourably perceived. This occurred in two of the four primary schools where the common factor in arousing their anxiety was the extent to which the teacher shouted. In one school the children were to transfer to a male teacher who had "a big voice." The children's perceptions were acquired from his lunch time behaviour where he was said to shout, tell people off and have them stand in a corner if they were naughty. As a result the prospect of transferring to his class held fears from some children. As one girl remarked, "I will feel horrible in his class." The teacher in the second school also had a reputation for shouting. "She's not as nice as Mrs X. She shouts a lot if they are naughty"; "Fiona says she shouts too much and Alison gets a headache." Here too the move was viewed with some trepidation.

Information was much scarcer among children who were to transfer to a new junior school. Even though the interviews were held late in the Summer term, children in two of the schools had not been told which teacher they were to have the following year although all knew which school they were transferring to. In the other two schools, the junior teachers had visited the classes but since none had experienced them as teachers, physical descriptions predominated—"tall, blue eyes, black hair, black skirt, black shoes and pink shirt"; "She's like a parrot, she speaks funny like a parrot." The rest was hearsay and as in all situations where there is a lack of information rumours abounded—"You get the cane and the slipper and there are lots of bullies." Nevertheless most children felt they would like it in their new class but that initially they would feel funny and a bit scared.

After transfer. Although it might be imagined that the transfer process would be smoother and less traumatic in the primary schools, the children's reactions were different in each school. In one school the junior class was perceived to be superior. Here the teacher was described as helpful and kind and all had settled in happily. In another, two-thirds of the children continued to express nervousness after one week either due to confusion regarding different working procedures or to the teacher's big voice, "cos when he shouts I nearly jump out of my skin." Apart from this class most children had settled in reasonably well although there were some general anxieties evident in all classes. These included concerns about being told off, providing a satisfactory standard of work, not knowing where things were and about work proving too difficult. Some problems were specific to individuals. For example one girl complained on being placed with all boys, and two children disliked being separated from their old class into a vertically grouped class containing mostly older children. These children continued to feel "strange" and had not settled in by the end of the first week.

Most of the children transferring to a junior school appeared to have settled in adequately. Teacher reaction was an important factor in children's minds, particularly whether she was kind or not and the extent of shouting. However in one class all the children preferred junior school even though their reactions to the teacher were lukewarm. Having two choices for lunch was particularly appreciated here. A few children continued to be nervous for reasons similar to those voiced by the primary children, e.g., concerns were expressed about different working procedures and, in one school, play times, were described as "a bit rough." This problem was alleviated in some schools by providing a separate playground for the younger junior pupils.

Differences in work procedures have been commented on in very general terms and these were clearly regarded as significant by the children. These are thus considered in greater detail under the headings of Classroom and Curriculum Organisation.

Classroom Organisation

The most striking and exciting feature as far as the children were concerned was that they sat at desks rather than at tables. All commented favourably on this, mentioning in particular that all their books and materials could be stored there rather than in boxes or trays—"You don't have to get up to get your work." Also, of course, this reduced movement in the class. One-half of the teachers re-grouped the children on entry. The children did not seem to mind this particularly if there was one child in the group from the old class. The major concern about the constitution of these groups was whether there was a "silly" boy or girl in it. The adjective "silly" was a common description in all the classes and was more usually applied to boys than girls.

In three schools, all junior, there were comments about differing behavioural demands. In one class children were not allowed to talk in class (to their apparent contentment), in another they could go to the toilet without asking and in the third the method of acquiring pupil attention was noticeably different. Their former teacher had stopped talking to attract attention: the new teacher clapped her hands. Additionally they had to put their hands on their heads if noisy.

Curriculum Organisation

The term curriculum is used here to refer both to content and work practices. With regard to content, changes in terminology clearly impressed the children, e.g., "The work here is called Maths and English not sums and writing. It feels more grown up." Others referred to science and handwriting lessons, and the increase in time devoted to PE and a wide variety of games, including dancing, skittleball, rounders, basketball and football. As one boy explained "its more like a boys' school, we have real boys' games. Infants is more girls everything." The most noticeable disappearance was toys. This was also seen as an indicator of maturity. "You feel older."

With the exception of one class, where the reading books followed the children from the infant class, all the children were allocated a different reading book. This usually, but not always, was assigned after they had read to the teacher. They also perceived the number work to be different even though most teachers began the term with revision work emphasising the four rules.

The impression given by a number of children was that this was the first time that they had done their work in "proper" lined exercise books. This was perceived as more "grown up" and better than "lots of pieces of paper which get smudged and dirty." Even for those children who had worked in exercise books the procedures demanded were somewhat different in relation to rules regarding margins, the specification of the date, underlining and so on. In a number of these classes items such as rulers, pencils and pencil crayons were allocated to each child thus obviating the sharing of such resources which is a typical feature of infant schools. Finally a feature specifically mentioned by children in one third of the classes was the requirement to wait for the teacher to tell them what to do and when to start.

With the possible exception of one class, the children's responses indicated that they had generally settled down by the end of the first week. But what experiences had they been exposed to in that time?

A fieldworker was present in each of the classes during the whole of the first week of term observing and interviewing target children in the same manner as in the infant classes. In addition to acquiring task descriptions fieldworkers also kept a record of classroom events and it is from these records that a picture of classroom practices can be drawn.

THE FIRST WEEK IN JUNIOR CLASSES

It seems part of the folklore of teaching that the first few days with a new class are extremely important in setting the tone for the whole of the coming year, yet few studies have focused on this process. Only two American studies, Emmer et al. (1982) and Tikunoff et al. (1978) appear to have reported findings at primary level, and both highlight the socialisation of children into the teacher's system of rules and procedures. The second study is of particular interest since it claims to have identified the features necessary for effective classroom management at this stage. In this view, effective managers describe their rules and procedures with clear explanations together with examples, reasons and rehearsals. Considerable time is devoted to this in the first week although care is taken not to overload the children with rules on any one day. Initial academic activities are simple but enjoyable with no undue haste in beginning workbooks and readers. Whole class activities predominate initially. Academic instructions are clear and written on the blackboard. Care is also taken of the children's physical and emotional well-being such that each child is accorded fair and consistent treatment by a sensitive teacher.

To what extent were these patterns of teacher behaviours manifest in the schools studied?

On entering the classroom on the first day all of the children were allowed the choice of where to sit. Subsequently these initial arrangements were changed in half the classes. The new groupings were usually on the basis of a reading test, although one teacher used a mixture of test and behavioural information. Where friendship groups remained, all were single sex. As far as the girls were concerned this was usually because boys were perceived as noisy and naughty.

In justifying their classroom rules, teachers claimed to be encouraging independence and responsibility. All children were exposed to a selection of these rules on the first morning. Classroom rules dominated on the first day with instructional or academic rules later as work got under way. A large array of rules was apparent, many of which were common across classrooms:

DON'T: Eat in class.
           Bang desk lids.
           Speak loudly.
           Call out.
           Rub out.
           Use the pencil sharpener without permission.
           Use the drink fountain when coming in from the playground.
           Whisper, chatter, talk.
           Jab, eat or bite pencils.
           Hit with, bang on desks with, break or bend rulers,
           or fire screwed up paper with them.
           Run in the corridor.

DO: Listen and do exactly as your told.
       Say "Yes, Miss" when replying.
       Have good manners.
       Produce good, neat work.
       Go to your place quietly.
       Put your hand up if you need anything.
       Put the date in the right hand corner.
       Leave a margin.
       and so on.

A number of these rules were demonstrated by teachers, from replacing chairs under desks and lining up outside the room, to class lessons on handling a pencil and a ruler. One teacher demonstrated the holding of a pencil by attaching one to her index finger with an elastic band before showing how it should be supported by three fingers, and not by holding the pencil "at the end of the bit that isn't sharpened."

There was a tendency to increase the pressure to conform to these rules over the first week, often using appropriate incidents to remind children. In one class, increases of noise level were dealt with by the order to "put hands on heads," and in another to "put arms behind backs" prior to repetitions of the rules about noise. Often children were reminded that their deviations from the rules were more typical of little infants than the big juniors they now were.

Many of the instructional rules concerned work layout and often these were different from their previous class. Confusion was therefore occasionally evident but most confusion was caused by their introduction, for the first time in their school life, to plain backed exercise books of lined paper. The apparently simple instruction to put their name on the front caused such anxious questions as which cover was the front? Did the front cover mean the first page? Were names to be in capitals? Did they have to write both Christian names? and so on.

In general the teachers took great care in phrasing their instructions on rules and procedures and in ensuring that the children felt at ease in their new environment. Not all teachers were equally sensitive, however. One teacher tended to be over forceful and erratic in responding to his own stated rules. His dealings with individual children were always carried out in a loud voice such that all interactions were public. Occasionally these were unfortunate. In responding to Sandra's writing he responded "that's a bit titchy isn't it? Was Ian your brother? He couldn't write properly either."

In this particular class, children were not allowed to use the pencil sharpener. This, combined with a sometimes unsympathetic approach, led to a great deal of anxiety about broken pencil points. One incident exemplifies this: Sara had broken her pencil and thus approached the teacher. His response was "What do you want me to do—put it back in? put a bandage on it?" At this point Sara was close to tears. Shortly after, another child had his pencil sharpened but found that when he got back to his desk the pencil point was loose. Rather than go back again he spent several minutes trying to tear the wood away from the end of the pencil.

Erratic responses to the teacher's own stated rules included praise on a number of occasions for work which clearly did not conform, yet criticism of other children's work which was indentical to that praised.

In addition to instructions regarding rules and procedures much of the first day was spent in learning children's names, occasionally by the use of games, giving out books and materials, and in formal and informal assessments by the use of reading tests or reading to teacher.

Normal teaching timetables were introduced gradually over the week and it was not until the second week that some children were given their reading books. In other classes diagnostic tasks were used prior to the introduction of the official scheme in the second week. This was particularly apparent in number work where there was a concentration on the four rules of number in the first week prior to the introduction of a structured mathematics scheme. This is reflected in the pattern of task demand which is considered in the next section.

In most classes there was a stress on whole class teaching and what has been termed a "skills and frills" or split day approach, whereby number and language work was dealt with in the mornings and craft, music and PE in the afternoons. As in the infant classes, queueing was a ubiquitous feature of classroom life with up to twenty children in the queue in one classroom. This was in part a consequence of the teacher's desire to mark work with the child present and only one teacher produced a solution for this. If a queue developed she collected in all the work to mark in the lunch break or the evening and allocated children other tasks.

Summary

If the description of effective managers provided by Emmer et al. is accepted as an adequate prescription for effectiveness in handling a new class of children, then most of the teachers in this study can be deemed successful.

Initial anxiety was allayed by allowing all children to sit next to a friend on the first day. Classroom rules and procedures were stressed in the early part of the week whereas instructional rules, relating particularly to work layout, were dealt with as work was introduced. Explanations of these were delivered with care and supported by rehearsals when this was felt appropriate. In most instances these rules were consistently applied. Whole class teaching predominated in this period utilising content that was generally familiar. In addition to socialising the children into the system of classroom rules, there was a stress on inculcating into children the belief that being a junior school pupil carried with it a more mature and responsible attitude to their work and peers.

TASK DEMAND

A total of 121 tasks were observed in the 11 classes during the first term of junior schooling. Five classes were in the junior department of four primary schools and six classes in four junior schools. The method was the same as that undertaken in the infant classes. Observation was carried out in three phases. The first phase comprised the whole of the first week of the new school year. This was followed by a two-day period before half-term and another two-day phase later in the term. Data gathering was limited to the same target children who had been observed in their infant classes. Where children in the same infant class had been split into two junior classes both of the latter were observed. This occurred in one primary school and two junior schools. Sixty tasks were acquired from junior schools and 61 tasks from junior departments of primary schools.

The distribution of actual task demands in number and writing are shown in Table 7.2 together with that from infant classes for purposes of comparison.

In number work the percentages of both incremental and practice tasks fell in the junior classes with a corresponding increase in the number of revision tasks. No enrichment or restructuring tasks were observed, which is not perhaps surprising at a time when junior teachers are attempting to ascertain the base from which to work.

The pattern for language tasks was quite different however. Here the percentage of incremental tasks increased by over ten per cent and the

TABLE 7.2
Actual Task Demand in Infant and Junior Classes in Number and Writing

	Junior			Infant		
	Number	Writing	Total	Number	Writing	Total
Incremental	16	18	34	72	32	104
Restructuring	0	0	0	2	0	2
Enrichment	0	2	2	14	10	24
Practice	22	31	53	93	156	249
Revision	15	16	31	21	3	24
Not known	1	0	1	10	4	14
Total	54	67	121	212	205	417

incidence of practice tasks decreased by thirty per cent. The ratio of incremental to practice tasks fell from almost 1:5 in infant classes to less than 1:2 in the juniors. This increase in incremental tasks would indicate a forward thrust in the acquisition of writing skills and was commented on by the pupils in their interviews.

The increase in revision tasks in both number and language work is hardly surprising at the beginning of a new school year and as Table 7.3 shows these were limited in the main to the first week of the new term.

In the first week of term over 50% of all tasks were revision but this fell away rapidly thereafter. It appears that revision of infant work gave way to practice of junior work. By late term practice tasks comprised three-quarters of all tasks. This increase corresponded with a steady decline in the proportion of incremental tasks suggesting that the work early in the term entailed rapid introduction of new work with little

TABLE 7.3
Task Demand in the Three Observational Phases

	Observation Phase			
Task Demand	First Week	Half Term	Late Term	Total
Incremental	17	10	7	34
Restructuring	—	—	—	0
Enrichment	—	1	1	2
Practice	8	21	24	53
Revision	28	3	0	31
Other	—	1	—	1
Total	53	36	32	121

TABLE 7.4
Task Demand by School Type

	School Type	
Task Demand	Junior	Primary
Incremental	21	13
Enrichment	1	1
Practice	23	30
Revision	14	17
Other	1	0
Total	60	61

opportunity to practice, whereas later in the term the rate of introduction of new work slowed in favour of additional practice.

Patterns of task demand also varied according to school type as Table 7.4 shows.

Children who moved to a junior school experienced a greater proportion of incremental tasks and a lower proportion of practice tasks. Here the ratio of incremental to practice tasks was almost 1:1. Where children moved within the primary school the ratio was 1:2.4—a very similar ratio to that experienced in their infant class. Changing school would thus seem to be associated with a sharp increase in the rate of meeting new skills or concepts and a related drop in the opportunity to practise them.

However this general finding should be treated with caution since there are marked differences in task demand between classes. The proportion of incremental tasks varied from less than 10% to over 70%; practice tasks varied from 26% to 70% and revision tasks from zero to 43%.

Sex Differences

Comparisons of task demand across levels of attainment and sex are presented in Table 7.5.

The differences between attainment levels are much more marked than those between the sexes. High attaining children experienced large doses of practice and revision, the average children received a balanced diet and the low children a diet of new skills and concepts with little opportunity to practise them. The only marked difference between boys and girls overall was the smaller proportion of revision tasks for girls—one-quarter, as opposed to one-third, of all tasks for boys. However as is clear from Table 7.5 this is totally accounted for by the very low proportion of revision tasks for low attaining girls.

These patterns do not reflect the infant experience where there were

TABLE 7.5
Actual Demand by Attainment and Sex (Juniors)

	Boys			Girls			Total	
	High	Middle	Low	High	Middle	Low	Boy	Girl
Incremental	1	5	11	2	5	10	17	17
Enrichment	—	—	1	—	—	1	1	1
Practice	12	7	8	13	6	7	27	26
Revision	4	5	9	5	5	3	18	13
Other	—	—	—	—	1	—	—	1
Total	17	17	29	20	17	21	63	58

very few differences between boys of differing attainment levels although it is worth noting that among girls the high attaining group were presented with the least proportion of incremental and greatest proportion of practice tasks. Overall however the differences between the sexes were slight.

Currently there is considerably interest in attempting to explain the common finding that boys are superior in number work and girls in the language area. The trends from this study are interesting and consistent but not large. In both the infants and juniors, girls received a higher proportion of incremental tasks in language and less practice and revision than boys. And in the larger infant sample, they received more enrichment tasks. This pattern is reversed in number where boys received more incremental, less practice, and in the infant sample, more enrichment tasks than girls.

Intended and Actual Demands

Language. As was argued in the analysis of task demand at infant level, it is important to know the extent of the discrepancy between the demand the teacher intended and the demand she actually made, and to gain some understanding of why such discrepancies occur.

Table 7.6 shows the frequency with which teacher's intentions corresponded with the demand actually made in language tasks.

The junior teachers intended an equal proportion of incremental and practice tasks, a pattern very different from infant teachers who intended a far greater proportion of practice tasks. However the actual demand made shows a very different pattern and almost twice as many practice as incremental tasks and a greater proportion of revision tasks than intended.

Overall 80% of teachers' intended demands were actually made but they were much more successful in some areas than others. For example all of the intended practice demands were made and all but one of the revision demands. Teachers were least successful in converting their intentions in

TABLE 7.6
Intended and Actual Demand in Language Tasks

Intended Demand	Actual Demand				
	Incremental	Enrichment	Practice	Revision	Total
Incremental	16	—	6	—	22
Enrichment	1	2	3	—	6
Practice	—	—	22	—	22
Revision	1	—	—	10	11
Not known	—	—	—	6	6
Total	18	2	31	16	67

incremental and enrichment tasks. (The intentions in the "not known" category are not considered in these analyses. These were all diagnostic tasks, the demands of which were not known for children the teacher was not yet familiar with. These were designed to ascertain what demands could legitimately be made in the future. From the table it can be seen that all turned out to make a demand for revision.)

Over one-third of all incremental tasks and a half of enrichment tasks turned out to make a practice demand resulting in children experiencing nearly one-third more practice tasks than intended. It will be recalled that this same pattern occurred in the infant classes.

Children of differing attainment levels experienced different patterns of demand however. Table 7.7 sets out the intended demand for each level of attainment together with a record of all discrepancies.

Thus, for example, a total of 7 incremental tasks were intended for high attaining children but 5 of these turned out to make a practice demand.

TABLE 7.7
Intended Demand and Discrepancies by Levels of Attainment in
Language Tasks

Intended Demand	High Attainers		Middle Attainers		Low Attainers	
	N	Discrepancy	N	Discrepancy	N	Discrepancy
Incremental	7	5 Practice	9	1 Practice	6	—
Enrichment	2	2 Practice	0	—	4	1 Incremental 1 Practice
Practice	9	—	5	—	8	—
Revision	2	—	2	—	7	1 Incremental
Not known	3	3 Revision	3	3 Revision	0	—
Total	23		19		25	

These, together with the 2 intended enrichment tasks which actua y made practice demands, meant that high attaining children experienc d some 80% more practice tasks than intended. Their actual task ex erience turned out to be just 2 incremental tasks, 6 practice tasks and 2 re vision (5 if the diagnostic tasks are included). Here the teachers' lack of bility to transform an intended incremental task into an actual demand indicates that this group of children experienced virtually no extension of skills or concepts in the language area.

Transformation of intent into actual demand was very much better for average children where only one discrepancy was recorded, one incremental task making practice demands.

Teacher's intentions for low achieving children were quite different from the other groups. This was manifested in larger proportions of practice and revision tasks. Also one enrichment and one revision task turned out to make incremental demands. Their actual experience was therefore 8 incremental, 2 enrichment, 9 practice and 6 revision tasks—a profile very different from their high attaining classmates.

It is apparent from the above that the major problem was the conversion of an incremental intent into an actual demand: a problem most apparent with high achieving children. How did this come about? Interestingly it was due to the same two factors found at infant level—either the child was already perfectly familiar with the work or the task means did not match the ends.

A common feature of such discrepancies involved high attaining children working on very familiar material because of the teacher's decision to base a whole class session on an exercise in a text book. These were often worked through exercise by exercise. In this approach the incremental intent was achieved for some at the expense of others.

This situation was often confounded by the choice of an inappropriate means for the intended ends. In one such task a teacher wanted to encourage the use of verbs as "action" words, but the actual task demanded only the matching of words to pictures—a very familiar task which was completed without any association with action words.

Number. Table 7.8 sets out the frequency with which teachers' intentions related to actual demand in number tasks.

In number there are less discrepancies between intended and actual demand than was found at infant level. The intended emphasis on practice and revision was retained with a slight increase in incremental tasks. This was brought about by intended enrichment and restructuring tasks making incremental demands. It is interesting to note differences between the language and number areas in diagnostic tasks. All such tasks made revision demands in language but incremental demands in number. However

TABLE 7.8
Intended and Actual Demands in Number Tasks

Intended Demand	Actual Demand					
	Incre-mental	Enrich-ment	Practice	Revision	Other	Total
Incremental	9	—	2	1	1	13
Restructuring	1	—	—	—	—	1
Enrichment	1	—	—	—	—	1
Practice	1	—	19	—	—	20
Revision	—	—	—	14	—	14
Not known	4	—	1	—	—	5
Total	16	—	22	15	1	54

in both areas teachers fulfilled their intentions in practice and revision tasks almost totally.

Did this pattern hold for all levels of attainment? Table 7.9 presents the intended demand for each level together with all the discrepancies.

These data present a similar pattern to that in language. The actual demands made of the high attainers included 1 incremental task, 9 practice and 5 revision tasks. Thus, as in language work, there was little indication of teachers developing new skills or concepts among these able children.

Transformation of intent into actual demand was very good for average pupils but, for low attaining children, teachers intended a much higher proportion of incremental tasks, and this proportion was almost doubled by failures to translate intended into actual demands. All diagnostic tasks turned out to have an incremental demand as did one practice and all of the restructuring and enrichment tasks. The demand actually experienced was

TABLE 7.9
Intended Demand and Discrepancies by Attainment Level in
Number Tasks

Intended Demand	High Attainment		Middle Attainment		Low Attainment	
	N	Discrepancy	N	Discrepancy	N	Discrepancy
Incremental	2	1 Practice	3	1 Not known	8	1 Practice
Restructuring	—		—		1	1 Incremental
Enrichment	—		—		1	1 Incremental
Practice	7		5		6	1 Incremental
Revision	5		5		4	
Not known	1	1 Practice	—		4	4 Incremental
Total	15		13		24	

thus 13 incremental, 6 practice and 5 revision tasks, i.e., much new input with little opportunity to practise it.

The failure to convert incremental intentions into actual demands was proportionally similar to the pattern at infant level. The two incremental intentions which made practice demands both occurred because of inappropriate means for the intended end. In the first case this was due to poor definition of the task in the maths textbook. The teacher's instruction did not help since it was a directive to carry out the next exercise. Thus the intention of estimating weights turned out to be a task simply requiring weighing without estimating.

The second case required the use of an abacus to understand place value but the actual task required only that the child be able to count to nine since the wooden beads had assigned place values on the abacus, and thus the task required practice of a technique well known to the child.

The only intended incremental task to have a revision demand was probably due to lack of adequate diagnosis. This task, an exercise from a maths scheme, had been covered in the infant school even though the task was observed over one month into the first term of the junior class.

Junior and Primary Compared.   Table 7.10 sets out the intended versus actual demand for tasks presented in junior schools and junior departments of primary schools.

Table 7.10 shows that teachers in primary schools plan more practice per incremental tasks than do junior school teachers, and when the actual demand achieved is considered, this gap widens considerably. The ratio of incremental to practice tasks in junior schools was almost 1:1 but nearer 1:3 in primary. Both sets of teachers were equally proficient at translating practice and revision intentions into actual demands but were less successful with incremental intentions. Primary school teachers attempted more enrichment tasks but only one in six were successfully translated.

It would appear that the children entering junior school were introduced to more new skills and concepts than their counterparts in primary schools.

Summary

The two most striking features of task demand in junior classes are the patterns of differential demand as the term progresses, and the very different demands achieved for high and low attainers.

The first week of term was dominated by revision tasks but these fell away rapidly thereafter to a mixture of incremental and practice tasks. Perhaps the most surprising aspect of the pattern is that the proportion of incremental tasks decreased as the term progressed whilst practice tasks increased. It might be expected that the introduction of new concepts or

TABLE 7.10
Intended and Actual Demand: Junior Schools and Primary Schools

School Type	Actual Demand						
	Primary						
Intended Task Demand	Incre-mental	Restruc-turing	Enrich-ment	Practice	Revision	Not Known	Total
Incremental	10	—	—	4	—	—	14
Restructuring	—	—	—	—	—	—	0
Enrichment	2	—	1	3	—	—	6
Practice	—	—	—	22	—	—	22
Revision	—	—	—	—	14	—	14
Diagnostic	1	—	—	1	3	—	5
Total	13	0	1	30	17	0	61
	Junior						
Incremental	15	—	—	4	1	1	21
Restructuring	1	—	—	—	—	—	1
Enrichment	—	—	1	—	—	—	1
Practice	1	—	—	19	—	—	20
Revision	1	—	—	—	9	—	10
Diagnostic	3	—	—	—	4	—	7
Total	21	0	1	23	14	1	60

procedures would increase as the term progressed but the opposite appears to have been the case.

The second major feature is the very different pattern of task demand actually achieved for high and low attainers. This was mainly a consequence of a failure to convert incremental intentions for high achievers into actual demands. Whole class teaching appeared to be a problem here whereby incremental intentions for average and low attainers were achieved at the expense of high attainers.

MATCHING

Judgements of the match between task and child in the junior classes were made in the same manner as outlined in Chapter 4. Table 7.11 shows the frequency of matching and mismatching in number and language tasks for children of differing levels of attainment.

It will be recalled that there was a consistent picture across both curriculum areas in the infant schools where approximately 40% of tasks

TABLE 7.11

Incidence of Matched and Mismatched Tasks in Number and Language for Children of Differing Levels of Attainment

	Number				Language			
	High	Middle	Low	Total	High	Middle	Low	Total
Match	2	8	6	16	8	9	11	28
Overestimate	2	4	11	17	2	4	12	18
Underestimate	11	2	7	20	12	3	1	16
Undecided	0	1	0	1	0	3	2	5
Total	15	15	24	54	22	19	26	67

were matched. This was not the case in junior classes where the incidence of matching was much better in language than in number tasks. 42% of language tasks were matched but only 30% of number tasks.

In number work mismatching was particularly severe for high attainers where nearly three quarters of all tasks were underestimates. On the other hand low attainers tended to be overestimated. The proportion here is very similar to that in infant schools. The middle achievers fared the best. One half of their tasks were matched.

A similar pattern was evident in language work but the incidence of the underestimation of high attainers was somewhat less at 55%. The degree of overestimation of low attainers was identical to that in number and, again, middle attainers were best served with a little under one-half of their tasks being well matched to their capabilities.

This general pattern masks differences both between type of school attended and between teachers. In junior schools for example, the low and average attainers were much more likely to be overestimated in number work than their counterparts in primary schools. Whereas in language, junior schools more frequently underestimated high attainers and primary more often overestimated low attainers.

However when classrooms are considered individually the differences are much more marked. The proportion of matched tasks varied from 71% in one classroom to 11% in another, and there were similar discrepancies in over and underestimation. It is of interest to note that the best and worst record of matching came from different classes in the same school. It was also apparent that some teachers were much better at matching in one curriculum area. For example the teacher with the best matching record achieved 100% match in language but 50% in number. Another gained 63% match in number but only 20% in language. The least competent teacher achieved no matches in number and 20% in language.

Similar differences were noted in overestimating. One teacher overestimated on 57% of number tasks but only 12% of language tasks whereas the opposite trend was apparent for another teacher who overestimated on 86% of language tasks but 29% of number tasks.

Task Demand

In the infant classes it was found, contrary to expectation, that better matching was apparent in incremental tasks than practice tasks. This was not so in junior classes as Table 7.12 shows.

Here the major types of task demand, incremental, practice and revision, are considered. The profiles are somewhat different but the incidence of match is similar in all three task types, i.e., slightly less than 40%. However, as in the infant school, incremental tasks were more likely to be overestimates, and practice and revision tasks to be underestimates. This is perhaps more understandable in revision tasks which tended to be diagnostic but this explanation does not serve to explain underestimation in practice tasks. The picture of mislocated practice tasks alluded to in Chapter 4 is even clearer in junior classes.

There are also indications that the quality of matching decreases through the term as Table 7.13 shows.

It will be recalled from the section on task demand that the incidence of revision tasks fell away rapidly after the early weeks, and that the proportion of incremental tasks also declined in favour of more practice tasks. This can be clearly seen in the ratio of incremental to practice tasks which was 2:1 in the first phase, 1:2 in the second and over 1:3 in the third. When incremental and practice tasks are considered in Table 7.13 it is apparent that the decline in the number of incremental tasks is associated with a diminution in the quality of matching. None of the incremental tasks observed towards the end of the term was matched; most were overestimates. Conversely the increase in the number of practice tasks is associated with an increase of underestimation.

This pattern, which would indicate that the quality of matching declined as teachers become more familiar with their new class, is disturbing.

TABLE 7.12
Match and Mismatch in Tasks of Differing Demands

	Match	Overestimate	Underestimate	Total
Incremental	13	18	3	34
Practice	21	9	23	53
Revision	11	8	12	31
Total	45	35	38	118

TABLE 7.13
Matching in Incremental, Practice and Revision Tasks in Each
Observational Phase

	Phase 1	Phase 2	Phase 3	Total
Incremental				
Match	8	5	0	13
Overestimate	8	5	5	18
Underestimate	1	0	2	3
Practice				
Match	3	10	8	21
Overestimate	2	3	4	9
Underestimate	3	8	12	23
Revision				
Match	10	1	0	11
Overestimate	7	1	0	8
Underestimate	11	1	0	12
Total	53	34	31	118

Teacher Assessment

Following the post task interviews with each child the teachers were asked to make a judgement about the child's progress with the task. This followed the same procedure as in the infant schools and by the same basic categories of "in difficulty," "getting by" and "doing well" were appropriate. Also, as in the infant classes, not one single task was perceived by any teacher to be too easy for a child. Table 7.14 relates these teacher judgements to categories of match and mismatch for number and language tasks.

It is clear from Table 7.14 that where teachers perceived children to be in difficulty most tasks were overestimates.

TABLE 7.14
Relationship Between Teacher Judgements and Matching
(Undecided Match Excluded)

Teacher's Perception	Number				Language			
	Match	Over	Under	Total	Match	Over	Under	Total
In difficulty	1	12	0	13	2	8	1	11
Getting by	10	5	3	18	16	7	7	30
Doing well	3	0	15	18	8	1	8	17
Vague/not sure	2	0	2	4	2	2	0	4
Total	16	17	20	53	28	18	16	62

TABLE 7.15
Next Steps in Number Work

	More of Same	Move on	Go back	Same Then Different	Other	Total
In difficulty	4	2	5	1	1	13
Getting by	6	8	0	2	2	18
Doing well	3	13	0	1	2	19
Total	13	23	5	4	5	50

This was true of both number and language areas where children in difficulty tended to be low attainers. Where children were perceived to be getting by, the majority of tasks were matched but in language tasks this perception was linked to underestimates among high attainers and overestimates among low attainers. Where children were seen to be doing well the majority of tasks were underestimates particularly among high attainers in number work.

That teachers perceived children to be working well on underestimated tasks is hardly surprising since teachers tended to base their judgements on a series of quick observations across the whole class, and children do work well on tasks that are too easy for them. At the level of classroom management this is a very satisfactory state of affairs. It is the cognitive consequences of this that are evidently not fully appreciated by the teachers.

Following the evaluation of the child's progress teachers were asked what their next step would be. Their major responses, in relation to their evaluations, are shown in Table 7.15 for number work and Table 7.16 for language.

For children perceived to be in difficulty the predominant response was to either give them more of the same or take them back a step. This latter strategy was much more prevalent in infant schools but the incidence of moving children on when in difficulty was similar (i.e., 15%). Children who

TABLE 7.16
Next Steps in Language Work

	More of Same	Move on	Go Back	Same Then Different	Other	Total
In difficulty	4	2	3	0	2	11
Getting by	9	13	0	3	6	31
Doing well	5	9	0	1	5	20
Total	18	24	3	4	13	62

were seen to be getting by were moved on in nearly 50% of cases, although one third got more of the same. Children who were seen as doing well were moved on in seven out of ten cases.

Decisions in language were slightly different, particularly with regard to perceptions of getting by and doing well (Table 7.16).

There was a greater reluctance to move children back here but the same pattern of decisions was apparent for both getting by and doing well. In both of these categories approximately one quarter of the children got more of the same and some 45% were moved on.

Summary

A somewhat disconcerting picture is presented when the finding that the quality of matching deteriorated as the term progressed is combined with the finding that junior teachers were less successful than their infant counterparts in matching number tasks to the capabilities of the children. In addition the same pattern of the underestimation of the high attainers and overestimation of the low attainers was apparent although there was evidence to indicate that this differed according to the type of school attended. It would seem that low attaining children transferring to a junior school were more likely to be overestimated.

8 Classroom Groups

So far the focus has been on the nature and type of classroom tasks and their appropriateness to childrens' capabilities. But tasks are performed in a social context which may aid or hinder their successful completion. In Britain the immediate social context of learning is generally the classroom group and this chapter investigates the impact of working in a group on task performance.

The practice of grouping children for instruction is widespread in Britain. Typically such groups contain four to six children but the basis for their composition varies from strict differentiation by ability to free friendship choice (Bennett et al., 1980; HMI, 1978). Such practices were encouraged by the influential Plowden Report (1967) where it was perceived to provide the best compromise in achieving individualisation of learning and teaching within the time available. "Sharing out the teacher's time is a major problem. Only seven or eight minutes a day would be available for each child if all teaching were individual. Teachers therefore have to economise by teaching together a small group of children who are roughly at the same stage (paras 754/5)."

Among the benefits envisaged for group work were that children would learn to get along together, to help one another and realise their own strengths and weaknesses, as well as those of others. They would make meanings clear to themselves by having to explain them to others and gain from such opportunities to teach and learn. It was also felt that the group would rouse apathetic children and allow able children to benefit from the thrust and counterthrust of conversation. The supposed benefits of small groups have recently been reiterated by HMI (1980) in calling for an increase in group work.

Recent research on classroom groups provides little support for such prescriptions, however. For example Boydell (1975) and Galton et al. (1980) both report similar findings with older primary age children. They found that most of the talk in groups was not related to the task, that conversations were not sustained, and that boys tended to talk only to boys and girls to girls. Boydell thus argued that seating children in groups "is no

guarantee that they will talk freely about anything, let alone their work."
Similar findings have been reported in America where Fisher et al. (1979)
for example, found that pupil involvement with work declined to an
average of 50% unless the teacher was interacting with or supervising the
group. Recent experimental studies have also shown that pupil
involvement and quantity of work completed rises significantly when
children are moved out of groups into rows (Bennett and Blundell, 1983;
Wheldall et al., 1980).

These studies indicate the possibility of a marked impact of the social
context on task performance but they provide no indication of the content
or value of group talk. To what extent do pupils provide explanations of
tasks to other pupils in the group? How much of this talk is distracting?
And in what ways and to what effect does teacher talk to members of the
group have an impact on their performance and understanding? These are
some of the questions which are dealt with here.

To respond to these questions two different approaches were necessary.
To ascertain types of talk, required the development of a category system
by which all talk could be classified. This was then analysed quantitatively.
The nature of that talk, on the other hand, particularly that relating to the
quality of pupil and teacher explanation, required a qualitative analysis.

TYPES OF TALK

In order to assess these, a complete record of all talk between pupils and
between pupils and teacher was required. Because of the problems of
audio-recording in classrooms, this necessitated fitting each member of the
target group with a radio microphone. However, this in itself would have
created a very artificial situation. To overcome this, dummy microphones
were fitted to every child in the classrooms studied. The advantage of this
was that the fieldworker was able to allocate the live microphones to a
target group without the pupils or the teacher being aware of which group
was being recorded. In pilot work prior to the actual study, it was
established that by the second day the novelty effect had largely been
overcome, i.e., little "microphone talk" was apparent, and thus all groups
wore the microphones for at least one day prior to recording.

Six of the sixteen classes were chosen for this part of the study to provide
a range of group composition in terms of sex and ability level (see Table
C.1, Appendix C). Most contained five children. In each recording a
fieldworker was present to provide a running commentary on details of the
classroom context, the tasks the children were engaged on and movement
from the group to the teacher or other parts of the room. In addition

another fieldworker observed in detail one target child within the target group.

Two tasks from each class were selected for analysis to provide a balance of number and language tasks. The following descriptions are therefore based on six number and six language tasks.

Categories of talk were derived by examining the type of talk apparent in the transcripts. In developing these categories the strategy was to start from the data and to work towards a category system. This involved reading through the transcripts, deriving tentative categories and testing them out on other transcripts.

The resultant system required first the categorisation of the participants involved, i.e., pupil-to-pupil, pupil-to-teacher or teacher-to-pupil and whether the talk related to the task or not. Non-task talk was not further differentiated. Teacher and pupil task talk was categorised in different ways (see Table C.2, Appendix C). Pupil task talk for example was subdivided into four main sections—instructional input, sharing information, materials and egocentric talk. These in turn were each sub-divided as is shown in Fig. 8.1. Definitions of all these categories are presented in Table C.3, Appendix C. However, short extracts of selected categories are provided below for illustrative purposes.

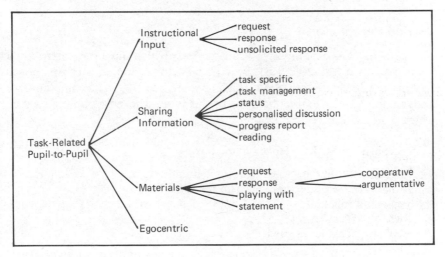

FIG. 8.1.   Major categories of pupil–pupil task talk.

Instructional Input

This category covers talk in which pupils provided explanations or answers to other pupils. In the following extract a group of boys were using an equaliser and the task required the balancing of this by different combinations of weights. Andrew did not understand how to do this and made a general request to the group.

Andrew: "Do you have to put three and two on one side?"
Stephen: "Shall I tell you what to do, Andrew? Why don't you use Unifix?"
Ian: "Come here. What is it? Where are you at?"
Andrew: "3 and 2 equals 4 and something."
Ian: "3 and 2 equal, and put them in that number."
Andrew: "Right. I'll put them in that number. What number is it? No, you've got to do what number it is."
Neil: "4."
Ian: "Is it?"
Neil: "No. 3 and 2."
Andrew: "Yeah, that one's . . . it's 4 and you've got to make it balance."
Neil: "Yes, it's not 3 and 2, it's 4."
Andrew: "Hey! I know where to put it. Put it in one."
Ian: "No, in 2. Yeah. And then . . . it's too light."
Andrew: "No, it isn't. Wait! Wait!"
Ian: "Yes, it's equal, Andrew."
Andrew: "That's right."

Sharing Information

This category has a number of subcategories which have in common talk about aspects of the task. Task-Specific talk, for example, is characterised by conversations about the task which have no bearing on its completion or understanding. The extract below is of this type, where two boys discussed which workcard to choose from a box.

Stephen and Richard looked in the box.

Stephen: "I'll find it."
Richard: "There's no more of them there."
Stephen: "Right."
Richard: "They're not."
Stephen: "That looks good."
Richard: "Yeah, but . . ."
Stephen: "But we can't do that and I don't know what to do."
Richard: "That's a bit hard. Why don't we do these? Oh, come on."

A few moments later.

Stephen: "No, this is what I like doing. Find the opposites. Yes."

Richard: "I got another one."
Stephen: "Hey, it's good, these, isn't it?"
Richard: "Yeah, they're good. . . . What are you up to? Rub it all out."
Stephen: "Oh no, I can do it on the side if I want."
Richard: "Just don't do it really fast. Just do it normally. . . . This is a long
word, beginning."

Task Management

This on the other hand, involves talk relating to the presentation of the
task. In the following excerpt, which also includes instructional input and
materials talk, Leah guided Craig on the way the task should be laid out.

Craig: "Oh, it's easy this. The last page's hard. You've got to use two
50p's and we've got to try how to do it . . . see if we can do it.
Right, take 50p. Buy one fruit cake."
Leah: "It's very hard. . . . Never mind. Fold the page in half."
Craig: "Why? Take 50p. Take 50p. Buy a packet of flour."
Leah: "Fold the page in half."
Craig: "Oh, yeah. Oooh, I did a margin and we're not supposed to.
Oooh. I'll have to . . ."
Leah: "I didn't."
Craig: "Can I borrow the rubber, please? Have you got the rubber?"
Leah: "Em, rubber."
Craig: "Oh, thanks. Thanks. Do we draw a line across?"

They started writing and sorting out the appropriate coins.

Leah: "Do that. Put out all the coins you need to buy all the groceries
shown in the pictures."
Craig: "Pardon?"
Leah: "Put out all the coins you need to buy the groceries shown in the
pictures."
Craig: "What? Do you need all the coins?"
Leah: "Yeah."
Craig: "Well, I don't need them all out yet. Now then, 22p."
Leah: "Where are you up to? Number two?"
Craig: "And a packet of flour. That's 14p."
Leah: "Packet of flour."
Craig: "14p. Put it in a list."
Leah: "Packet of. . . . what?"
Craig: "You put it in a list."
Leah: "Yeah, I know."

Progress Reports

These contain instances in which children compare the amounts of work completed. This talk was fairly common and occasionally lead to arguments as in the following extract.

> Ian: "Have you started your second? I am doing my second."
> Neil: "You're finishing up yesterday's."
> Ian: "This isn't yesterday's. This is today's."
> Neil: "That's your first one of today's, isn't it?"
> Ian: "Yeah."
> Andrew E: "Daniel has done two cards all on his own."
> Ian: "I know 'cos I saw him writing it. Well, I've done more than you."
> Andrew: "You haven't done more than me."
> Ian: "Well, I'm there,"
> Andrew: "I'm on my fourth card."
> Ian: "You're not 'cos you've only done two today."
> Andrew: "I am. 1, 2, 3, 4. I'm on my fourth."
> Ian: "Well, 'cos you're counting those that you did yesterday."
> "I'm on my third."
> Ian: "You're on your second today, aren't you? But not your fourth today."
> Andrew: "Yeah. I'm on my fourth."
> Ian: "You're not 'cos you're counting the ones you did Yesterday."

In Status talk children compare their abilities or aptitudes in relation to the task being performed.

> Ian: "I'm doing them in my head now."
> Neil: "I bet you get them all wrong."
> Ian: "Stephen has to count on his fingers."
> Stephen: "It's best doing it with them."

The Materials Category

This has a number of sub-divisions. Requesting and responding to requests for rubbers or pencils are common facets of classroom life although cooperation was not always forthcoming, as is shown in the following extract.

> Andrew E: "Hey! Don't mess them up, Ian. Hey! Stop it. I'm putting them in."
> Andrew R: "No, I need it."
> Ian: "Two and one. You have to wait now because I'm doing it."
> Andrew E: "No, get them out of the other one, Andrew. Leave them, Andrew."

Andrew R: "I'll need them for a bit."

(30 seconds later)

        Ian: "Andrew. Stop it."

Andrew E: "Hey!"

          (Observer reports physical confrontation here).

        Ian: "Andrew!"

Andrew R: "I'll tell."

        Ian: "We're using them."

Andrew E: "You idiot!"

        Ian: "We're using them. We can have these."

Andrew E: "Well, you can't have this . . ."

        Ian: "Andrew! Get off!"

Andrew E: "Or these."

        Ian: "Mrs T."

      Neil: "See, he's a baby 'cos he went to tell."

Mrs T.: "What do you want, Ian?"

        Ian: "I'm doing the measuring, and Andrew is taking them back out."

Mrs T.: "Oh dear! We have only got one of these. This, Andrew?"

        Ian: "No, that."

Mrs T.: "Andrew E? Why not just take them out when someone else is using it? Or they all get all mixed up. Just one person at a time use it."

Egocentric Speech

This, as the term implies, refers to children talking to themselves as they complete the task.

Definitions of categories not illustrated here can be found in Appendix C.

Most of the illustrations are in fact taken from the transcription of one group to show that the full range of the categories was often apparent in the performance of one task.

CATEGORIES OF TALK

All talk that occurred between children in the group, and between these children and others outside the group, including teachers, was recorded. Most of the interactions with the teacher actually took place at the teacher's desk as the children either read to the teacher, had their work marked or asked questions. Very little teacher talk to children in the group context occurred.

The number of words spoken during the tasks observed varied greatly as Table 8.1 shows.

TABLE 8.1

Average and Range of Number of Words Spoken in Number and Language Tasks

Focus of Talk	Number	Language
Pupil–Pupil	2809	1813
(range)	(2195–3422)	(335–3095)
Pupil–Teacher	240	164
(range)	(93–359)	(23–408)
Teacher–Pupil	887	610
(range)	(395–2138)	(166–1617)

In language tasks, for example, an average of 1813 words were exchanged between pupils but this varied a great deal between groups. The extent of pupil–pupil talk was some three times greater than teacher-to-pupil talk, which in turn was some three times greater than talk initiated by pupils to the teacher. However, these averages are confounded by the fact that the tasks were of different length. Number tasks varied from 37 to 45 minutes, and language tasks from 27 to 44 minutes. Nevertheless, when this is taken into account by calculating the number of words per minute, the range is still extremely wide. The number of words per minute exchanged between pupils, for example, varied from 50 to 86 in number work and from 12 to 74 in language activites (see Roth, 1983, for full details). In recognition of this problem of different task length, all the following tables are presented in percentages.

Table 8.2 presents a breakdown of all talk into the two major categories of task and non-task talk for number and language tasks.

The percentage figure shown in the boxes is the average for all six

TABLE 8.2

Average and Range of Types of Talk in Number and Language (% rounded)

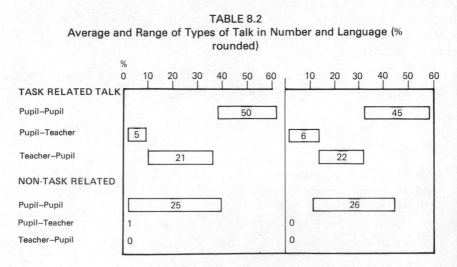

groups and the extremes of the box show the range. For example, in number tasks an average of 50% of all talk was pupil-to-pupil task-related, but in some groups it was as low as 38% and in others as high as 58%. If this is compared with pupil-to-pupil non-task talk (25%) it is apparent that there was twice as much task-related as non-task-related talk among pupils.

Pupil–teacher talk was limited to some 5% of all talk in both number and language. Teacher–pupil talk, on the other hand, was more extensive; but as was indicated earlier, the great majority of this took place when members of the group were at the teacher's desk. Social talk between teachers and pupils was very rare.

Overall, three-quarters of all talk was task related, a very different picture from that painted by previous research on older children. Neither was there any indication of sex differences. Boys and girls at this age appeared to converse freely and frequently with members of the opposite sex. The crucial question, however, is whether this talk is equally useful and beneficial to work on the task at hand. Is, for example, the child's explanation of a concept to another child (instructional input) to be regarded as of equal value to a child arguing with another about who should have the unifix cubes (materials talk)? In previous studies these have been accorded equal weighting but a useful distinction could be made between task enhancing talk, i.e., that which enhances a child's understanding, and task related talk, i.e., that which might aid production but not understanding.

Table 8.3 sets out the proportion of pupil talk in the four major task-related categories.

The pattern of talk across the categories was similar in both number and language. Over half was in the Sharing Information category whilst the remainder was equally spread across the other three categories. The average for Instructional Input which is most likely to be task enhancing was 8% of all talk, although this varied across the twelve groups from zero to 20%. The nature and content of this is dealt with fully in the qualitative analysis.

The large block of Sharing Information talk was shared among the four sub-categories as shown in Table 8.4.

TABLE 8.3
Percentage of Talk in the Four Major Task-Related Categories

Task-Related Talk	Number	Language
Instructional input	8	8
Sharing information	27	26
Material	6	5
Egocentric	9	7
Total	50	46

TABLE 8.4
Percentages of Talk in the Sharing Information Sub-Categories

Sharing Information	Number	Language
Task-specific	38	37
Task-management	16	30
Progress reports	25	10
Status	7	14

The proportion of task specific talk was the same in number and language lessons, but the other sub-categories varied markedly between these types of task. Talk about the management or presentation of the task was much higher in language but comparisons of progress were more extensive in number work. Apparently the number of calculations or work cards completed was more salient in children's minds than the number of lines written in a story. Status talk was more limited than the other categories but was twice as frequent in language than number.

Only 5% of talk was about materials, and the major reason for such talk was requests. There was noticeably more talk devoted to such requests in number work, which is perhaps not surprising since many tasks required weights, cubes, artificial money or rulers. There was more argument about materials in number tasks. Such arguments were illustrated in an earlier extract. There was a discrepancy in the amount of talk used in requesting and responding here simply because requests were often fulfilled without comment.

As was shown in Table 8.1 the amount of pupil–teacher talk was small. Two-thirds of this took the form of requests for help of some kind or referred to the management of the task. This is dealt with in detail in the qualitative analysis where it will be seen that in language, requests for spellings dominated. The nature of teacher–pupil talk is also considered later.

Finally, within the confines of the small sample, an attempt was made to ascertain whether group composition related in any consistent manner to different patterns of talk. There were no differences related to sex composition but fairly strong indications that attainment mix did have an effect.

The sample was divided into those groups consisting of children of average to high attainment, average to low attainment and one group with both high and low attainment. Table 8.5 shows the resultant profiles across the major categories. The high/average groups produced a much higher level of Instructional Input, less Task Management and more Progress comparisons. One tentative explanation for the latter finding might be that such groups are more competitive. It is interesting to note that the

TABLE 8.5
Profiles of Talk for Groups of Differing Composition (%)

	Group Type		
	High/average	*Average/low*	*High/low*
Sharing Information			
Instructional input	15	2	3
Task-specific	40	35	39
Task-management	17	26	42
Progress report	23	14	4
Status	11	11	8
Materials			
Requests	44	27	21
Response			
Cooperative	17	4	0
Response			
argumentative	13	2	0
State	23	28	41
Play	0	6	32

combination of high and low ability children provided a profile more like the average/low groups.

THE NATURE OF INSTRUCTIONAL INPUT

Pupil-to-Pupil

The picture emerging from the quantitative analyses is that the amount of instructional input is low, being some 16% of task related talk and approximately 8% of all talk. Differences in type of talk were noted in language and number tasks such that a higher proportion of requests and responses were apparent in language and more unsolicited help in number work. These findings represent the bare bones of group talk but tell us nothing of the exact nature of it. In order to provide this flesh, all talk in the instructional input category, which might be considered to be the most task enhancing talk, was analysed qualitatively.

It will be recalled that such talk was categorised broadly as requests and responses, but requests embodied different demands and responses were of differing complexity. In respect of this, a distinction was made between higher order and lower order talk. More specifically, higher order requests were defined as requiring an explanation of how to obtain a solution, e.g., "Will you show me how to add fractions?," whereas a lower order request simply required an answer without explanation, e.g., "What is 14 take 7?," or, "How do you spell *whale*?" Responses were similarly categorised.

Analysing requests and responses in this way showed up clear differences in language and number tasks which are presented separately below.

Number

In number work the great majority of requests were lower order. These tended to be short and specific—"Which coin has the biggest value?"; "What is the price of half a kilogram of carrots?"; "How many two's in fifty-four?" Sixty per cent of such requests elicited a lower order response and one response in six was incorrect.

> Amy: "You can do shares . . . like three shared nine. Three shared nine is four . . . see?"

Of the lower order requests that did not gain a similar response many were simply unheeded or were occasionally rejected.

> Fiona: "Amy, are you on 7?"
> Amy: "What that one?"
> Fiona: "Yes, I don't know how to write it down."
> Amy: "I'm not telling you. I'm doing my maths."

Lower order requests eliciting a higher order response were very rare.

One response in four was unsolicited, i.e., children helped, or attempted to help, without being asked to. The majority of these were of lower order and were not always correct. Sometimes they were rejected.

> Fiona: "Can't you do your second one?"
> Amanda: "No, it's the fourth one."
> Karen: "Do you know what the fourth one is? Do You? 17."
> Fiona: "It might not be for all you know."
> Karen: "All of them. Three—17, four—17, five—17."
> Fiona: "Amanda, I wouldn't believe Karen 'cos she nearly got them all wrong."

Not all unsolicited help was taken seriously even when an adequate explanation was offered.

> Andrew: "I'll show you with this four. Right. And one more."
> Ian: "Yeah."
> Andrew: "Join them together."
> Ian: "Five."
> Andrew: "Five. And then add three."
> Ian: "Five."

Andrew: "Add three nitwit. And then what do you do?"
Ian: "Put them in the toilet and flush it."

Less than 10% of requests were higher order. These often took the form of a general implied request which appeared to be recognised by the group as explicit, e.g., "I can't do this" or "I don't know how to do this." Over one-half were unheeded or pupils were unable to help, or were incorrect. Some had a status sting in the tail.

David: "Suzanne, Suzanne. I don't know how to do this."
Suzanne: "How many less than 14 is 7? What's 7?"
Lisa: "God, it's 7!"
Suzanne: "See all you have to do is that less that. Mrs S. has done that one on the board before hasn't she?"
Lisa: "Yeah, it's the same as takeaway isn't it?"
David: "Oh yeah."
Suzanne: "He doesn't know anything does he?"

Finally it was not always clear whether children working on individual tasks were allowed to seek help from the others in the group; the children's confusion over this is exemplified in extracts taken from two different groups in the same classroom:

Hayley: "Stuart, Stuart. What's that one? What is it? Ten take away one leaves . . .?"
Stuart: "Ten take away one?"
Hayley: "Ten?"
Craig: "Hayley, you're not allowed to let people help you. Don't help her Stuart."
Stuart: "But she's done the right answer and Mrs D. crossed it."
Hayley: "She crossed it and it was the right answer."
Victoria: "Well you have to go and learn yourself. Not allowed . . . so you'll have to do it yourself Hayley."
Craig: "I'll tell if you help her."

This can be compared to the following extract from a different group in the same classroom where Jonathan, himself unable to help Liz, directed her to someone who could. Liz and Jonathan were "stuck" on different problems and engaged in a trade-off.

Liz: "I know. If I tell you that will you tell me this?"
Jonathan: "Alright . . . right then, what is it?"
Liz: "4p."
Jonathan: "Oh thanks."
Liz: "Will you tell me this?"
Jonathan: "I know who knows this—Craig does."

Language

The low incidence of higher order requests and responses was even more marked in language tasks. Lower order demands comprised nearly 90% of all requests and most of these were for spellings. The type of response gained varied markedly in different groups. In one group five such requests resulted in two "no responses", one refusal and two incorrect answers.

> Phillip: "How do you spell panda?"
> Scott: "p, a, n, d, r."
> Phillip: "P, a, n, d."
> Scott: "P, a, n, d, e, r." (emphasising "er" sound)
> Phillip: "d, r?"

Similarly

> Phillip: "Is there an 'r' in monkey?"
> Verity: "No it's 'a'. It's 'a' you silly."

In another group all eight requests were attended to even if it caused some exasperation.

> Stephen: "Let's ask her for that word." (her being Lisa).
> Richard: "Found, found."
> Lisa: "Frouned."
> Amanda: "Frone, frone, let's see."
> Lisa: "Frowned because look you frown like that. (giggles). I can't do it."
> Amanda: "Frone."
> Lisa: "It's frowned isn't it?"
> Stephen: "Is that frown?"
> Richard: "You got it wrong."
> Stephen: "I got it right."
>
> (later)
>
> Stephen: "What's this again? Frowned?"
> Lisa: "I'm not telling you."
> Stephen: "Frowned. Frown."
> Lisa: "Let's have a look. Which one? We told you that."
> Stephen: "We've forgotten again."
> Lisa: "Frown.'
> Stephen: "Frowned."
> Lisa: "Not frowned, frown."

Occasionally the answer was refused but the method was provided, e.g., the child was handed a dictionary or referred to the blackboard.

Very occasionally the original lower order request was amended in light of the response. In the following extract for example, a general plea for help received a lower order response which in turn led to a further higher order response.

Lisa: "I'm stuck. I'm stuck Amanda."
Amanda: "Are you?"
Lisa: "This one." (Lisa's task is to find the odd man out in a list of words—a pan, plate, sink, car, saucer).
Amanda: (Pointing to the word car) "That one there."
Lisa: "It isn't because sink and cars . . . and they're not like them."
Amanda: "Easy, some are in something. The other one is in a different place, isn't it?"

The few occasions in which unsolicited help was offered, all concerned the spelling of words.

Summary

Previous research on teaching in general, and on classroom groups in particular, has implicitly assumed that task-related talk is somehow superior to other kinds of talk. However the quantitative analyses showed that talk typically categorised as task related is extremely varied and, at face value, differentially useful for the task at hand. It was therefore felt that a useful distinction might be drawn between task related and task enhancing talk and that the latter would be manifested in the instructional input categories. Webb (1982) for example found that engaging in helping behaviour and receiving help correlated with achievement, but this was limited to help which involved explanation or elaboration, i.e., what has been called higher order talk. Thus the finding that the great majority of requests and responses were of lower order is disappointing in this regard, although it might be expected that lower order responses would, if correct, further the completion of the task, and thus achieve savings in teacher time. Whether such responses lead to a better understanding is open to question.

Teacher–Pupil Interaction

Number Work. The nature of the interactions between teachers and pupils does not lend itself to the categorisation of requests and responses. The focus here is therefore on the different strategies teachers used to present tasks, and equally important, how they dealt with children's errors and misunderstandings. In other words, on the nature of teacher explanations.

In all the classrooms observed the children were working their way through a sequenced number scheme. They sat in groups but worked on independent tasks. Tasks were usually presented by a directive to "carry on" from where the children had left off. Following this, teachers seated themselves at their desks where they dealt with individual children. Thus, virtually all of the talk initiated by teachers occurred at their desks. The reason behind this strategy was the teachers' insistence on marking work in the presence of the child. This is a laudable objective but carried with it certain organisational consequences. The most pressing of these was queueing. Queues were a constant feature of all the classrooms studied. The teachers were aware of this problem but felt unable to suggest an alternative which did not destroy their underlying objective. In some classrooms teachers operated a dual-queue system whereby they listened to children reading at one side of the desk at the same time as marking and correcting other children's work at the other side. The effect of this practice is taken up later.

As stated above, most teachers, in presenting the task, simply directed children to "carry on." Only one teacher adopted an alternative strategy. In this class the teacher was concerned to assess whether the children actually understood the task directions and engaged in both class and group exchanges to this end. The question and answer format used is demonstrated in the following short extract.

> Teacher: "Underneath you will find there are three shaded in . . . three shaded in, and some are not shaded in. How many are not shaded in? Anyone?"
> Children: "Seven."
> Teacher: "Seven, so we can find out from counting that three and seven make?"
> Children: "Ten."
> Teacher: "Ten. Now look at the other side. Fill in the answers. Three and . . . you'll have to put in the numbers that are missing. Three and what value ten? Well we counted them."
> Children: "Seven."

This was followed by a similar explanation with an example of a take-away sign.

This same teacher also brought together members of different groups who were working on the same workcard to assess their understanding.

> Teacher: "Take 50p. Buy a packet of flour. Twelve . . .?"
> Craig: "Ten bags."
> Teacher: "And one . . .? What does kg mean?"
> John: "Kilograms."

Teacher: "Kilogram of sugar. Bring me your books and then we can show how to set it out."

She then took the children through how the task should be presented. Following this they were told to "have a go" but to come and ask if they got stuck. The children returned to their various groups, and the teacher to her desk after checking that all children understood the task.

The directive to "carry on" was sometimes modified by requiring the class to complete a number of problems written on the blackboard. The number presented was usually small, some five or six. This seemed to exacerbate the queueing problem since a constant stream of children required these to be corrected before they could carry on with their work card.

An analysis of the interaction at the teacher's desk raises a number of interesting issues. For example, how do teachers deal with mechanical or procedural errors, or with lack of understanding of the concept required, and with the competing demands of children in the dual queue system?

Dealing with mechanical or procedural errors tended to lead to short interactions. The most common strategy was to take the child step by step through the problem. The following two extracts are typical.

Teacher: "Right. Come on let's try another one. Do your units. Two nothings are?"
Jonathan: "Nothing."
Teacher: "Two one's are?"
Jonathan: "Two."
Teacher: "Two. Now go and do these on this piece of paper."

Teacher: "You've got 13 less 9."
Edwin: "Take away 9."
Teacher: "Yes. Leaves you with how many?"
Edwin: "2,3,4, 2,3,4,5,6."
Teacher: "Well how about getting some unifix and working it out?"

In a number of such extracts it is unclear whether the child actually understood the procedure because the teacher simply provided it rather than ascertaining if the pupil comprehended it. In the following extract Craig could not complete the problem 15×2, which involved carrying, and asked the teacher.

Teacher: "Now, this time you're going to carry your ten. Now watch. Two fives are ten. Nought down. Carry one. Like your add sums, yes? Two ones are two and one makes . . .?"
Craig: "Three."

Teacher: "Well, go on. Two sevens are . . .? Martin you're being silly on that table. Stop it. Two sevens are . . .?"
Craig: "Nine."
Teacher: "No, it's not nine. Look. Two sevens are . . .?"
Craig: "Fourteen."
Teacher: "Four down, carry one. Two ones are . . .?"
Craig: "Three."
Teacher: "No, it's not two and one. It's two times one. Two times one . . .?"
Craig: "Two."
Teacher: "Two ones are two, and that one makes . . .?"
Craig: "Three."
Teacher: "Yes. Do these on this piece of paper first."

Since the teacher actually told Craig the procedure "four down carry one," it is difficult to assess Craig's actual understanding. In other instances the level of understanding was later ascertained by the fieldworker. Edwin was one such example.

Edwin: "Miss L."
Teacher: "Will you please sit down and wait for me."

The teacher spent half-a-minute writing out five sums.

Teacher: "Now I've written all this out. Now before we look at this, let's think about it. Should we try the first one?" (10 less _____ → 6).
Edwin: "10 less nothing . . . add . . . 6."
Teacher: "Leaves you with 6, doesn't it? 10 less something leaves you with . . .? Now then, you've got 10, and you've got to have how many left?"
Edwin: "Six."
Teacher: "Six left. So we've got to have six left. So how many do we need to take away from that 10 to leave us with 6? 10 less 6 . . . 10 less something leaves us with 6, I'm sorry. Now then, how do you think we could work it out?"

Edwin did not reply.

Teacher: "Well shall we try it with the unifix? Would you like to go and get me 10 unifix?"
Edwin: "10. 1, 2, 3, 4, 5, 6, 7, 8, 9, 10." (getting the unifix).
Teacher: "Read it through. It's the easiest one of the lot. So we've got 10 less something leaves us with . . .?"
Edwin: "Six."
Teacher: "Six right. So we want to find out what that something is—don't we? So what are we left with?"

Edwin: "Six."

Teacher: "We're left with 6, so you leave yourself with 6 from those." (pointing to unifix).

Edwin: "1,2,3,4,5,6."

Teacher: "So that's what left, isn't it? So that belongs there, doesn't it?"

Edwin: "Yes."

Teacher: "With the 6 there. So what do we have to take away from this full 10 to leave us with 6?"

Edwin: "Four."

Teacher: "Now how can we check that? Do you know?"

Edwin: "Hmm."

Teacher: "Put your four in there. Can you think of a way? Well how many did we have altogether? Ten and we wanted six of them left, so that told us how many we had taken away from it, yes?"

Edwin: "Yes."

Teacher: "So how can we check? How much do that and that add up to? How much do that and that add up to then?"

Edwin: "Ten."

Teacher: "Well see if it does. Count them all."

Edwin begins to move some of the unifix.

Teacher: "No. You've no need to put them together."

Edwin: "1,2,3."

Teacher: "Could you start at four?"

Edwin: "4,5,6,7,8,9,10."

Teacher: "Right. So that's right, isn't it? We've checked it. Not too sure about that? Well, try and do this next one with me then. What do we want first of all?

Edwin: "Ten less nothing."

Teacher: "Less something. We just said that 'cos we don't know what that is yet, do we? Leaves us with . . .?"

Edwin: "Five."

Teacher: "Right. Now then, we want how many left?"

Edwin: "Five."

Teacher: "Right."

Edwin: "1,2,3,4,5." (counting out the unifix).

Teacher: "So we've got 5 left. That's what we wanted left, isn't it? So what do we get rid of to leave us with five from the ten?"

Edwin: "1,2,3,4,5." (counting the unifix).

Teacher: "Oh, so 10 less 5 leaves us with . . .?"

Edwin: "Five."

Teacher: "Right. Now see if you can write the others out. O.K.?"

Edwin's initial misconception that the ＿＿ equated with nothing "10 less nothing . . . add . . . 6" was not corrected by the teacher. The first problem was completed mechanically only with explicit guidance from the teacher who did not ascertain whether Edwin understood the checking process. His initial misconception was repeated in the second example and the instructional process was repeated. Edwin was later interviewed by the fieldworker at the end of his task where it became clear that he had no understanding of the process.

The impression gained from this extract is that there might be more value in teachers providing less direct instructional input and adopting a more diagnostic stance thus allowing the child to exhibit his errors. Teachers often seemed to devote large amounts of time instructing pupils but to little effect. The next extended extract between a teacher and Victoria further supports this. (Two thirds of all the teacher's talk during this lesson was with Victoria.) A fieldworker was also observing the same girl.

9.25   The teacher helps Victoria: "Oh dear, you did get in a muddle yesterday, didn't you? Let's try it again here shall we?. . . We've got a multicoloured one, look. A blue ten and a red unit. Can you do it without your bundles?"

Victoria: "Yes."

Teacher: "Mmm. Take six from three. Can you take six from three?"

Victoria: "Yes."

Teacher: "No. What do you do?"

Victoria: "Borrow."

Teacher: "Where do you get it from?"

Victoria: "There."

Teacher: "What does that make it into?"

Victoria: "A three."

Teacher: "Where do you put your extra ten? (No reply from Victoria) Next to the . . .?"

Victoria: "Three."

Teacher: "What number does that make?"

Victoria: "Thirteen."

Teacher: "Thirteen. Thirteen take away six. Put six in your pocket."

Victoria: "6 . . . 7,8,9,10,11,12,13 . . . five, six, seven." (counting her fingers).

Teacher: (Almost half a minute after Victoria's answer). "Yes. Now will you just do that one there and come and show me."

Victoria: "It's right."

Teacher: "I'm sorry. That one. That one there."

Victoria: "Yeah."

Teacher: "But do it down there carefully and come and show me before you do any more.'

Victoria: "Is that a five?"
Teacher: "That's a fifty one take away forty three."
Victoria: "Right. 'Scuse Craig'."

Victoria returned to her table and began on her work.

9.32   Victoria went back to the teacher with her work.
        Teacher: "You've done that right at the top there, and then you
                said eleven take away three leaves nine (the
                fieldworker explains that Victoria used her ruler to
                count back three, but started with eleven as the first
                number—hence the answer nine). Put three in your
                pocket. Go on and count on."
        Victoria: "3,4,5,6,7,8,9,10."
        Teacher: "It's eleven, isn't it? So how many is that?"
        Victoria: "Eight."
        Teacher: "We'll cheat a little bit this time and turn that into an
                eight. But be careful next time. You're going to do two
                next time, one there and one underneath. Right?
                Think what you're doing. You're quite capable."

Victoria returned to her table. She worked quietly alone, once asking Hayley
to move, then went to the teacher. The teacher looked at Victoria's work:

9.37   Teacher: "You've done this wrong again. Now look at this one.
                Do you need to carry a ten on that one? Can you take
                two away from nine? I told you to watch the top number
                didn't I? (The sum is $49 - 22$). Nine. Can you take
                two away from nine? Can you not? If I had nine sweets,
                could I not give you two of them?"
        Victoria: "Yes."
        Teacher: "Yes. So you don't need to carry ten, do you? That's
                put in there as a little trick to see if you're thinking
                what you're doing. Now this you did right. ($46 - 27$).
                But look here. Sixteen take away seven. Put seven in
                your pocket. I think you went wrong there. Start again.
                Put seven in your pocket."
        Victoria: "Seven."
        Teacher: "Go on."
        Victoria: "Seven, one, two, three . . ."
        Teacher: "No. You said seven, one, two, three. What comes
                after seven?"
        Victoria: "Eight."
        Teacher: "Right. Start again."
        Victoria: "7; 8,9,10,11,12,13,14,15,16."
        Teacher: "Right, and what have you got?"
        Victoria: "Nine."

Teacher: "And what should be there then?"
Victoria: "Nine."
Teacher: "Have you got a rubber?"
Victoria: "Yes."
Victoria: "Are you going to alter that one? Do you know why now? Right, go and do that one again. Be careful."

Later the teacher turned her attention to Victoria again:

Teacher: "Right, Victoria. Let me have a look at what you're doing. Good girl, you've got it the right way round this time. Where are you up to now?"
Victoria: "Done that one."
Teacher: "You've done that one. And that one. Can you be more careful and do two this time?"
Victoria: "Yes."
Teacher: "Can you manage that? Look at the top number each time."
Victoria: "Right."

Subsequently Victoria waited in the teacher's queue so that the six sums she had just completed from the blackboard could be marked. She commented to someone in the queue, "I hope I get them right. One, two, three, four, five, six. 'Cos if I don't, I'll have to do them again." She also explained that she had finished her book and that she had got to see the teacher as she was giving out the books today.

9.58   The teacher marked Victoria's work. The first $(45 - 16)$ was wrong:
Teacher: "Can you take six from five? (No reply from Victoria). No. Well what do you do?"
Victoria: "Carry some over."
Teacher: "Well, have you done it?"
Victoria: "No."
Teacher: "Well, what made you do that silly sum? 'Cos it is a silly sum. 'Cos if you add that to that you have forty six, and you don't even have forty six to start with. Well, I just don't know. I'm sorry Victoria, you do one wrong and then one next to it right and then here you've done it wrong again. Look. Can you take four from nothing? (No reply). If there's nothing can I take four from it?"
Victoria: "Yeah."
Teacher: "Look. There's nothing in my hand. Can I take four out of there?"
Victoria: "No."
Teacher: "No. And what should you do?"

Victoria: "Carry a ten over."
Teacher: "Carry a ten." (She then asks Victoria to do the two corrections and to bring them back).
10.00   Victoria: (returning to her seat) "Haliborange. Haliborange."

The teacher asked Victoria to do the tables sums on the blackboard and the child rushed through them, using her fingers to add sums such as 2×7, for which she made the answer nine. She did all multiplication as addition.

Despite the large amount of time and effort the teacher devoted to Victoria she did not diagnose the child's underlying problem. The fieldworker was able to do so by watching her perform her task. As was shown in the extract, the fieldworker explained Victoria's error with the ruler, but the major source of Victoria's problem was that she subtracted the tens column before subtracting the units column. This was not diagnosed by the teacher because she, in common with most of the teachers observed, reacted solely to the answers the child provided. Had the teacher asked Victoria to work out the problem in her presence, the error in procedure might have been more apparent.

Reacting to the product of a child's performance rather than adopting a diagnostic stance and ascertaining the process or strategy which the child used was typical. The outcome was often to perpetuate and perhaps accentuate the child's misunderstanding, and on other occasions it led to children moving on in the maths sequence without a proper understanding. For example, on occasion children were seen to alter their answers in the queue either after seeing other children's work or on discussing their answers with others in the queue. Because teachers reacted only to answers, these were marked correct and the child moved on to the next work card.

The problem was exacerbated by the insistence of some teachers to stick to the mechanics of a problem even when it was clear that the child did not understand either the underlying process or the explanation offered.

The following extract illustrates this. Here the notion of carrying, and the transformation of the carried ten into units, was totally ignored, despite Fiona's obvious lack of understanding.

Fiona: "Miss, I can't work out the fourth and fifth. $2\overline{)54}$: $3\overline{)51}$.
Teacher: "Well you ought to be able to oughtn't you. And your pencil's thick and black for a start. That's squashed together. You've forgotten how to do this? You'd better practice at home this weekend. How many two's in five?"
Fiona: "Two."
Teacher: "Where does the two go?"

Fiona: "In there."
Teacher: "Write it down at the top. How many left over?"
Fiona: "One."
Teacher: "Now what do we say? How many two's in . . .?"
Fiona: "Four."
Teacher: "In what? How many two's in . . .?"
Fiona: "One."
Teacher: "No."
Fiona: "Five."
Teacher: "How many two's in . . .?"
Fiona: "Four."
Teacher: "But that isn't four. What number is that?"
Fiona: "One."
Teacher: "But you can't say how many two's in one can you? Because
           there aren't any, and that's your number. How many two's in
           . . .?"
Fiona: "Fourteen."
Teacher: "Yes now come on. You were busy talking and you're stopping
           other people from working as well. You're getting into a bad
           habit of talking Fiona. You're doing far too much. Right come on.
           Do this one $(3\overline{)51})$."

It is apparent that Fiona did not know the rules concerning carrying
which led her into a series of guesses. However, rather than dealing with
these, the teacher attempted to gain the correct response by repetitive
questioning, "How many two's in?"

Queueing. There is a second issue relating to the above illustration
which is not apparent in the extract. Throughout this interaction another
child, Katy, had been reading to the same teacher, but had been ignored.
This was a direct result of the dual-queue system operated in this and
several of the other classrooms. Elsewhere Karen experienced the same
situation.

Teacher: "Right, well, we'll have a look at the words shall we?" We've got
           plenty of time."
Karen: "Drive."
Teacher: "No."
Karen: "Drove."
Teacher: "Drove, yes."
Karen: "River . . ."
Teacher: (to Howard while Karen continues reading). "How many two's in
           fourteen? Not 4, Oh Howard you really are painful with your
           sums. . . . Oh wait a minute Karen I wasn't watching those. Let's
           have them again."

Shortly afterwards the teacher threatened to shoot Howard for not knowing his 2× table and for not looking it up on the chart. Karen continued to read her list of words for about ten minutes but was ignored by the teacher. In an attempt to gain attention she repeated the word "sell" three times.

Teacher: (to Howard) "Go and find out how many two's there are in fourteen."
Karen: "Sell."
Teacher: "Sell, that's right."
Karen: "Shall I get (book) 11a?"
Teacher: (tapping Howard on the head with a book) "Go home this weekend and tell your mummy that you need to learn your 2× table and you need to practice your sharing sums. You're the worst in the class."
Karen: "10c?"

Gaining no response, Karen left the teacher's desk and chose a book.

Situations such as these only occurred where a dual-queue system was operated. It would appear to be an organisation in which it is impossible to provide satisfactory attention to both children. And constant claims for attention from both sides of the desk may contribute to the teacher's levels of frustration apparent in both of the above extracts.

There is yet another major consequence of queueing. This is that it affords the teacher no opportunity for adequately supervising children's work in groups. This is important in the light of evidence that the extent of on-task behaviour in groups falls significantly when teacher supervision is lacking (Fisher et al., 1979).

Teachers regularly complained about the queues but appeared to be victims of their own aims, being unable to experiment with any alternatives. The only alternative found in this study was practised by the teacher who only occasionally sat at her table but spent much more time supervising groups, and assessed the correctness of tasks by questions and answer sessions in the group setting.

Teacher: "Quickly, put it down. Right I'm going to read it to you. I want you to follow because I'm not writing all the answers . . . ready? Point to the next one. Which two cakes can be bought for one five pence?"

(This continues through the list of questions with members of the group responding in the following manner).

Teacher: "What is the total cost, that means altogether, of a fruit cake and a rock bun? How much is the fruit cake? Look at the list."
Otto: "5p."

> Teacher: "How much are the rock buns?"
>   Otto: "9p" (this is wrong).
> Teacher: "So how much is it altogether?"
>   Otto: "9p."
> Teacher: "How much for two scones?"
>   etc. etc.

The only criticism of this teacher was in the lack of specificity with which she defined key terms.

> Teacher: "Which of these coins has the least value?"
>   John: (puzzled).
> Teacher: "That means you wouldn't be able to buy very much with it."
> (later)
> Teacher: "What is the dearest? In other words which will take up a lot of your money to buy one of these cakes?"
> (later)
> Teacher: "What is the cheapest? Which doesn't take up very much of your money?"

Summary

This analysis of teacher–pupil interaction in the category of instructional input has highlighted a number of issues relating to the utility of teacher explanations. The most central is the strategy of reacting to children's answers rather than basing diagnoses on the strategy employed by the child. At face value such a change in practice would seem likely to achieve significant savings in time for the teacher and improvements in understanding in children.

Teachers were clearly conscious of and unhappy about the extent of queueing but appeared unable to develop alternatives. The one alternative observed appears to have the advantage of improving the supervision of groups in addition to allowing time to assess whether the children are clear about the requirements of the tasks set.

There were also indications that some teacher decisions actually exacerbated the problems of queueing. One was the practice of setting "daily five" or "daily ten" sums on the blackboard to be completed before children continued with their workcards. The evidence gathered would indicate that this increased queueing. Finally, the decision to adopt a dual-queue system would seem to lead to a very unsatisfactory situation for both teacher and taught.

Language. Teacher–pupil talk in language was dominated by teachers providing or correcting spellings. However there were distinctly different strategies for handling such requests. Some teachers simply provided the correct spelling, some directed pupils to dictionaries (although there was often teacher help), others helped with explanations whilst another refused to provide the spelling preferring to try and elicit it from the child. The following extracts illustrate these different responses.

A direct response to a request for a spelling was fairly common: Kerry went to the teacher for a spelling.

> Teacher: "What do you want? Let me have a look at what's going on."
> Kerry: "Fitted."
> Teacher: "Eh?"
> Kerry: "Fitted."
> Teacher: "Who?"
> Kerry: "Fitted."
> Teacher: "You can do that yourself. F,i,t,t,e,d."
>
> Nicholas: "Help."
> Teacher: "Help?"
> Nicholas: "Help."
> Teacher: "That's not a hard one. You should be able to manage that."
> Nicholas: "Help."
> Teacher: "Hel.p."
>
> Phillip: "Mrs B. I can't spell elephant."
> Teacher: "You're not so bad but it's a 'p' and an 'h', like ph for Phillip. It's the ph in elephant. So that's right up to there. That should be p.h.a."

Children were provided with some kind of dictionary in a number of the classrooms but the regularity with which children were referred to them varied. The amount of teacher input required when this strategy was used is demonstrated in the following longer extract.

> Amanda was stuck on the first question: "A person who ex . . . plores . . . is an . . . eh? Oh, it's hard, this." She worked out the answer to the third question . . . soldier . . . then read the first one again, saying once more, "Oh, this is hard." She read it yet again and finally said, "Oh, this is hard. I'm going to tell teacher." The teacher explained to her: "Well, I thought I'd give you something that would just make you think a little." She checked that Amanda could read the instructions, and then told her the first answer, instructing her to "Look it up in the dictionary."
>
> 9.39   As "explorer" was not in the classroom dictionaries, Amanda was sent to the headmistress to borrow "the big dictionary."

9.42   The teacher came over to the table to help Amanda, and explained
        how to look first for the "e's" in the dictionary, then "ex" in order
        to find "explorer." While Amanda was looking for the right page,
        the teacher was interrupted by another child but continued to help
        Amanda: "I would look down, starting there, can you see?"
        Amanda spotted "explore" and was asked to start reading the
        definition. She read, "To search, in, inq . . . uire. Inquire into. To
        investi. In . . . ves . . . ti . . . gate. Investigate," and so on. She read
        many of the words with difficulty, though she sounded them out
        carefully. The teacher had turned her attention to the other child.

        (later)

Teacher: "Right Amanda. What do you think an explorer is?"
Amanda: "A person who explores."
Teacher: "Yes, but what does exploring mean? If you are exploring
          something. Read what it said in the dictionary."
Amanda: "Looks for monsters and that."
Teacher: "Looks for monsters? I suppose so, yes. Looks for what? It said
          to . . . and there was one word that began with 'in', two words
          began with 'in,' in the dictionary. To investigate and to inquire.
          That means to find out really, doesn't it. I know that's a bit hard
          for you, but you did very well to find that in that big dictionary,
          because that's a grown-ups dictionary. Good girl."
Amanda told the teacher that soldier was not in the blue dictionary, and she
was given a clue, "it begins with s,o,l,d" and was told to look in the green
one.

In this task the words required were beyond the child's understanding
and much time was devoted to finding the word "explorer" in the
dictionary. No one would doubt that this is a useful skill to develop but the
experience was somewhat tarnished by the teacher's acceptance of
"looking for monsters" as an adequate definition. This acceptance was
probably in part due to the teacher's view that children should rarely be
told that they are wrong. The problem of finding "soldier" was
circumvented by the provision of the first four letters of the word.

Other teachers would provide more explanation for the spelling of
words and these accounts were often cast in a mystical vein.

Scott: "I don't know how to spell it."
Teacher: "It's a funny word. It's got a secret 'h' in it."
Teacher: (turning to Verity) "Now let's have a look at your spellings.
          What's 1? What animal's that?"
Verity: "Rhino."
Teacher: "Oh, what does rhino start with? What letter sound?"
Verity: "'r'."
Teacher: "'r', well what have you put a 'h' for? You're a silly billy. 'r', and

then here's a 'h'. You don't hear it. It's a silent 'h'. Rhin-o. The rest of it's right. Tiger's right. Gor-i-lla. Two 'l's, l,l,a. . . . You looking?"

Verity: "Yeah."

Teacher: "Now, six is whale, silent 'h' again. Magic 'e' changes 'a' into . . .?"

Verity: "'a' (ay)."

Teacher: "'a'. Whale. You've not been thinking, have you. Elephant is right, apart from a capital 'a' where it shouldn't be, and panda. Which one are you going to choose to write about?"

Verity: "Um . . ."

Teacher: "Mm?"

Verity: "The whale."

In these extracts two different children required the same spelling. To one the "h" was "secret" but to another it was "silent". The magic "e" was also prominent in this classroom but whenever the teacher used the term its function was always explained. This can be seen in a later episode with Verity.

Verity: "Race."

Teacher: "Are you sure you can't spell race?"

Verity: "I can't spell it."

Teacher: "Well we've had this sound you know. What does it start with?"

Verity: "'r'."

Teacher: "What do you think comes next?"

Verity: "'e'."

Teacher: "Race? How do we make an 'a' sound. (No reply.) What letter is it the name of?"

Verity: "'A', 'a'" (hard vowel sound).

Teacher: "'a' right. So if we put an 'a' there we need something at the end to change the 'a' into 'A'. What do we put on the end?"

Verity: "An 'e'."

Teacher: "Magic 'e'. Now all you're short of is the 'c'. Remember the magic 'e' changes that into an 's' sound."

The final strategy apparent was the decision not to give the spelling directly but to try and coax it from the child without providing any clues. The success of this process was variable as the following extract shows.

Teacher: (standing by the group) "How much have you done Joanne?"

Joanne: "I can't spell mend."

Teacher: "Mm?"

Joanne: "Can't spell mend."

Scott: "m,e,n,d."

Teacher: "Yes, that's an easy one Scott. Just like it sounds."

> Joanne: "m,e,d."
> Teacher: "No, that's med. Mend. What comes after the 'e'?"
> Joanne: "A 'd'."
> Scott: "I spelt it right."
> Teacher: "No, not yet. Mend. m,e. . . . Let her have a little think, Sarah. Mend."

Sara and Scott listened and watched the teacher who was still talking to Joanne. "Come on Joanne. That's very simple. What do you think is the next letter? (No reply). You've said it's not 'd' 'cos that would be med and you want mend. Come on, have a go. (No reply). Come on, be quick. There's Peter waiting for me to hear him read." (The teacher sat down beside Joanne). "Well, is it 'a'? Is it 'b'? Well come on. Go through the letters and decide which one it is that comes next. . . . Well, say something. You're not usually short of words as a rule. You've got such a lot to say. Come on Joanne. What's the matter? What's the matter with you? Just tell me what's the matter. Why aren't you speaking. Well, read what you've put."

> Joanne: "My daddy is special because he . ."
> Teacher: "What are you going to tell me he mends?"
> Joanne: "Cars."
> Teacher: "Oh well, come on, He mends cars, Then come on, put the next letter. Where's your pencil? . . . Come on. Put something. Tell me something even if it's wrong and then I can tell you what's right. Look at all these people waiting for me, come on. Joanne come on, put a letter down there. I'll come back in a minute. . . . Yes? (The teacher is now back at her table).

The three of them had just settled to work again when the teacher asked: "Now then Joanne, have we got that word? Did she ask somebody? I thought she would do. m,en, n, m-end. It's exactly as it sounds."

> Scott: "She wanted me to tell her."
> Teacher: "And did you?"
> Scott: "I had to. She . . ."
> Joanne: (interrupting Scott) "No, He put the, he put the 'd' the wrong way round."
> Scott: "Yeah."
> Teacher: "Well, you weren't thinking, young lady. You can manage that. My daddy is special because he mends, you want a 's' on the end don't you? He mends cars and mends . . ."
> Joanne: "Engines."
> Teacher: "Well you want a 's' on the end of mends there. Otherwise it doesn't say mends, does it. And mends engines. Then a full stop, good, and a capital letter. Right. He put . . ."
> Joanne: "He puts exhausts . . ."
> Teacher: "Oh that is a hard word. I'll give you that."

Spelling dominated teacher–pupil talk in the language area but there was also a smaller amount on sentence structure and grammar. Here there seemed to be a marked tendency to tell rather than to explain. Three short extracts illustrate this.

Kerry went to the teacher who corrected her writing: "Baby animals, full stop. Let's have it by itself. There are lambs at the farm. Now that's very careless 'cos farm is on the blackboard. Now think what you're doing. Born . . . born . . . Not at spring, it's in spring. Now put 'we saw' and do a little list of what we saw."

Craig: "He read it to me. I didn't think it made sense."

Teacher: "We see baby animals on the farm. Now that makes sense, doesn't it? You read the sentence."

Jonathan: "We see baby animals on the farm."

Teacher: "That's right. You've not finished the sentence, look. We see the baby animals. There are a lot on the farm. You see, you've got all in a muddle."

Jonathan: ". . . on the . . ."

Teacher: "We see the baby animals. Yes. With . . . their . . . mother . . . on . . . the . . . farm. Always try and read it through carefully."

Jonathan: "Yes."

Teacher: "Well I don't know whether he wants mend or mends. He'll put the 's' on if he wants it. Finger spaces (between words). You've remembered it there."

Scott: "I've remembered it here."

Teacher: "That's better. My daddy is special because he can mend cars and . . ."

Scott: "He's."

Teacher: "He's, and he's. What are you going to say next?"

Scott: "Earned a lot of money."

Teacher: "Well you don't want the 's' then do you. You want he earns. Now earns is a difficult word. I'd better give it to you in your book."

In each of these extracts the teacher changed either the tense or the sentence structure without informing the child why this was being done. It is not clear therefore whether Scott, for example, will know for future work why there is no apostrophe "s" on "he" or the reason for shifting from the past to the present tense.

Summary

Teacher instructional input in the language area was mainly in providing or correcting spellings. It has been shown that differing strategies were adopted. These data do not allow one to ascertain which is the best strategy but it might be thought that there are advantages in providing explanations rather than simply giving the answer.

9 The Quality of Teacher Diagnosis

> *If I had to reduce all of educational psychology to just one principle I would say this: the most important single factor influencing learning is what the learner already knows. Ascertain this and teach him accordingly.*
>
> (Ausubel, 1968).

In previous chapters it has been shown that teachers have problems in matching tasks to pupils' attainments. Frequently, these problems have at their root, the misdiagnosis (or non-diagnosis) of pupils' skills and knowledge. When mismatching was observed by teachers it was shown that they rarely went back to isolate the pupil's cognitive problems. Teachers appeared to focus on the product of children's work rather than the processes by which it is produced. This was illustrated in the chapter on working in groups. There, instructional input was predominated by teachers' persistence with procedural matters in the child's work.

It thus seems unlikely that matching will improve until teachers are more adept at diagnosing the problems children have with designated tasks. Whilst schemes of work could doubtless be improved in respect of sequence and structure there seems to be an infinite number of ways in which children can misinterpret task requirements. In establishing children's learning there is only one appropriate response to childrens' misinterpretations: that is to perceive them for what they are and diagnose their source in the child's intellectual invention. Any other response stores up problems for later stages in the child's learning.

Easily said, this remedy might not be so easy to practise. There are some obvious and formidable problems. Most evident is that teachers are so grossly outnumbered by pupils in classrooms. Diagnostic interviewing takes time and time is at a premium. It could be argued that teachers cannot afford the time to conduct individual interviews with children to discern the intellectual processes they use to complete their work. However, given the evidence of the previous chapters, and general evidence on the subsequent and long term limitations that many pupils evinced, it could be argued that teachers cannot afford not to ascertain children's misconceptions as early as possible.

Rather than considering the problems and advantages of teacher diagnosis in a polemical fashion, it was decided to explore the value and problems of teacher-conducted diagnostic interviewing.

To this end a second phase of research was planned. This phase took the form of an in-service course for infant teachers. One of the aims of the in-service course was to explore further some of the problems related to matching in the classroom and in particular the problems related to diagnostic interviewing.

Through the auspices of the local advisory service, seventeen experienced teachers of top infants were recruited. The aims of the course were made clear to the teachers. It was emphasised that whilst they might expect to improve their own matching behaviour in their own classrooms, the primary aim was, with their collaboration, to explore the professional problems which were entailed in matching.

The course was prepared by the research team and conducted by a very experienced ex-College of Education tutor. The teachers met on eight half-day sessions. Each session involved the discussion of either materials from the research study (four sessions) or of the teachers' practical work in their own classrooms (four sessions). The practical work involved the conduct of diagnostic interviews. In preparation for this work all the participants discussed the problem of the match in the light of their own experience and of data and case studies from the project. Discussion was provoked by descriptive materials and leading questions. The following is an example of an exercise from the first session of the course.

SESSION 1. EXAMPLE 3

John is a "low achiever" in the class.

Teacher's Instructions to the Class

"Get out sum books, 'Starting Points' and a pencil. Turn to the back of your sum books and, at the top of the page, write '× 2.' Write out your two times table." The whole class were then asked to recite the table.

After a break for a story the teacher continued by saying "Turn to page 28 and read the page to yourself. Does everybody know what to do now? Count the dots and put the number in the box. Read what it says together."

The children were shown a picture of a square and two half squares and were told to dot the squares as they counted them. The class then examined shapes in the book to see the half squares.

e.g.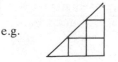

The teacher then said "The first one is done for you."

i.e. $1 + 1 + 1 + \frac{1}{2} + \frac{1}{2} + \frac{1}{2} = 4\frac{1}{2}$

Finally she asked "Who thinks they can finish these off?" and, on more than one occasion, reminded the children "Don't forget to count the half squares." (No mention was made as to how to count them).

Task History

The teacher indicated that related work had been done previously.

Description of John at Work.

9.50	John started two times table.
9.53	He worked slowly and cross checked with other children at the table.
9.56	Completed table with $10 \times 2 = 20$.
9.57	Listened to other children recite the table but did not volunteer to say it on his own.
9.58	Recited table with class but seemed to be half a syllable behind everyone else.
10.00	(Break for story related to writing).
10.15	Followed the teacher's instructions to put finger on half squares.
10.17	Listened to the teacher's instructions.
10.19	John did the sums very quickly but only added up the whole squares hence all the sums were wrong.
10.20	Joined the queue at the teacher's desk.
10.21	Left the queue and altered one sum quickly before rejoining the queue. Talked to some other children and returned to his table on discovering his answers were wrong.
10.23	Rubbed out all his answers and started again. Counted all the half squares as whole ones.
10.25	Joined the queue again.
10.27	The teacher rubbed out all John's answers and went over the first sum with him. With the teacher's help he did two sums correctly.
10.29	Sent back to finish the remaining sums on his own. Joined the queue again.
10.32	The teacher marked all his work correct.

Fieldworker's Description of John at Work.   John wrote out the two times table by cross checking with other children at the table. He was very hesitant when reciting it with the class. During the teacher's introduction on area he appeared to be only half listening. He did the exercise very quickly but only added up the whole squares and thus all his answers were wrong. When he joined the queue the feedback from other children convinced him that his sums were incorrect and so he returned to his desk before seeing the teacher. On redoing the sums he counted all the half squares as one and therefore they were all wrong again. The teacher went through his work with him and showed him how to count the squares properly. She watched him do two sums and then told him to complete the others on his own. He managed to get all the sums correct.

In response to this account the teachers were asked to comment on the following questions.

1. What salient points strike you about the above example?
2. In your view, did anything go wrong with this task? If so, please give details.
3. What do you think John got out of this task?
4. Would you say this task was matched to the child's attainment? Please give reasons for your opinion.
5. If you noted any problems under questions (2) and (4) above, how might they have been prevented?
6. What number task would you have done next with this child? Please describe and explain your reasons.

The teachers took their written responses to each session and these were used as the basis for discussion of issues related to the quality of provision of the pupil's experience.

Language tasks were equally closely studied during the course. The following exercise is a typical example.

SESSION 5. EXAMPLE 2

The Teacher's Intentions for Elizabeth

"We will be doing spelling. I select words that are linked with the children's weaknesses. Today we will probably deal with the "oi" combination. We did "oy" two days ago."

Reasons for Teacher's Intentions

"This exercise will help with phonic word building."

A Description of the Lesson

9.40   The Teacher: (Mrs Brown)
                    "Everybody get out your sound books, pencils and crayons. What sound did we do last time?"
           Tony: "Oy."

Mrs Brown: "Good. Have a look at it. Which two letters make
the sound?"

Sam: " 'o' and 'y'."

Mrs Brown: "Who can give me a word with 'oy'?"

(Mrs Brown wrote "oy" on the blackboard)

(Various children suggested words with "oy" in them but
Elizabeth did not contribute.)

Mrs Brown: "What did I say we would do next time? Make 'oy' a
different way. Which two letters this time?" (Mrs
Brown wrote "oi" on the blackboard and
continued) "Write this in your book. Can you give
me any words?"

The following words were written on the blackboard as the children
volunteered them. Elizabeth copied them down but made no attempt to
suggest words.

coin	moist	soil	point
oil	noise	Android	choice
join	foil	voice	
boil	coil	spoil	

After each word there was a brief discussion as to its meaning.

10.00   The whole class (including Elizabeth) sounded out the words on
the blackboard.

Mrs Brown: "Write a sentence of your own today using as many
words as you can."

10.01   Elizabeth attempted to write a sentence.

10.15   Elizabeth completed her work after listening to the children read
out the sentences they had written.

A Copy of Elizabeth's Work

oi

coin	coil
oil	Android
join	voise
boil	spoil
moist	point
noise	choice
foil	

A Android lost hiz voice is oil and soil

A discussion with the Fieldworker and Elizabeth Following the Task

Fieldworker: "Would you read the words you wrote down?"

Elizabeth then proceeded to read all of the words—with the exception of "choice"—incorrectly, e.g., she read "Astronaut" for "Android."

Fieldworker: "Does the sentence you wrote make sense?"
  Elizabeth: "No."
Fieldworker: "Does it matter?"
  Elizabeth: "No. If Mrs Brown writes you have to write words she writes."
Fieldworker: "What does 'moist' mean?"
  Elizabeth: "When it's slimy."
Fieldworker: "What does 'foil' mean?"
  Elizabeth: "Like paper foil."
Fieldworker: "Is foil paper?"
  Elizabeth: "Like wool but rather smooth."
Fieldworker: "Can you remember any words from last Tuesday?"
  Elizabeth: "Toy, boy, write."
Fieldworker: "Do you have to learn these spellings?"
  Elizabeth: "Yes, sometimes in the morning and sometimes in the afternoon."
Fieldworker: "Do you use any of the words in your stories?"
  Elizabeth: "No."

Finally the fieldworker asked Elizabeth to write down the following words: "join," "soil," "noise" and "voice." Her attempts were:

ion
soil
nois
voice.

Questions Following Session 5, Example 2

1. Is Elizabeth ready for this task? Please explain.
2. What did she get out of it? Please explain.
3. Can you suggest other ways, which you would have preferred, of achieving the teaching aim for Elizabeth.

In the discussion following this exercise the emphasis was on the role of practice in learning.

The value of the fieldworkers' diagnostic interviews was discussed in detail and many instances were critically evaluated. It was agreed by the teachers that the interviews were very short and appeared, at least in experienced hands, to be a practical proposition. Efforts were then made to train the participating teachers in the conduct of such an interview.

By using examples in script and on video tape it was emphasised that diagnosis, in this form, had several phases. The first is an observation phase in which the child is watched whilst performing the task. This leads to the formation of a provisional hypothesis or hunch as to what the child's problem (if any) might be. The third phase demands that this hunch be tested by presenting the child with appropriate tasks related to the performance of that originally assigned. In this phase additional questions have to be asked and (as has been described earlier) new hypotheses formed and tested as necessary.

After demonstrating these techniques, several logs of tasks were then presented to the teachers in order for them to practise the generation of possible, tentative hypotheses and to design first moves in an interview. It should be emphasised that this pencil and paper exercise was planned as a preliminary to actual practical work. The following are examples of materials used in training.

MATERIALS USED IN TRAINING: EXAMPLE 1

Peter is a high achiever in his class.

The Teacher's Intention for Peter

He is to write a story about "Fred the Dragon." The objective is to enrich language, especially with reference to animal homes and animal noises. The teacher is working on an "animal" theme building up to a visit to the zoo.

The teacher suggests that Peter does not like doing free writing and that he is difficult to keep on task. She intends to make him persevere.

A Description of the Lesson and of Peter at Work

9.52   Teacher shows class a book, "Spider Silk." She asks them to count the spider's legs and to look at the pictures. She reads the captions. Peter attends closely.

9.54   Teacher talks about making cocoons, hatching eggs and the movement of baby spiders.

9.57   She tells the class where spiders live, what they eat and how they make their webs.

10.01   Teacher asks, "what is a magnifying glass?" Peter says "You look through it to make things bigger."

10.04   Teacher talks about grass spiders, house spiders and hammock spiders.

10.08   She revises many of the points made.

10.10   She says, "This is not what we were going to do but since we have started we'll go on. She puts the date on the board. Peter says, "We've got a holiday on Thursday." The teacher begins writing on the board. Peter is not looking.

10.16   Teacher still writing. Peter is not paying attention. The teacher says, "when you have done that, I want you to write some more yourself—where spiders make webs, lay eggs etc. Now it is break time."

10.55   Children back in class. Peter copies date from the board and begins to copy story. He changes seat, moves back, looks at neighbour's work and chews his pencil.

10.58   Peter is writing. Now on his second line.

11.01   Looks at glazier replacing broken windows.

11.04   Still watching the glazier.

11.05   Changes pencil. Returns to writing. Teacher says, "Peter, you'd see better if you moved round here." He says, "I don't like it round there." He stays put.

11.10   Peter has finished copy writing. He takes his book, shows his friends and goes to the teacher who says, "Go and sit down." He goes slowly back to his seat.

11.11   He begins his own writing. The teacher makes the general announcement, "If you need words, come to me."

11.13   Peter wanders out to the blackboard and the teacher sends him to his place.

11.14   Peter has written only two words of his own.

11.15   Peter begins writing. Writes one word. Sits down with one finger up each nostril. Gazes into space. Watches glazier.

11.18   Still gazing around. Teacher says. "If I've to tell one more person to stop looking at that man, I'll be very cross."

11.20   Peter resumes writing. Writes one word. Teacher says, "Peter would you rather write about a man putting in windows." Peter nods enthusiastically. Teacher says "When you've finished that work."

11.22   Peter has now done one line of his own writing.

11.27   Peter picks his nails and begins his second line of writing.

11.28   Peter sharpens pencil. Returns to seat. Writes one word. Chews finger nail. Goes to teacher and says, "I can't think what to write." She says, "Read me what you have written." He does so and she asks what happened next. He replies, "Little eggs hatch out into baby spiders," and she tells him to write that.

11.32   Peter has written one more word.

11.36   Goes back to teacher who asks him again what happens next and tells him to write out his reply.

11.40   Peter is writing again. Writes half a line and joins queue at the teacher's desk. She asks him to read his work and he recognises an error saying, "Oh, I weren't thinking." Peter goes back to his place and changes "blow them go" to "blow them away."

11.43   The teacher asks him why spiders make webs. He says "To catch flies" and she asks him to write that.

11.47   The teacher asks, "have you finished yet?" and Peter shakes his head.

11.48   He writes quickly and re-joins the teacher's queue.

> Teacher: "What kind of webs and where do they put them?"
> Peter: "In the bushes."
> Teacher: "What do they catch?"
> Peter: "Insects."
> Teacher: "What do they do with them?"
> Peter: "Eat them."
> Teacher: "Go and write that."

11.50   Peter writes one word. He then swops pencils with another boy.
11.51   Teacher announces dinner time.

A Copy of Peter's Work

From the board he wrote:

Tuesday 5th May
We saw a little spider drop from the ceiling all the way down to the cupboard
on a very fine silk thread. We looked at a book about spiders silk.

In his own words he added:
mother spider macks a cocoon round the little egges and wen the little eggs
hatch the little spiders com out and make a silk and let the wind blow them
(go) away spiders spin a web for a trap.

An Account of the Post-Task Interview Between Peter and the Fieldworker

Fieldworker: "Can you write this for me?" (She dictates the first sentence
from the board).
Peter writes: "We saw a little spider drop from the ciling all the way down to
the cupboard."
Fieldworker: "Can you read your story to me?"
Peter: Does so.
Fieldworker: "Can you finish your story for me?"
Peter writes: "They spin a web for food a spider (long pause) bilt a wed
("Oh, I've done it wrong." Rubs out and writes "web") (long
pause) "on bushes" (pause, "that's all I can think of.") He
then said, "I've got a sore gum and that's why I can't think of
any more."

MATERIALS USED IN TRAINING: EXAMPLE 2

James is a high achiever in his class. He is 6.5 years old and has a maths age of
10.3 years.

The Teacher's Intention for James

"James will construct a number square using the three times table."

The Reasons for the Teacher's Intentions

"The children have not actually learnt the table by rote but I have done a lot of work on building it up and this exercise will provide further consolidation and general understanding."

The Task History

Prior to the task James had done a lot of work building up the table including sums of the following type:

$$1 \times 3 \underline{\quad} \underline{\quad} \underline{\quad} 3$$
$$2 \times 3 \underline{\quad} \underline{\quad} \underline{\quad} 6$$
$$3 \times 3 \underline{\quad} \underline{\quad} \underline{\quad} 9$$

and $18 \div 3 = 6$ and $3\overline{)63}$

$9 \div 3 = 3$ $\qquad$ $3\overline{)39}$

A Description of James at Work. At the start of the lesson the teacher addressed the class:

"Put the numbers 0 to 10 in squares across the top of the page. Put the numbers 3, 6, 9 etc. down the side jumping in threes. One times three makes three so colour in that square (see figure 9.1). Two times three is six so colour in that square. I want you to go up to ten times three."

11.11	James ruled a vertical and a horizontal line. He then wrote the numbers 1 to 10 very quickly across the top.
11.12	James looked at the blackboard and copied the numbers from the left hand side of the table (see Fig. 9.1).
11.14	He went to his tray to fetch some crayons.
11.15	He coloured in the first square, swopped crayons and coloured in the next square (see Fig. 9.2). The fieldworker noted that James appeared to have seen the pattern already and made no attempt to work out the answer.
11.16	James completed colouring in his seventh square.
11.20	He completed his work and took it to the teacher for marking.

A Discussion Between James and the Fieldworker. The fieldworker asked James to reconstruct the 3 × table from memory. He did so very easily and quickly.

The fieldworker then told James to refer to his number square when answering the following questions:

Fieldworker: "How many threes in twelve?"

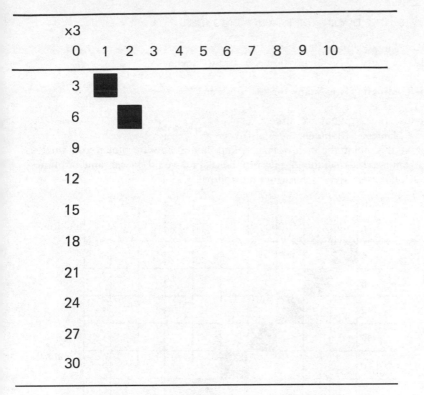

FIG. 9.1 A copy of the teacher's work on the blackboard.

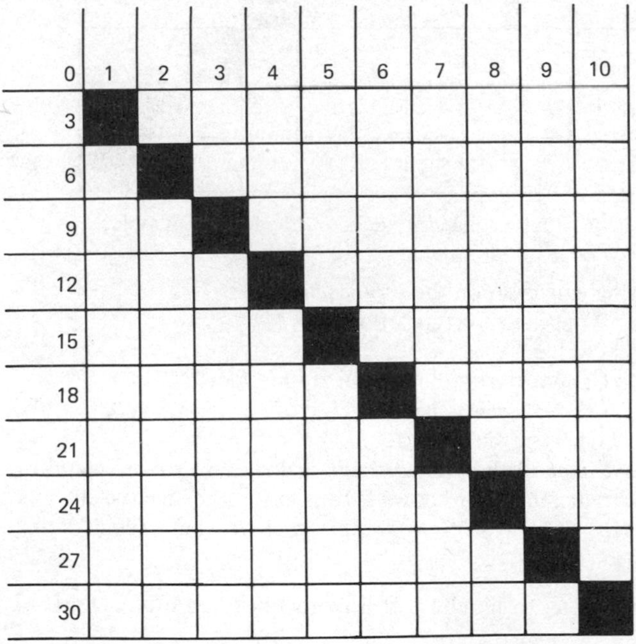

FIG. 9.2 James' number square for the three times table.

James: "Four."
Fieldworker: "How many threes in twenty-seven?"
James: "Nine."
Fieldworker: "How many threes in fifteen?"
James: "Five."
Fieldworker: "What are three sixes?"
James: "Eighteen."

At this point the fieldworker asked James how he would construct a pattern for the 4 × table. James replied that he would do the same but times four and proceeded to construct the following table:

	0	1	2	3	4	5	6	7	8	9	10
4		■									
8			■								
12				■							
16					■						
20						■					
24							■				
28								■			
32									■		
36										■	
40											■

FIG. 9.3   James' number square for the four times table.

The following conversation then took place:
Fieldworker: "What are four times three?"
James: "Twelve."
Fieldworker: "Can you write the answer to this sum 20 = 4 × ?"
James: "Oh dear, this is hard. It is five."
Fieldworker: "What are six times four?"
James: "Sixteen I think but I don't really know."
The fieldworker then wrote down "40 ÷ 4 =   " and asked James to complete it. His reply was, "I know this is shares but I don't know the answer."

The instructions to teachers following these examples were:

Discuss the following questions with your colleagues in your group and write your responses in the spaces provided. i.e. You might or might not agree with your colleagues in discussion. Please write *your* view *after* the small group discussion.

1. What was the fieldworker's hunch about the child's task performance: did the fieldworker think that the task was too hard, too easy or about right. What led you to your conclusion?
2. Do you think she changed her view during the course of her interview with the child?
3. What might the fieldworker have concluded at the end of the task?
4. Are there any questions that you would have liked to have seen added to the interview? Why?
5. Are there any questions that you might have omitted from the interview? Why?
6. What task would you do next with the child?

Throughout all the training sessions discussions were recorded in full knowledge of the teachers and with their permission. Additionally, and again with their permission, all written responses to set exercises were collected.

Analysis of the first attempts to generate hypotheses and design suitable tasks to test them showed that the teachers made no use whatsoever of the notion of hunch or hypothesis. On reading the manuscript of a lesson they saw all problems as self-evident and rushed directly from observation to judgement and thence to prescription. All problems were to be solved by direct teaching. Efforts on the part of the course leader to get the participants to be more tentative in their conclusion and circumspect in their proposed resolution were not so much rejected as ignored. In the light of this it was decided to proceed to having the teachers conduct their own diagnostic interviews with children in their own classes.

Teachers were given a set of procedures for the conduct of such interviews and asked to select a child who appeared to be having problems with a maths task and to attempt to ascertain the nature of the child's difficulty. They were also asked to bring a record of the interview to a subsequent session of the in-service course. In this setting it was to be evaluated.

Analysis of these teachers' interviews and the group discussion of them revealed a number of interesting features. Above all else the teachers were preoccupied with the practicality of conducting a discussion with a child whilst at the same time managing the rest of the class. Three-quarters of the teachers raised this issue as a serious problem. Despite making special working arrangements for the rest of the class (and thus subverting their normal daily work) these teachers were subjected to constant interruptions. These interruptions were perceived as an acceptable fact of classroom life. The interviews were seen to be the fly in the ointment. Indeed it appears that these teachers not only accepted and permitted such ad hoc exchanges but actually encouraged them as a form of management of learning. They expected to be the provider of immediate solutions to any and all problems. Since teachers comment that this form of management limits any careful reflection on problems it is interesting to ask what they feel children get out of it. According to the participating teachers it is a form of responding to children's needs.

In the light of the apparent practical problems in the management of the interviews, the teachers were asked to comment on the utility of the technique. One quarter of the teachers found it quite useless and a further quarter found the interview useless but the preliminary period of observation very important and useful. For these, the period of observation told them all they wanted to know. The children's problems were obvious and the remedies self evident.

In one case, for example, a child was given a revision task in adding tens and units. Several examples of the procedure were worked on the blackboard. First, examples which did not need carrying, e.g., t.   u.

$$
\begin{array}{cc}
2 & 2 \\
+ & 5 \\
\hline
\end{array}.
$$

Then examples demanding carrying, e.g., t. u.

$$
\begin{array}{cc}
1 & 7 \\
+ & 9 \\
\hline
2 & 6 \\
\hline
1 &
\end{array}.
$$

It was emphasised that the units should be added first, the units column completed and the ten put below the answer box in the tens column. The child in question was then given eight examples to work on. The teacher observed that she did not use cubes, a number line or her fingers. Her first four sums are shown below:

$$
\begin{array}{cc}
\text{t.} & \text{u.} \\
1 & 1 \\
+ & 9 \\
\hline
2 & 9 \\
\hline
\end{array}
\qquad
\begin{array}{cc}
\text{t.} & \text{u.} \\
1 & 3 \\
+ & 9 \\
\hline
4 & 9 \\
\hline
\end{array}
\qquad
\begin{array}{cc}
\text{t.} & \text{u.} \\
1 & 5 \\
+ & 9 \\
\hline
6 & 9 \\
\hline
\end{array}
\qquad
\begin{array}{cc}
\text{t.} & \text{u.} \\
1 & 7 \\
+ & 9 \\
\hline
8 & 9 \\
\hline
\end{array}
$$

The teacher immediately observed that the child "appeared to have added each row horizontally." This, considered the teacher, was "quite unexpected. I thought the task was well within her capabilities . . . I had expected her to use the correct procedure." It took the teacher very little time to get the child to use the correct procedure but there was no effort made to understand why she had not done so in the first place.

In respect of the actual conduct of the interviews the teachers were not adept at forming provisional hypotheses. In three-quarters of the interviews no form of comment represented the teachers' speculations. In three cases, some attempt was made to comment on preliminary observation but these took the form of conclusions about the child's work rather than hypotheses to be considered. In the above case for example, the teacher concluded that the child had added the numbers horizontally and did not speculate on the origins of this error.

In the absence of hypotheses it might be expected that analytical interviewing did not take place. This expectation was fulfilled. In almost all cases there were very few questions asked. Teaching predominated. Sometimes this took the form of asking questions to direct the pupil's thinking. For example, one teacher had observed that one of her pupils sometimes had trouble in remembering the previous day's teaching. The teacher's interview was intended to see what problems this child had in making up sums of money using coins of different value, a task the child had done previously. The teacher drew three purses and wrote '6p' alongside each of them. She also set out a tray containing a mixture of coins of different denominations (50p, 10p, 5p, 2p and 1p). The interview aimed at ascertaining the child's problem then proceeded as follows:

    Teacher: (pointing to 6p) "How much is that?"
      Child: "6p."
    Teacher: "Will you put six pennies in this purse?"
      Child: (put six coins in the purse: $3 \times 50p$; $2 \times 10p$ and $1 \times 5p$).
    Teacher: "What colour is 1p?"
      Child: "Brown!"
    Teacher: "Sort out the brown coins."
      Child: (sorted out the 2p and 1p coins).
    Teacher: "Now which are the 1p? Can you see the '1' on the coin?"
      Child: "Yes."
    Teacher: "Can you put six '1p' in the purse?"
      Child: (did as she was asked).

The interview ended there. The teacher was satisfied that the child now understood although the same child had apparently understood this task previously. It is impossible to say from this interview quite why the child responded in the way she did initially. The teacher's interview quickly re-established a procedure whilst avoiding entirely the child's misunderstanding. This was set aside in favour of pressing home a routine.

From these first efforts on the part of teachers to use diagnostic interviewing to ascertain children's learning problems some conclusions seemed striking. The teachers directly interpreted observations. The meanings of observations and the related pedagogic treatments were self evident. Secondly, the teachers did not interview; they taught. They did not diagnose, conjure alternatives or check possibilities. Third, they managed the interviews as a special concession to the general approach of crisis management. They expected to be the provider of instant solutions to a constant stream of problems: the interviews got in the way of this form of management.

Against these forceful impressions it must be recognised that these were the teachers' first attempts at this task. It would be reasonable to see these teachers, who, it will be recalled, were all very experienced and committed to improving their matching, as novice diagnosticians. In this spirit the teachers, under the chairmanship of the course leader, subjected the interviews to critical analysis. They concluded that they were disappointing, particularly in respect of the articulation of provisional hypotheses about the origins of children's problems and in the exploration of the foundations of those problems.

The teachers recognised what one called the "make do and mend" response to children's errors. The course leader provided further guidance in the conduct of such interviews. It was emphasised that the interviews should not take more than 5 minutes and that, to this end, typical written responses from pupils might be set aside in favour of verbal responses. Further examples of project interviews were used for critical appreciation. Individual feedback and evaluation was provided to each teacher on the basis of her first interview.

The teachers then made another attempt. Again they concentrated on number tasks. On the surface, these cases differed considerably from the first efforts. All the interviews were rated very positively by the teachers and they reported that they revealed problems which were "fascinating" and "eye opening." One teacher remarked that she "would not have believed it had she not seen it with her own eyes." The interviews also proved much more practicable. Half of the teachers found them perfectly straightforward to conduct within the limitations of the classroom and quarter had only minor problems. One teacher however concluded that she "could not cope at all." Most of the teachers found it possible to produce a tentative hypothesis regarding the child's work.

Whilst the teachers were much happier with the formalities involved in interviewing, examination of the content of the interviews revealed that no progress had been made in analysing children's problems. Indeed, it could be said that these interviews revealed more profound problems in this respect than the initial attempts made by the teachers. For example, in the following interview, the teacher was trying to ascertain the origins of John's specific mathematical error. John was a middle achiever in the class. He was following the school maths scheme and was doing addition of hundreds, tens and units without carrying. Prior to this he had done addition of tens and units with carrying. These had been done successfully. The teacher moved him on to the next step which was addition of hundreds, tens and units with carrying in the units column.

He started well with the following:

$$
\begin{array}{ccc}
\text{h.} & \text{t.} & \text{u.} \\
1 & 1 & 4 \\
+2 & 2 & 5 \\
\hline
3 & 3 & 9
\end{array}
\qquad
\begin{array}{ccc}
\text{h.} & \text{t.} & \text{u.} \\
1 & 4 & 1 \\
+2 & 3 & 8 \\
\hline
3 & 7 & 9
\end{array}
$$

and then proceeded:

$$
\begin{array}{ccc}
\text{h.} & \text{t.} & \text{u.} \\
1 & 4 & 7 \\
+2 & 1 & 4 \\
\hline
 & & 510 \\
0
\end{array}
\qquad
\begin{array}{ccc}
\text{h.} & \text{t.} & \text{u.} \\
2 & 0 & 7 \\
+1 & 3 & 8 \\
\hline
 & 1 & 0
\end{array}
$$

He rubbed out the last two answers and did them again using red and blue counters (the code was that reds were units and blues were tens).

The first one he got wrong again and in the second he added the unit column only using red counters. He then went to the teacher to say that the sums were not coming right.

It is worth emphasising that the teacher was surprised at his difficulty because of his facility at previous examples requiring carrying in the units column.

The teacher then started her interview as follows:

    Teacher: "Why do you think they are wrong?"
       John: "Because there is a ten in the column and there should not be."
    Teacher: "Good. Go and get some counters."
       John: "Reds and blues?"
    Teacher: "Yes. Now write the sum down again. What do we do first?"
       John: (He wrote the sum down:

$$
\begin{array}{ccc}
\text{h.} & \text{t.} & \text{u.} \\
1 & 4 & 7 \\
+2 & 1 & 4 \\
\hline
\end{array}
$$

).

       John: "Add the units first."
    Teacher: "Go on then."
            (John took four and seven red counters).

Teacher: "Now what?"
   John: "Add them up and see if I have ten."
Teacher: "Go on then."
   John: "Do I put a nought then for ten?"
Teacher: "Count off ten. What do we do with the ten reds?"
   John: "Keep them."
Teacher: "What do ten reds become?"
   John: "Add them."

It seems to the outsider that John was lost here and he was trying to read the teacher's mind. She was trying to give him verbal hints. She was not giving him new or different empirical experiences to deal with. She tried a new verbal hint:

Teacher: "Why have you brought blues and reds?"
   John: "Because I thought I needed them."

The hint failed and the teacher was at a loss as to what to do. She altered her tack and decided to teach him.

Teacher: "Should I help you?"
   John: "Yes."

It must be recognised at this point that this interview was conducted in a classroom under the usual circumstances. Some children were painting and others were writing. The teacher reported later that she "got some spilt water and some painted faces" and she had a queue of children wanting spellings for their writing.

Additionally she was concerned about John. She was of the view that "he really had tried, he is a very conscientious little boy." For this reason she felt she ought to delay teaching no longer. Later she was of the opinion that she had jumped in too soon. She felt that she had not gone back far enough to fathom out John's problem.

The exchange then continued as follows:

Teacher: "Add together four and seven and make a red stick. These are units. We always count in tens."
   John: "Eleven make one red and one blue."
Teacher: "Where do we put the one unit?"
(John put the one unit in the units column).
Teacher: "What do we do with the one ten?"
(John put the carrying figure under the answer box).
Teacher: "Now what do we do?"
   John: "Add the tens: $1 + 1 + 4 = 6$."
Teacher: "Have we got ten tens?"

John: "No. The six goes in the tens column."
Teacher: "Good. Where does the six go?"
John: "In the answer box."
Teacher: "Now what?"
John: "Add up the hundreds." (This he did correctly.)

It appears here that with a few reminders, John got back into a routine he had been familiar with previously. We do not know how he went wrong. The teacher suggested that he would need more practice. It could be that she is right. Otherwise it could be that John's small piece of aberrant behaviour was a symptom of something more profound, that he did not understand the routine he was to practice.

What is vividly shown here is the temptation, later recognised by the teacher, to stop diagnosing and start teaching. Equally revealed is that the child was playing "read your mind" with the teacher. Her questions were not seen as mathematical questions. They were interpreted by John in their social context. In trying to teach in a Socratic fashion ("Why did you bring red and blue counters?") she, in the event, was interpreted by the child as leading him by a series of nudges and winks—which he endeavoured to comprehend. This feature was shown very clearly in another interview which might, at first sight, appear to be a sound attempt at Socratic probing.

In this case, the child, Harriet, had been given a revision task as an assessment test. The task and Harriet's responses are shown in Fig. 9.4.

The teacher observed that Harriet did the first six examples with evident ease but became increasingly distracted as the task became more difficult. Harriet eventually brought the paper out for marking and the interview proceeded as follows (the lines have been numbered for ease of later reference).

Teacher: "Why do $2 + 2 + 2$ make 8?"   1
Harriet: No response.
Teacher: "Did you use cubes?"   2
Harriet: "Yes."   3
Teacher: "Where are your cubes?"   4
Harriet: "I put them back."   5
Teacher: "Go and get them again."   6
          (Harriet brought back cubes.)   7
Teacher: "Do that again for me." (Pointing to incorrect sum.)   8
          (Harriet obtained three cubes and two cubes).   9
Teacher: "You have three cubes and two cubes. Why?"   10
Harriet: "Because it's for that." (Pointing to sum.)   11
Teacher: "What does it say?"   12
Harriet: "Three groups of two." (Child corrected to "3 sets of 2.")   13
Teacher: "Is that correct?" (Pointing to cubes.)   14

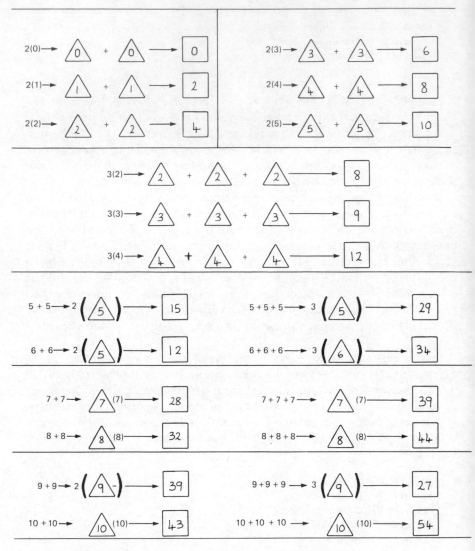

FIG. 9.4.   Harriet's number task showing her working (Harriet's responses are handwritten).   Adapted from *Mathematics for Schools* (Addison-Wesley).

Harriet: "Yes."	15
Teacher: "Yes?"	16
Harriet: "Yes."	17
Teacher: "Read it again."	18
Harriet: "Three groups of two."	19
Teacher: "Look at cubes. Are they correct?"	20

Harriet: "No."	21
Teacher: "What's wrong? What have you got?"	22
Harriet: "Three and two."	23
Teacher: "So what is wrong?"	24
Harriet: "Nothing."	25
Teacher: "Nothing is wrong?"	26
Harriet: "I have three groups of two."	27
Teacher: "Have you?"	28
(Harriet obtained three groups of three and a two).	29
Teacher: "Count how many in that group" (pointing to a three).	30
Harriet: "Three."	31
Teacher: "Is that a group of two?"	32
Harriet: "No."	33
Teacher: "Make a group of two." (Did so.) "Can you make three groups of two?" (child did so). "Now what have you got?"	34
Harriet: "Two groups of two."	35
Teacher: "How many altogether?"	36
Harriet: "Six."	37
Teacher: "What is wrong with that?" (Pointing to original answer.)	38
Harriet: "It says eight."	39
Teacher: "What did you do wrong?"	40
Harriet: "I didn't count properly."	41
Teacher: "Can you get three groups of three?" (Child did so.)	42
Harriet: "Nine."	43
Teacher: "5 + 5 can be . . ."	44
Harriet: "Written as two groups of five."	45
Teacher: "What is the answer?"	46
Harriet: "Ten."	47
Teacher: "What does it say $7 + 7 \rightarrow 7\ (7) \rightarrow 28$."	48
Harriet: "7 + 7 can be written as seven groups of seven."	49
Teacher: "Can it?"	50
Harriet: "No."	51
Teacher: "So what is wrong?"	52
Harriet: "It should be two groups of seven."	53
Teacher: "How many is that?"	54
Harriet: "Fourteen."	55

The most interesting feature of this interview is that whilst it has the trappings of the Socratic method it is hardly diagnostic at all. Rather than exploring the child's thinking, the line of questioning was used as a series of winks and nudges to put the child right.

Examination of lines 14–20 provides the first example of this. The teacher asked Harriet if what she had done was correct. Since the child thought it was, her teacher repeated the question. This is usually seen as an appeal to social processes: a repeated question indicates something was wrong with the answer. This device was used by the teacher again (ll. 24, 26, 28) and, again, to no avail. This type of question is a nudge or a wink or hints that "something is wrong." It is a rhetorical device to get the child to admit something is wrong. It cannot tell us why the child did what she did. At best it may be seen as an attention directing device but it can only be this if the child reads the teacher's mind and recognises the social convention. If the teacher wanted to direct attention she might have been better simply doing so. This she eventually did in l. 30.

The technique up to that point was devoid of empirical content. The teacher did not attempt to link her questions to concrete materials. The teacher then directly taught Harriet how to compose a group of six (ll. 34, 36).

Eventually (l. 38) she had to tell the child her original answer was wrong. We have no reason to believe up to that point which of the two answers the child thought might be wrong. The teacher, again directing the child, missed an opportunity to look at the quality of her thinking. She then asked (l. 40) how the child went wrong and accepted (or at least did not challenge) the child's account (that she mis-counted). But from the preceeding exchange this almost certainly was not how the child got this problem wrong. That is to say that both the child's processes and the teacher's line of questioning suggest that the child did not have three sets of two in the first place. What she had was three and two. How she got this to be "eight" might have included mis-counting but that is not the whole or even the kernel of the problem.

Another line of evidence which is consistent with the view that the teacher was preoccupied with putting the child procedurally straight is that her probing began and remained with her attention to one wrong answer and she focused her line of questioning on getting the right answer. But on the lower half of the page Harriet had all her answers wrong. Inspection of these errors permits two suspicions. One is that she always assumed the unknown quantity to be the size of the set. In examples such as $5 + 5 \rightarrow 2$ $(\triangle)$ / this view worked for her to a point.

However, in examples in which the quantity of sets was required she continued to put in the set size., e.g., in $7 + 7 \rightarrow \triangle$ (7) she inserted seven instead of two.

It would have been interesting to know if this was her rule and if so why. One might argue that it is a very reasonable rule given the repeated use of the symbol $\triangle$. Its use inside and outside the bracket appears not to have been interpreted by Harriet. Had she been asked to explain how she did these and to contrast written examples with concrete examples her views on this might have been made clearer.

The second suspicion is that Harriet was adding all instances of the set in any one sum rather than seeing the sums as two separate, equivalent processes, e.g., in, $7 + 7 \rightarrow \triangle (7) \rightarrow 28$ she appears to have added the four sevens. Similarly in $8 + 8 \rightarrow \triangle (8) \rightarrow 32$.

This hypothesis fits the other cases if we accept that as the numbers got bigger she made adding errors on the large quantities of blocks entailed.

It seems that this teacher wanted the child to think. She required the child to think. But the content of the thought provoked was less mathematical than social. The questions were not straight in a mathematical way. They were not related to empirical experience, the operations of rules and the evaluation of mathematical outcomes. The questions were socially loaded. In the end we do not know what Harriet's problem was or how it came about. We do not know, therefore, how it might be avoided in the future. We do not know whether Harriet understood her original error or her new process.

Inspection of the end of the interview may be interpreted as encouraging—Harriet, with minimal help, put another sum right. But had she merely learned a chant? What would happen when she met similar but unfamiliar questions in the more informationally noisy context of her maths book?

More generally, what did Harriet learn about how to proceed in maths, how to resolve errors, how to check procedures? It might be inferred that learning to read the teacher's mind would be her best bet for getting the procedures right. This more general question is critically relevant to describing and understanding the quality of learning experience.

If attention is focused on the teacher it might be asked what explanation there is for her behaviour. She certainly seemed devoted to having thoughtful children. But why did her questioning focus on only one (the first) wrong answer? Why did she use so little empirical evidence in her interview? Why did she use her authority? (i.e., in hinting that the child was wrong). Why did she not operate a more wholistic interpretation of Harriet's errors?

The following remarks are speculative:

1. She focused on the first wrong answer simply because it was first. This is consistent with a view that she was intent on sorting out procedures rather than establishing understanding.
2. She used a social signalling interview because they are gentler and permit the negotiation of emotional tone, i.e., clashes of facts can be upsetting: they are non-negotiable.
3. She could not teach Harriet how to proceed mathematically in cases of error/dispute/check because she did not know herself, i.e., "doing" maths and "understanding maths general procedures" was not only a problem for Harriet. It was a problem for her teacher.

The point of these speculative remarks (and given the evidence available they are only speculative remarks) is to draw attention to the serious problems which may be met if diagnosis is seen as the road to better matching. Whilst such a solution to the problem has logical merit and intuitive appeal it seems that diagnosis poses problems of management, role, skill and knowledge for the teacher.

The first problem, that of management, is rather obvious and probably easily soluble as the teachers in this project discovered. The remaining problems are both less obvious and less easily resolved. At least in the limited data available here, teachers found it extremely difficult to resist the urge to put pupils right. If they saw something wrong and a solution was apparent they could not delay teaching. Teachers teach. Even if that role is adaptable, the desire to withhold teaching until the child's problems or understanding is ascertained is only the first step in the conduct of diagnostic interviewing. Such interviews require considerable social and intellectual skill, the former to retain a cooperative, productive relationship with the child and the latter to produce an incisive line of questions. Finally, they require an understanding of both the processes to be attained and experience of the manner in which children can and typically do misinterpret these processes.

This skill and knowledge was not evident amongst the teachers in our sample. Whilst in conventionally accepted standards these were able and experienced teachers they did not display the skills necessary to ascertain children's misunderstandings as a basis on which to build foundational work in number. Nor might they have been expected to. It is unlikely that such skills would be acquired in initial training or by mere experience.

INTERVIEWS FOLLOWING LANGUAGE TASKS

It will be recalled that in the discussion periods of the in-service course, there had been as much attention paid to language tasks as to number tasks. It was emphasised that the role of the interview was either to ascertain the problem of a struggling child or to extend the range of performance of a child who found the task easy.

As with number tasks, in the practical phase of the course teachers selected to interview children in their own class. They made their own records and brought these for discussion. These interviews showed features similar to those evident in maths post task interviews.

In one instance, for example, the teacher designed a class task intended to encourage imaginative writing. She showed the children a glass paper weight in the form of a prism. The children each handled and talked about the prism. The teacher encouraged them to consider what it looked like, what it felt like and what it reminded them of. She put these ideas on the board and all the class started work on their writing.

The teacher's observation focused on Mari who started to write immediately, wrote industriously for twenty minutes and paused only to get two spellings ("diamond" and "pointed") from the teacher.

She produced the following passage:

> Green red blue and purple are the colours of the diamond. The diamond shined like a star. It is pink and white too. It looked like a diamond. It is a little diamond. The glass is sharp and pointed too. It is like the rainbow, pink yellow green and blue.

The post task interview ran as follows:

Teacher: "Have you seen a paper weight like this before?"
Mari: "Yes, but I couldn't touch it."
Teacher: "Did you like to touch this one?"
Mari: "Yes."
Teacher: "What did it feel like?"
Mari: "It felt hard and cold like a piece of ice. Well, not as cold as that."
Teacher: "Was it a diamond?"
Mari: "No not really. It was a piece of glass cut in a special way."
Teacher: "Why did you call it a diamond?"
Mari: "It was so beautiful."
Teacher: "What did you think about when you looked at and felt the paper weight?"
Mari: "The blue reminded me of the sky and the white of the stars glittering at night."
Teacher: "Why did you write the word shined? Would 'shone' or 'was shining' or 'shines' have been better?"
Mari: "No, shined is better."

It is noticeable that most of the interview was not about writing and much of it detracted from imaginative experience. For example, the teacher asked "was it a diamond?" and, later, "Why did you call it one?" Additionally Mari was taken up on her use of English in a puzzling way. Mari's somewhat poetic use of "shined" was challenged but her choice not explored.

A second teacher set out to encourage imaginative writing. Her main aim was to get children to create ideas. In her report she strongly emphasised that "grammar and punctuation are never mentioned by me." The children had been doing scientific work on shadows and the teacher asked them to write a story called, "The magic shadow." She wanted them to let their imagination "run riot." She asked the class to consider the sounds and feel of shadows and what a shadow would be like if they could pick one up. The teacher's observation then focused on Louise who worked at great speed to produce the following:

My magic shadow

One lovely Summers day I was looking at my shadow and along came a little fairy dressed in white silk. When I was not looking the fairy sprinkled some magic powder on my shadow and quikly ran of and the moment she was gone my shadow changed colour and it changed a lilac and a very light lilac and it started to talk to me and it said hello so I said hello back to it and it said what is your name so I said Lou and my shadow said that a nice name and just at that moment my mum called me in and I said wont be a sec and I said to my shadow do not talk so after tea it changed back to normel

Notwithstanding her preliminary protestations, the first thing the teacher observed about this piece of work was that the punctuation was not up to Louise's normal standards. Additionally the teacher noticed that Louise had not stopped to think if she could add to the descriptive value of her story, a consideration which does not fit well with the notion of a riotous imagination. The teacher asked Louise to read her story and noted that she did so with fluency, "pausing where the full stops should have been."

In the interview the teacher decided to try to get Louise to add to her descriptions. The interview proceeded as follows.

> Teacher: "If you picked your shadow up what might it feel like?"
> Louise: "Slimy."
> Teacher: "Slimy things are usually wet. Can you tell me anything else that would feel slimy?"
> Louise: "Worms. Mud."
> Teacher: "Well do you think a shadow would be slimy?"
> Louise: "No, not really."

It seems that the teacher did not want Louise to be over-imaginative. In the above excerpt she appeared to be putting Louise right on the reality of shadows! The teacher then asked Louise to feel her dress and asked her, "Do you think a shadow would feel like that?" Louise agreed it would. Later the teacher asked Louise to write just one more sentence describing a shadow and Louise obliged with: "a shadow is a purple-black it would feel silkey and very light like a feather it would float." It appears that she gave what the teacher asked for—although not at all what she wanted. The teacher appeared to have rejected Louise's imaginative responses and asked for more detail of a constrained sort.

These examples are consistent with the other language interviews collected by the teachers. They suggest that the teachers, even after considerable training and selection of their own cases, had little to add to children's writing experience and, in many respects actually seemed to detract from them.

CHILDREN'S RESPONSES TO DIAGNOSTIC INTERVIEWING

It was argued in a previous chapter that children seek to please teachers by delivering the goods teachers appear to want. Children learn what teachers want by monitoring what they reward. Thus, neat work, full pages, procedures evidently followed—all these attract teacher's praise.

It was further suggested that part of the reason teachers proceed in their own knowledge of mismatching is that the children are happy and interested in their work—at least for the most part. In the light of these considerations it could be argued that the children play an important role (if indeed they do not bear considerable responsibility) in the continuation of mismatching in the classroom. In their desire to obtain praise their life is much easier if the teacher's demands are specific and concrete. Following procedures to get a row of ticks is easier than puzzling out the precise meaning of place value in tens and units sums. In several of the examples of teachers' diagnostic interviews the child appeared to be reading the teacher's mind in order to please her. It is worth noting that it is not only young learners who behave in this way. There is plenty of evidence which suggests that students of all ages endeavour to deliver what their teachers will rate highly. Life is made easier for all parties if the teacher is clear and concrete about what she wants. Being clear is, of course, a self evident good thing. Being concrete however usually entails the description of procedures and routines rather than the description of the cognitive objectives, of more fundamental understanding, which underlie such procedures.

With this in mind it is possible to see an additional dimension to the diagnostic interview. Such an interview provides the teacher with an opportunity for strongly rewarding the child for displaying his thinking, for showing the teacher his interpretation of what he is doing, i.e., rewards not necessarily for getting things right but for communicating his point of view. In this way pupils might learn that there is something to be said for taking responsibility for their own learning and for diminishing the age old demarcation issue in classrooms, i.e., that teachers think and pupils learn.

It is noteworthy that in all the cases of teacher interviews collected there was no instance of praise. Additionally, in the teachers ratings of the interviews, none suggested that they might be of use to the child or that the child could have conceivably profited from reflecting on his work. This lacuna is perhaps another facet of the teacher's role as teacher.

In the view developed here it is a facet well worthy of examination. If the diagnostic interview is seen as the sole responsibility of the teacher, the prospects of implementing improvements in matching in this manner seem remote. If however, by the judicious and just administration of rewards for cooperation in the demystification of learning processes, the child can be brought to learn that they must play an active role in such an exchange, the prospects seem brighter. They seem brighter still if the above suggestion is seen as a small but significant change to the ecological balance of the classroom. What the children might learn is that they can expect to be asked to give an account of their thinking about a task (as opposed to expecting to hand in a full sheet of work). They might learn to expect rewards not for being right but for being thoughtful. Adaptation to this small shift in teacher behaviour could have implications for the quality of learning experience which goes beyond mere matching.

10 Conclusion

The focus of this study has been on task processes in classes of 6 and 7-year-old children whose teachers were rated as better than average by the advisory service in the education authorities concerned. Working closely with these teachers showed clearly that they were dedicated and conscientious people. Few with experience of working with infant teachers would doubt this description. The questions posed in this study relate to how such dedication is harnessed in attempts to provide appropriate learning experiences for their pupils.

In appraising the quality of learning experiences the demands on the children of the tasks set were first ascertained. Although there were often marked differences in the classrooms studied, tasks demanding practice of existing knowledge, concepts or skills predominated. This was particularly apparent in language work where over three quarters of all tasks set demanded practice. A typical task was a request from the teacher for the class to write a story, usually accompanied by exhortations on neatness and appropriate grammar. Here the demand was for the practice of well-understood routines and rarely did such tasks impart or demand the acquisition of new knowledge. This staple diet of little new knowledge and large amounts of practice was rarely varied to include tasks which required either the discovery or construction of new of different ways of perceiving problems, or the application of existing knowledge and skills to new contexts.

The teachers studied held strongly to the philosophy of individualisation and it was therefore expected that differential demands would be intended for children of differing levels of attainment. High and low attaining children certainly received different curriculum content but they experienced similar patterns of task demand. Thus similar ratios of incremental to practice tasks were planned for both groups of children. This pattern was further confounded by the fact that teachers found it much more difficult to transform an intended incremental into an actual incremental task for high attainers. In reality therefore high attaining children received less new knowledge and more practice than their low attaining peers. This is the

213

opposite pattern to what might have been expected with the probably consequences of delays in progress for high attainers and lack of opportunity for consolidation for low attainers (cf. Brophy & Evertson, 1976).

The main reasons for teachers failing to implement intended demands were twofold; poor or misdiagnosis, and failures in task design. Many mismatches in demand occurred because the teacher did not ascertain that the child was already perfectly familiar with the task content. Poor or non-diagnosis thus underlay the fact that many incremental tasks actually made practice demands. Task design problems were also relatively frequent. In such cases the requirements for the performance of the task did not match the teacher's intention.

Little improvement in patterns of task demand happened as a result of transferring to a junior class or school. Here the pattern changed markedly as the term progressed. Revision tasks predictably predominated in the early weeks as the teachers ascertained the base from which to start. Thereafter incremental and practice tasks were the most prevalent.

Here too there were marked differences in the classrooms studied but in general there were more incremental and few practice tasks in this term than in the infant classes. This pattern was more apparent in junior than primary schools and particularly so in the language area. This would indicate a quickening pace in knowledge acquisition. However this general pattern hid the rather surprising trend that the number of incremental tasks decreased, and practice tasks increased, as the term progressed. Thus children were rapidly introduced to new concepts and skills early in the term with little opportunity for consolidation, whereas later in the term knowledge acquisition fell away to be replaced by more and more practice.

Teachers' task intentions during this term were similar to those found in infant schools. They planned large amounts of practice and revision for high attainers and a high input of new knowledge with little opportunity to practice for low attainers, with the same predictable consequences.

High attainers also experienced, as they had in the infant classes, tasks which did not make the intended demand. Thus they received 80% more practice tasks than intended, indicating little extension of concept acquisition, whereas low attainers experienced equal amounts of incremental and practice tasks which left little opportunity for consolidation. In number work the pattern was even more notable. Here low attainers received three times more incremental than practice tasks. The same problems of mis- or non-diagnosis and task design underlay the mismatching of intention and actual demand.

The quality of a pupil's learning experience is also related to the match between the intellectual demand of tasks and the pupil's attainments. In both number and language work at infant level teachers were able to provide a match on approximately 40% of tasks. About a third were too difficult for the child and a little over a quarter were too easy. This general pattern masks marked differences in the classrooms studied. There was also an indication that teachers in the infant schools were somewhat better at matching than those in infant departments of primary schools. It was also very clear that the quality of matching varied in relation to the children's intellectual standing in the classroom. High attainers were underestimated on over 40% of tasks assigned to them, a pattern similar to that reported by HMI (1978). But an equally clear pattern of overestimation was found for low attainers. Of their assigned tasks 44% were overestimated in both language and number work.

Matching was worse in the first term of junior schooling where the proportion of matched tasks in number work fell to 30%. The incidence of mismatching was particularly severe for high attainers since three-quarters of the tasks they received were underestimates. Low attainers again suffered from overestimation, a trend which was more marked in junior schools than junior departments. It was also interesting to find that the quality of matching declined as the term progressed. In the last observation period for example most of the incremental tasks were overestimates and practice tasks underestimates.

Teachers were adept at recognising a task that was proving too difficult but were totally blind to tasks whose demands were too easy. The reasons for this are at least twofold. Firstly the teachers' typical management style required them to be seated at the front of the class, and as a result supervision was limited to quick observational sweeps of the classroom. The usual image was of a class working cheerfully and industriously. This, indeed, is the second reason for a teachers' lack of recognition of too-easy tasks. Children always worked in this way irrespective of appropriateness of the task set. From the teachers' point of view, children were busy, and busy work equated with appropriate demands.

Thus in the short term, inappropriate work appeared to have little direct emotional or motivational consequences for children of this age. Although cognitive problems, which manifested themselves in unproductive or confusing learning experiences, were all too clearly apparent in the post task interviews, this cognitive confusion was masked from the teachers by the children's cheerfulness and industry. The teachers avoided the immediate consequences of such confusion by rewarding individual endeavour, and by restricting their considerations of children's work to the product, not the process of such work, a facet taken up later.

Intended classroom learning is embedded in the content of the tasks teachers provide for children. A detailed analysis of the structure of curriculum content was therefore carried out for number and language.

In number, all teachers used some kind of sequenced scheme. Children worked through these schemes "at their own rate," although the teachers perceptions of "rate" in this context appeared to refer to rate of mechanical progress through the scheme rather than rate of understanding. The content of the task, often in the form of work cards, was thus individual-ised, even though task demand was not. Little teaching was undertaken. Children were usually told to carry on from where they had last left off.

In contrast no sequential schemes appeared to be used in language. Most tasks were generated from the teacher's source of ideas. Most tasks were designed to develop writing skills, the typical approach being to introduce the topic as a class lesson involving discussion prior to its specification as a common class task. There was therefore no differentiation of task demand for children of differing levels of attainment. And as was stated earlier the great majority of such tasks required only the practice of established con-cepts and skills for high attainers. Writing was thus characterised by a lack of sequence and a lack of development.

It is also of interest to note that there was a clear differentiation in the tasks presented between reading and writing skills. Writing tasks were for the development of writing skills, and reading skills were to be enhanced by phonics and comprehension exercises. As such there was no integrated language approach.

Although different in source, presentation, demand and sequence, number and language tasks had in common a teacher stress on procedural rather than cognitive aims. They were interested in the production and presentation of work rather than in the identification or discussion of cog-nitive processes.

Although an accurate general picture, enormous differences in content provision were observed between classes, and within the classes, studied.

In mathematics some classes covered almost twice as many areas as others. Further, the "work at your own rate" philosophy precluded many low attainers from experiencing a wide range of content met by their more academically advanced peers even in the same classroom. Only half of the low attainers experienced division and money problems for example. The fineness of the sequence of development within any specific area, e.g., subtraction, also varied widely. In some classes the content was covered in a series of giant, sometimes quite mystifying leaps, whereas in others the same operations were developed in finely graded stages.

The width of the curriculum also varied greatly. In some classes a very narrow range of content was covered yet in the same period of time other teachers managed a much wider range with apparent success. These wide differences in provision appear to result from the selection of the particular mathematics scheme used. But within-class differences stem more from the teachers' decisions regarding individualisation of instruction. 'Covering the basics' thus has a bewildering variety of meanings, but as yet there is no evidence of what implications these may have for subsequent mathematical understanding. What is clear however is that generic phrases such as "the basics," "the four rules of number" or "own rate" are almost meaningless in practice.

A wide variety of provision was equally evident in language work. But here it was the common and predictable features of writing experiences which attract attention. Teachers had uniform and restricted aims which, in three quarters of tasks observed, were to practice writing with particular attention paid to quantity and grammar, especially full stops and capital letters. Teacher evaluation focused on quantity, neatness and grammar irrespective of how the task was specified, or the attainment level of the child.

The children did little to focus the teachers' attention on to their bland and uniform diet. As well as the ubiquitous cheerfulness and industry they were totally clear about how to please their teachers irrespective of their overt demands. Thus, for example, the exhortation to "write me an exciting story" was clearly interpreted as a request for a given number of lines of neat writing with due attention to full stops and capital letters. And in this interpretation they were correct.

Despite this diet however some progress was made in writing. When this was assessed after 6 months the children wrote, on average, more words, generated more ideas and used more connectives. They also wrote stories which were judged to be better on quality and organisation. On the other hand there was little or no development of those aspects which teachers stressed the most. More than half the children failed to use full stops appropriately and correct usage of capital letters remained almost static. The overt encouragement by teachers for exciting stories appeared to have no impact since no change in imaginative content was recorded over the 6 month period.

The failure of children to deploy correct grammatical usage when not under the direct supervision of teachers could result from lack of appropriate teaching or it could be that such exhortations were premature. Only future studies will tell.

It was shown earlier that poor, or misdiagnosis, underlay many failures to transform an intended into an actual task demand. Another crucial role for diagnosis is in delineating children's cognitive confusions prior to the provision of adequate explanations. The evidence shows that here too diagnosis is a central problem. The teachers did not diagnose. They reacted to the product of a child's task performance rather than to the processes or strategies deployed in attaining the product. Thus procedural matters, such as taking the child through the rules of carrying numbers or providing spellings, predominated, rather than diagnosis of the nature of the child's cognitive misconceptions. This was usually undertaken at the teachers' desk in an atmosphere of "crisis" management as teachers' attempted to attend to the queues whilst simultaneously supervising the class visually. Their evident frustration was an obvious consequence, and, given their chosen managerial style, unavoidable. Often the only individual teaching that children received was at the teacher's desk, but teaching within the above context hardly seems designed to enhance individualised learning, although it must be recognised that classes of thirty children impose severe constraints on teachers time and attention.

Nevertheless teachers cannot afford to disregard children's misconceptions. This maxim, together with the all too obvious problems teachers had with diagnosis, led to the development of an in-service course from which it was hoped to gain a better understanding of this from another group of experienced teachers. The ultimate aim was to provide practical advice for teachers which took into account normal classroom contraints.

Through the use of actual case studies and transcripts, followed by training in the use of diagnostic interviewing in their own classroom, teachers came to understand and accept the utility and necessity of diagnosis. Over time they learned to derive tentative hypotheses or hunches about the nature of the children's misconceptions. But they simply could not sustain an analysis of the child's responses. They fell back to direct teaching, stressing procedure rather than understanding.

A number of reasons accounted for this failure. The interviews were conducted within the framework of the typical crisis management style, i.e., that teachers are the providers of instant solutions to a constant stream of problems. As such the interviews got in the way of management. The second reason was that teachers could not stop teaching. There was a constant urge to rush into direct teaching at the first sign of error, before the misconception had been properly diagnosed. The third reason was that conducting a good diagnostic interview requires considerable skill. Teachers are not trained in such skills and find it difficult to acquire them. No doubt accumulated experience is hard to discard. And finally to conduct an effective interview requires an understanding of the processes to be attained, and experience in the manner in which children can, and typically, do, misinterpret processes.

Focusing on classroom tasks, and the influences of teachers, pupils and classroom context on their quality and performance, has brought into sharp relief a number of concerns, some serious, relating to the demands and appropriateness of tasks; to decisions regarding curriculum content; to the adequacy of teacher diagnosis and explanation; and to classroom management strategies. Most of these receive scant attention in the research literature (cf. Rosenshine, 1983) but are central factors in achieving and maintaining the quality of pupil learning experiences.

What has emerged in general terms is an increased understanding of the formidable problems teachers face as they strive to implement the laudable philosophy of individualising instruction, and the equally formidable array of skills that are required to carry this out effectively. The objective here however is not to criticise teachers for not being perfect but to provide a clear specification of the apparent problems with a view to improvement.

What follows therefore is an exploration of ways and means whereby this improvement might be sought whilst recognising that the issues are complex and interactive. Nevertheless two major problem areas arise, classroom management, and teachers' knowledge and understanding of content and pupils' typical responses to it.

It has been shown that teachers typically adopt what has been termed a crisis management style. This requires that they be all things to all pupils at all times. The consequences of this style include constant interruptions, divided teacher attention, lack of adequate class supervision, lack of opportunity for adequate diagnosis and explanation and, in many instances, teacher frustration. In short, a learning environment which is far from optimal for teacher or taught.

It has been claimed that teachers often sacrifice a concern for learning in favour of a concern for management (Doyle, 1979) and the findings reported here would seem to lend some support for this view. Nevertheless the essence of any good management strategy is to provide a system of rules and procedures which will optimise the main purpose of the work setting. In classrooms therefore management should provide the framework for the teachers' learning intentions. One of the main failings in the crisis management style is that it does not allow for the creation, or the flexible use, of time necessary to fulfil these intentions adequately. Evaluations of alternative managerial techniques must therefore recognise these as central criteria.

A number of suggested alternatives emanate from observed practice. The first is the abandonment of dual queues, a system which has been shown to benefit neither the teacher nor the pupils. This need not require the modification of the teachers' stated aim of marking work with children present although the operationalisation of this aim certainly requires amendments to cut down the ubiquitous queueing. One method would be the creation of a clear set of classroom rules regarding queueing which could profitably be used in conjunction with changes in the function and operation of groups.

Much of the teachers' time was taken up by their willingness to react to low order requests. In language work for example they were constantly harrassed for spellings. This represents a great deal of wasted time as well as breaks in continuity of working, and is, perhaps, a result of a lack of clarity in teachers' objectives for this kind of work. It seems unlikely that children of this age are capable of error free writing. Teachers must thus decide whether they want error-free work, in which case copy writing would seem more appropriate; or whether they wish for imaginative, expressive writing, in which instance spelling could be neglected in the short term. In the latter case this would provide an opportunity for teachers to acquire a more coherent understanding of patterns of children's errors which are currently masked by ad hoc provision. In the language work observed teachers' intentions appeared to fall awkwardly between these two stools.

Teaching to groups of children rather than to the class or individual is currently prescribed by HMI (1980). This report reiterated the suggestions made in the Plowden Report (1967) concerning the utilisation of groups since it was recognised that teachers could not be expected to individualise instruction in large classes of children. Unfortunately the use of classroom groups in practice has emerged as no more than a convenient seating arrangement rather than as a specific site for teaching.

Here too teachers need to clarify their aims. The assumption appears to be that simply sitting children together will further intellectual and social development. Research on groups does not support this assumption and neither do the findings reported in this study, where it has been shown that interaction is usually of dubious quality. Classroom groups do have potential as teaching and learning contexts, and many schemes are available (Slavin, 1983), but this potential is far from being realised.

Nevertheless if properly managed teaching to groups, regardless of whether the rest of the class is engaged on the same content area, could hold advantages in terms of extended contact, the opportunity to fine tune task demand and provide adequate diagnosis. A further stage in this process could be the implementation of peer teaching, although more research in normal classroom settings is required in this area.

Teachers would of course benefit greatly from additional assistance in the classroom, but teacher aids in Britain are not common. An increasing number of schools are however inviting the participation of parents in the teaching process both in school and at home with evident success (Tizard et al., 1982). The encouragement of this trend, which might perhaps be extended to suitable unemployed school leavers for example, would create the time necessary for teachers to concentrate on individual pupils.

These suggestions by no means exhaust the possibilities. The purpose here is not to provide comprehensive solutions but to indicate that possibilities do exist for the creation of teacher time. But when created a second step is necessary—the development of teacher skills. In order for adequate diagnosis and explanation to be afforded by teachers additional knowledge and skill in curriculum content areas, and in interacting with individual pupils, is required. Teachers need to be knowledgeable about the schemes available, their differing content, assessment procedures and implications for the management of learning. Crucially they need knowledge of how a wide range of pupils typically respond to this content, their common errors and misconceptions. On the basis of such knowledge they need to develop a range of strategies designed to overcome them.

Attention needs to be drawn to the cognitive complexities of content, rather than concern with mechanical progress; and to the processes whereby pupils arrive at products, rather than to the products themselves. In order to fulfil this change in focus, skills require developing in diagnostic interviewing and the phrasing of explanations. The problems experienced in this study provide a guide in this area although it is likely that training at pre-service level may not meet these same issues. Training at in-service level has the additional difficulty of attempting to overcome established routines.

There is an increasing demand, in Britain at least, that prospective teachers should undertake the academic study of a single specialist subject area for at least 2 years of their course. If this is interpreted by teacher educators to mean the provision of courses on esoteric academic content and theory then such study is unlikely to have implications or meaning for subsequent classroom practice. The findings of this study would indicate that for the training of teachers of young children additional time should be provided for students to develop their own pedagogic theories based on increased contact with pupils working on typical curriculum contents. A large and regular amount of time spent with different pupils throughout the course developing their knowledge and skills in content, diagnosis and interaction, bolstered by a closer examination of the continuity of learning experiences in the longer teaching practices, seems more appropriate.

At in-service level, skill based courses in this area need to be supplemented by initiatives designed to reduce the isolation of teachers with respect to their decisions on curriculum content. A detailed sharing of information through the exchange of their own case studies with teachers in other schools might be considered, perhaps extended by case conferences of individual children or curriculum decisions within their own school. The current trend towards the creation of posts with specific curriculum responsibility should help this process with the specialist post holder taking a key role.

The philosophy of individualised instruction has informed the education of young children for many years. We do not doubt the validity of this but, like all ideals, it is easier to theorise about than practise. Nevertheless teachers of this age group have made significant steps towards its successful implementation. Learning environments have been created which are characterised by good social relationships, expert utilisation of resources, happy and industrious pupils. What this study has revealed is that a number of cognitive aspects of this environment appear to have been hidden from teachers. These have been carefully specified, and their possible consequences outlined, not to carp or criticise, but as a basis for improvement. Teachers will, we hope, accept them in this spirit, for their information, reflection, maybe even inspiration. For improving the quality of pupil learning experiences is as much their aim as ours.

REFERENCES

Anderson, L. M. (1981) *Student responses to seatwork: implications for the study of student's cognitive processing.* Paper presented to AERA, Los Angeles.

Atkinson, R. C. (1976) Adaptive instructional systems: some attempts to optimise the learning process. In D. Klahr (Ed.), *Cognition and Instruction.* Hillsdale, NJ: Lawrence Erlbaum Associates Inc.

Ausubel, D. P. (1968) *Educational Psychology: A Cognitive View.* New York: Holt, Rinehart & Winston.

Ausubel, D. P., & Robinson, F. G. (1969) *School Learning: An Introduction to Educational Psychology.* New York: Holt, Rinehart & Winston.

Bassey, M. (1977) *Nine Hundred Primary School Teachers.* Nottingham Primary Schools Research Project. Trent Polytechnic.

Bennett, N., Andreae, J., Hegary, P., & Wade, B. (1980) *Open Plan Schools: Teaching, Curriculum, Design.* Windsor: NFER.

Bennett, N., & Blundell, D. (1983) Quantity and quality of work in rows and classroom groups. *Educational Psychology*, **3.2.**, 93–105.

Berliner, D. C. (1976) Impediments to the study of teacher effectiveness. *Journal of Teacher Education*, **27**, *(1)*, 5–13.

Blumenfeld, P. C. (1980) An initial model of the relation between work, form, content and process. In P. C. Blumenfeld et al. (Eds.), *Ecological Theory of Teaching*, Research Report ETT 80–85. San Francisco: Far West Laboratory.

Boydell, D. (1975) Pupil behaviour in junior classrooms. *British Journal of Educational Psychological*, **45**, 122–9.

Bronfenbrenner, U, (1976) The experimental ecology of education. *Teachers College Record*, **78**. 2, 157–204.

Brophy, J., & Evertson, C. M. (1976) *Learning from Teaching.* Boston: Allyn & Bacon.

Bruner, J. S. (1964) Some theorems on instruction illustrated with reference to mathematics. In E. R. Hilgard, (Ed.), *Theories of Learning and Instruction.* Chicago: National Society for the Study of Education.

Cockcroft, W. H. (1982) *Mathematics Counts.* Report of Committee of Inquiry into the Teaching of Mathematics. London: HMSO.

Davis, R. B., & McKnight, C. (1976) Conceptual, heuristic and algorithmic approaches in mathematics teaching. *Journal of Children's Mathematical Behaviour*, **1**, 271–86.

Denham, C., & Lieberman, A. (1980) *Time to Learn.* Washington: National Institute of Education.

Doyle, W. (1979a) Classroom tasks and student abilities. In P. L. Peterson and H. J. Walberg (Eds.), *Research on Teaching: Concepts, Findings and Implications.* Berkeley, Ca.: McCutchan.

Doyle, W. (1979b) Making managerial decision in classrooms. In D. L. Duke (Ed.), *Classroom Management.* Chicago: University of Chicago.

Doyle, W. (1980) *Student Mediating Responses in Teacher Effectiveness.* Denton, Texas: North Texas State University.

Duckworth, E. (1979) Either we're too early and they can't learn it or we're too late and they know it already: the dilemma of 'applying Piaget'. *Harvard Educational Review*, **49**, 3, 297–312.

223

Dunkin, M. J. (1976)   Problems in the accumulation of process–product evidence in classroom research. *British Journal of Teacher Education*, **2** (2), 175–87.

Emmer, E. T., Evertson, C. M., & Anderson, L. M. (1982)   Effective classroom management at the beginning of the school year. In Doyle, W. and Good, T. (Eds), *Focus on Teaching*. Chicago: University of Chicago Press.

Fisher, C. W., Filby, N. N., Marliave, R., Cahen, L., Dishaw, M. H., Moore, J. E., & Berliner, D. C. (1978) *Teaching Behaviours, Academic Learning Time and Student Achievement*. Beginning Teacher Evaluation Study. San Francisco: Far West Laboratory for Educational Research and Development.

France, N. (1979) *Primary Reading Test: Level 1*. Slough: NFER.

Galton, M., Simon, B., & Croll, P. (1980) *Inside the Primary Classroom*. London: Routledge & Kegan Paul.

Glazer, R., Pellegrino, J. W., & Lesgold, A. M. (1977)   Some Directions for a cognitive psychology of instruction. In A. M. Lesgold et al. (Eds), *Cognitive Psychology and Instruction*. New York: Plenum Press.

Haertal, G. D., Walberg, H. J., & Weinstein, J. (1983)   Psychological models of educational performance: a theoretical synthesis of constructs. *Review of Educational Research*, **53**, 75–92.

HMI (1978) *Primary Education in England: A Survey by H.M. Inspectors of Schools*. London: HMSO.

HMI (1980) *Education 5–9*. London: HMSO.

Hughes, J. M. (1972) *Phonics and the Teaching of Reading*. London: Evans.

Jackson, P. W. (1967) *Life in Classrooms*. New York: Holt, Rinehart & Winston.

Jensen, A. R. (1974) *Educational Differences*. London: Methuen.

McNamara, D. R. (1981)   Teaching skill: the question of questioning. *Educational Research*, **23**, 2. February.

Norman, D. A. (1978)   Notes towards a complex theory of learning. In A. M. Lesgold et al. (Eds), *Cognitive Psychology and Instruction*. New York: Plenum.

Plowden Report (1967) *Children and Their primary schools*. London: HMSO.

Posner, G. J. (1978) *Cognitive Science: Implications for Curriculum Research and Development*. Paper presented to the AERA, Toronto, March 1978.

Rosenshine, B. (1983)   Teaching functions in instructional programs. *Elementary School Journal*, **83**, 4 335–52.

Roth, E. (1983) Group processes in the primary school. Unpublished MA dissertation, University of Lancaster.

Schwebel, M., & Raph, J. (1974) *Piaget in the Classroom*. London: Routledge & Kegan Paul.

Slavin, R. (1983) *Cooperative Learning*. New York: Longman.

Sullivan, E. (1967)   Piaget and the school curriculum. *Bulletin of the Ontario Institute for Studies in Education*. Toronto.

Tikunoff, W. J., Ward, B. A., & Dasho, S. J. (1978) *Volume A: Three Case Studies*. (Report A78–7). San Francisco: Far West Laboratory for Educational Research and Development.

Tizard, J., Schofield, N. N., & Hewison, J. (1982)   Collaboration between teachers and parents in assisting children's reading. *British Journal of Educational Psychology*, **52**, 1–15.

Webb, N. M. (1982) Student interaction and learning in small groups. *Review of Educational Research*, **52**(3), 421–451.

Wheldall, K., Morris, M., Vaughan, P., & Yin Yuk Ng (1981)   Rows v. Tables: An example of the use of behavioural ecology in two classes of eleven year old children. *Educational Psychology*, **1**, 2, 171–83.

Wilkinson, B. (in preparation) *The Development of Children's Writing*.

Young, D. (1970) *Group Mathematics Test*. Sevenoaks: Hodder & Stoughton.

APPENDICES

Appendix A

Curriculum Cover: Mathematics

Steps worked by target children in each school in the Spring and Summer terms in:

Table A.1   Addition   228
Table A.2   Subtraction   230
Table A.3   Multiplication   231
Table A.4   Division   233
Table A.5   Sums involving more than one of the four rules   235
Table A.6   Fractions   236
Table A.7   Money   237
Table A.8   Time   238
Table A.9   Length and area   239
Table A.10   Shape   241
Table A.11   Weight   241
Table A.12   Capacity   242
Table A.13   Conceptualisation of numbers   242
Table A.14   Number language   243
Table A.15   Graphic representation   244

TABLE A.1
Addition

Addition								Class								
	1	2	3	4	5	6	7	8	9	10	11	12	13	14	15	16
Counting on, more than	H	M/L	L	A	H	H/M	A	H/M		M/L		L		M	H/M	A
Missing number in a sequence		H/M			H/M	H/M	M/L	L	L	H/L			H/M			A
Number bonds (sum to 10)		L			H					L		H/M	H/L		L	
Horizontal addition of 2 figures (sum to 10)	A	L	M/L	M/L	A	L	A		A	A		H/M	A	A	L	A
Horizontal addition of more than 2 figures (units only)			H	A		H/L	A		A	M/L		H/M	A	A	A	M/L
Vertical addition (units only)									M/L						M/L	
Mapping	L	L		A			M/L		L	A						A
							H/M									
Number bonds (up to 20)	A	L	M/L	M/L	A	L	A	M	A	A	A	A	A	A	L	A
Horizontal addition of 2 figures (sum to 20)	A	H/M	H/M	M	A	H/M	A	A	H	A	A	A	A	A	H/M	M/L
More than, less than and equal to	H/M	H/M	H/M	H/M	A	H/M	A	A	A	M/L	A	H/M	A	A	H/M	H
Vertical addition of tens and units (no carrying figure)		H/M	A	H	A	H/M	H	A	A	A		A	H	A	H	
Horizontal addition of tens and units (no carrying figure)				H	A	H/M	A	A	A	H	A	A	A	H/M	H	
Vertical addition of tens and units (with a carrying figure)	A	H	H	H	A	H/M	A	A	H/M	M/L	A	A	A	A	H	
Horizontal addition of tens and units (with a carrying figure)	H/M	H/M	H	M/L	A	H/M	A	A	A	H	A	H/M	H/M	H/M	H/M	
Problems involving addition of tens and units				A	H						A	M		A	H/M	H
Composition of hundreds, tens and units					H											

228

TABLE A.1
(Continued)

Addition	|— Class —|															
	1	2	3	4	5	6	7	8	9	10	11	12	13	14	15	16
Vertical addition of hundreds, tens and units (with carrying figure)	H															
Vertical addition of 3 units			H/M				H	H				H/M	M/L			
Missing number "addition" sums, e.g., 5 + ___ = 7 (horizontal layout)	M	M/L		A	H/M	A	A	H	H/M	M/L				A	A	M/L
Equalisers, e.g. 2 + 4 − 3 = ___	L							A							A	
Double missing number sums, e.g., 3 + 7 + ___ = 10 + ___				H	H				H							
Missing number addition sums (vertical layout)																
Problems involving units only (picture aids)				A		H/M	H/M		A			A				
Problems involving units only (no picture aid)										M/L						A
Vertical addition of multiples of ten			H/M												L	
Horizontal addition of multiples of ten			H/M		H									A	H	
Composition/decomposition of tens and units, e.g., ___ tens and ___ units	H/M	M		A		H/M				M/L					A	A

229

TABLE A.2
Subtraction

Subtraction	1	2	3	4	5	6	7	8	9	10	11	12	13	14	15	16
Counting back, less than		M/L		A	H	H/M	A	H/M		A					H/M	A
Problems involving units (with picture aids)										M/L						
Horizontal subtraction (units only)	A															
Vertical subtraction (units only)						A			L	M						
Horizontal subtraction (maximum number 20)	H	M/L	A	A	H	A	A	M	A	M/L		A	A	A	A	
Vertical subtraction (maximum number 20)			H/M			H/L						H/M	M	A	H/L	H
Missing number sums, e.g., 6-___=2 (horizontal layout)	M	H		H			A	H							A	M
Missing number sums (vertical layout)					H	A									H	
Subtraction of multiples of 10 (horizontal layout)			H/M										A			
Subtraction of tens and units (no carrying) horizontal layout		M	A	H	A	H/M		A	A	H	A	A	H/L		H	H/M
Subtraction of tens and units (no carrying) vertical layout	H/M		H/M	M	A	H/M	H/L	A	A	H		H/M	H/M	A	H	
Subtraction of tens and units (carrying) horizontal layout					A				A	H/M		A		H/M	H/M	
Subtraction of tens and units (carrying) vertical layout	A		H		H/M	H/M	H		H/M	M		A	A	A	H	
Problems involving units (no picture aids)				M/L		H				H		M/L			L	A
Problems involving tens and units			H/L	H/L	H	H				A	A				H/M	H

TABLE A.3
Multiplication

Multiplication	1	2	3	4	5	6	7	8	9	10	11	12	13	14	15	16
Pairs												M/L		H/L	H/M	H
Counting in twos, fives and tens			M/L		M/L	A	M/L		A			M/L				
Counting in 2s, 3s, 4s and 5s with numbers available, e.g., circle every 3rd number in 1, 2, 3, 4, . . . etc.		L		L												
Counting in 2s, 4s, or 6s					M/L	L	A									
Repeated addition related to multiplication, e.g. 7+7=7 2=							A		A	H/M						
Doubling		L														
Simple multiplication using notion of "sets of"					A		H			H		H/M				H
Number squares up to 100			M/L		A		A					M/L				
Routine practice of single tables (2–9) (horizontal layout)	A				A	A	A	A	A	H/M			A			
Vertical multiplication of units by a unit multiplier					A	A		A	A			A	A		M/L	H
Horizontal multiplication of units by a unit multiplier								M/L					H	A	L	

(Continued)

TABLE A3
(Continued)

Multiplication	Class															
	1	2	3	4	5	6	7	8	9	10	11	12	13	14	15	16
Vertical multiplication of tens and units (no carrying figure)	H/M												A	H/M	M/L	H
Missing number multiplication sums (horizontal layout)				H/M		H/M	H					H/M			H/M	H
Horizontal multiplication of tens and units (no carrying figure)			M/L		A	M/L			A				M	H/M	H/M	H
Bracket sums			H/M		H/M					H			A	H/M	H	
Vertical multiplication of tens and units (with carrying)	H/M											H/M	A	H		
Horizontal multiplication of tens and units (with carrying)					H/M						A				H/L	
Multiplication of fractions (vertical layout) with carrying															H.	
Problems involving multiplication of units (no picture aid)				H/M				H		H/M	A	M/L	A		L	
Problems involving multiplication of tens and units							H	M/L			A				H/M	

TABLE A.4
Division

Division	Class															
	1	2	3	4	5	6	7	8	9	10	11	12	13	14	15	16
Sharing												H/M				
Repeated subtraction												H/M				
Problems involving division of units (with picture aid)			H		H		H		H	H						
Division of units (vertical layout) no remainders	H/M	H		H		H/M				H						
Division of units as table practice (horizontal layout)					M				H/M				A	H/M		H
Missing number division sums, e.g., ? ÷ 3 = 3								L								
Division of units (vertical layout): with remainders							H			M/L					M/L	
Grouping, e.g., Group 8 in 3s = 2 groups of 3 + 2													A			
Division of tens and units: horizontal layout, no carrying, no remainder				H/M		A		A	A			H/L	H/M	H/M	H/M	H
: vertical layout, no carrying, no remainder									A				H/M	H		
: horizontal layout, no carrying, with remainder					H	H/M		H	H			M/L	A	A	M/L	
: vertical layout, no carrying, with remainder					H	H/M			H/M				M/L		A	

(*Continued*)

233

TABLE A.4
(Continued)

Addition										Class						
	1	2	3	4	5	6	7	8	9	10	11	12	13	14	15	16
: horizontal layout, with carrying, no remainder					H/M											
: vertical layout, with carrying, no remainder											A				H/L	
Problem involving division of units (no picture aid)		H		H	H/M			A					H/M	A	L	
Problems involving division of tens and units				H		M			H			A			H/M	

234

TABLE A.5
Sums Involving More than One of the Four Rules

Sums Involving More than One of the Four Rules	Class															
	1	2	3	4	5	6	7	8	9	10	11	12	13	14	15	16
Mixture of horizontal addition and subtraction of multiples of ten							H									
Number sentences involving addition or subtraction (up to 30)					A											
Missing number sums involving addition and subtraction				M												
Mixture of horizontal addition and subtraction within the same sum, e.g., $6 + 4 - 3 =$			A	A			H					M/L				
Addition and subtraction sums with brackets				H/M								H/M				
Identifying and inserting appropriate sign in four rules computation, e.g., 6 0 4 = 2							A									
Simple problem sums involving more than one of the four rules				M	A											
Groups of sums showing the relationship between the four rules, e.g., $4 + 4 + 4 = 3 \times 4 = 12$					H							H/M				
Sums involving a combination of the four rules, e.g., $(4 \times 6) - 2 + 4 =$				H												

235

TABLE A.6
Fractions

Fractions										*Class*						
	1	2	3	4	5	6	7	8	9	10	11	12	13	14	15	16
Fractions: halves			A	H/M	A	A		A	H	H	A		A	A	A	H
Fractions: quarters			A		A	A		H	H	H				A		
Fractions: thirds						H/M		H							A	
Fractions: fifths								H								

236

TABLE A.7
Money

Money	Class															
	1	2	3	4	5	6	7	8	9	10	11	12	13	14	15	16
Coin recognition	H/L		A				A		L	L	A					
Composition of coins		H/L		A	A	H	A	M/L		A	A	H/M			A	
Converting pence to two pence and vice versa								H								
Converting pence to half pence and vice versa					H			H				H/M			H	
Addition and subtraction of pence	M/L		A	A	M/L		A			M		H/M		M/L		
Addition and subtraction of sums involving half pences	H		A			H		H				H/M	A	H	H	A
Simple bills	M			A	H/L	H	H		H/M	A	A		H/M		H	A
Simple bills with change				M/L	M/L	H	H/L		A	H	A	A				
Shopping: problem sums, no fractions		H		A		H/M						H/M				
Bills involving multiples of a given item(s), e.g., 3 buns at 2p per bun	H		H	A	H/M	H	H	H/L	H	M/L		H/M		L		A
Bills involving fractional multiples of an item(s), e.g., 1½ kg of sugar at 20p per kg				H	H/M					H						

237

TABLE A.8
Time

Time		1	2	3	4	5	6	7	8	9	10	11	12	13	14	15	16
	Class																
Days of the week					H/L	A				M							A
Months of the year					A	A											A
Recording the times of the day that various things are done			M/L														
Earlier/later		A		A	A	A	H	H	A	A	A		A	L		A	A
O'clock		A	L	A	A	A	A	H	A	A	A		A		A	L	A
Preparing work for telling the time, e.g., colouring the quarter sections of a clock face			M/L														
Half past		A	H/L	A	A	H	H/M	H	A	A	A	A	A		M	M/L	A
Quarter past		A		A	A	A	H/M	H	A		A	A	A			M/L	A
Quarter to		A		A	A	A	H/M		A		A	A	A			M/L	A
The 5 minute intervals past the hour		A	H/L	H/M	H/M	H			M		H	A	H/M			H/M	A
The 5 minute intervals to the hour		A	H/L	H	H/M	A					H	A	H/M			H/M	A
Timing activities, e.g., how many seconds to do things			M												M		
Time duration, e.g., How long is it from breakfast to dinner time					H/M						H		H/M				
Different ways of reading the clock, e.g., 5 to 6 = 5.55									H		H						
The 24 hour clock																A	A

TABLE A.9
Length and Area

Length/Area								Class								
	1	2	3	4	5	6	7	8	9	10	11	12	13	14	15	16
The vocabulary of measurement, e.g., width, height and length		A	A		A	A	H	A	M		A			A		H/M
Measuring objects using non-standard lengths		L									A					
Estimations of length					H		A				A					
Measurement of dimensions of objects (centimetres)		A	A	A	A	A		A	A		A			A		
Measurement of objects (metres)				H	L		H				M/L					
Conversion of centimetres to metres (or decimetres) and vice versa		H									M/L					A
Measurement of lines (centimetres)	H	H	A	A	A	A	A	A			A	A		H/M	A	A
Construction of lines (centimetres)			A	L			H		A		H	A				
Perimeters											H/M				A	
Simple problems involving measurement											A					
Relationships between length, width and area											A					A
Estimations of area using regular shapes											A					

(Continued)

239

TABLE A9
(Continued)

Length/Area		Class														
	1	2	3	4	5	6	7	8	9	10	11	12	13	14	15	16
Finding out the area of items using regular shapes		H				H					A					
Finding the area of objects using standard units											A					
Estimations of area using irregular shapes											A					
Finding areas using irregular shapes											A					

TABLE A.10
Shape

Shape	|	1	2	3	4	5	6	7	8	9	10	11	12	13	14	15	16
										Class							
Circles and squares		M	L	A	A	A	A	A							A		A
Rectangles and triangles		M	L	A	A	A	A	A									A
Complex symmetrical shapes (e.g., hexagons)					H	H											
Simple 3D shapes						H				H/M		H					A
Construction of 2D shapes						L							A				A
Symmetry							H/M										A

TABLE A.11
Weight

Weight	|	1	2	3	4	5	6	7	8	9	10	11	12	13	14	15	16
										Class							
Lighter than/heavier than		M/L			A												
Estimating weights						H						A	A		A		A
Balancing using non-standard weights			M/L	H		H		A				H/M					
Balancing using standard weights					H					M	M/L	A	A				
Problems involving weights												H/M					A

241

TABLE A.12
Capacity

Capacity								Class								
	1	2	3	4	5	6	7	8	9	10	11	12	13	14	15	16
Full/empty etc.			A								M					A
Capacity: an introduction using non-standard units							A				M					A
Capacity: millilitres and litres					A					H						

TABLE A.13
Conceptualisation of Numbers

Conceptualisation of Numbers								Class								
	1	2	3	4	5	6	7	8	9	10	11	12	13	14	15	16
Counting objects/cardinality		L		H	A	L			M/L							
Ordinal numbers		M/L	H/M			H			H							
Odd/even numbers		L			H	H/M	M/L	H					H			A
Sets and subsets							A		H/L							
Equivalent sets		H/L			H	H	A	H	L	H/M				A		A
Partitioning sets									H	H						

TABLE A.14
Number Language

Number Language	Class															
	1	2	3	4	5	6	7	8	9	10	11	12	13	14	15	16
Thick/fat/thin			A													
Large/small big/little			A													
Long/tall/short			A	A												
Narrow/wide			A													
Many/few			H													
Straight and curved lines			H		H	H	H									H/M
Number language: equivalent terms, e.g., plus = add					H			H/L	A							A

243

TABLE A.15
Graphic Representation

Graphic Representation																
Class	1	2	3	4	5	6	7	8	9	10	11	12	13	14	15	16
Recording relationships, e.g., hair colour. A yellow B brown C black		M														
		H/M														
Graphs					A	H/M	M/L	L						A	A	
Reading gauges																
Games and Puzzles											A					
Map puzzles																
Number codes, e.g., A B C 1 2 3 etc.		H/M														

Appendix B

Language: Stimulus Stories

1. Zap and His Flying Machine   245
2. The Sail Away Island   246

1. ZAP AND HIS FLYING MACHINE

*[1]Zap was a happy little fellow. He hadn't a care in the world. *[2]One day he found a pair of goggles, so whistling to himself, he sat down to design himself a machine to go with his new goggles.

*[3]He decided that it must be a cheerful machine. He lay down to think what sort of gaily coloured machine he would make. A boat would be nice, but it wouldn't be much use on land, unless it had wheels. *[4]A boat with wheels and sails would be good, but what would happen if it came to a precipice? Clearly wings and a propeller were needed as well. Yes this machine would be something special. An aeroboat car.

*[5]First Zap started with the boat, which he made from an old plastic oil drum. Then he started to make the chassis with some old pram and bicycle wheels. He thought that he would use these wheels like an aeroplane—two big ones at the front and a smaller one behind. *[6]Next he put a wheel on a long handle into the cockpit, for steering, and a piece of wood for his feet to rest on. That would steer well, he thought.

*[7]Zap sat in the drum to test it, so far. He tested the levers and they worked perfectly. The next job was to make the wings and tail and he made some legs, which went down to the wheels, and *[9]last of all, he found a piece of deckchair material and made a sail. *[10]He was pleased with his work. What shall I call my magnificent machine?, he wondered. Shall I give it a name? I know, Zapmobile. That's it! Zapmobile.

---

*Position of slides.

245

*[11]Now at last Zap's machine was ready. He was very excited. He thought, if it works, I can fly away, off over the houses and into the sky. *[12]So he climbed into the cockpit, pressed the starter and whir . . . whoopee! It works he shouted! Up, up, up went the Zapmobile. Zap did two loop the loops—his adventure was just beginning.

(This story was adapted from "Zap goes flying" by Cephas Howard, Transworld Publications Ltd., 1972.)

2. THE SAIL AWAY ISLAND

*[1]This is a story about a family of mice. The Mother was called Hannah and the Father, who was big and strong, was called Bouncer.

They were really a very happy family, *[2]but they were constantly being chased by the ginger household cat, who liked to eat mice for his dinner. They became so frightened of him *[3]they decided to borrow a boat and sail away to find a peaceful island.

I'll be the ship's Captain, declared Bouncer. It took the mice most of the night to load the ship and launch it into the harbour. *[4]Ignoring the crowd at the pier, they sailed bravely out to sea.

*[5]One morning, Captain Bouncer cried—Land ho! On the horizon was an island. *[6]They sailed up to it and the mice waded cautiously ashore and tied up their boat.

*[7]I claim this land, cried Bouncer, as a place where all mice can live without fear. We will build a great kingdom, dedicated to the freedom of mice, and I will be kind!

*[8]After unloading their supplies, they somersaulted on the beach through the long brilliant sunset. How wonderful it was to be on land again. *[9]Finally, as the last rays of daylight faded, they climbed back aboard the ship to spend the night.

*[10]At dawn, they discovered an enormous footprint in the sand. It looks like a bear track, said Hannah. Stand aside, ordered Bouncer. We'll use my grandad's favourite trick. First dig a deep hole, then cover it with straw and bait it with honey. Tonight the beast will smell the bait, stumble into the trap and the island will be ours.

*[11]By evening the trap was completed. The mice spent a sleepless night in a nearby hole. The next morning they discovered that the trap was still empty. Look! shrieked Hannah. Someone has cut the rope. The ship has gone.

That night the mice hid behind a sand dune and kept watch over the honey jar. *[12]Just after dawn a shadowy figure appeared on the beach.

---
* Position of slides.

(This story was adapted from "The Island of the Skog" by Kellogg Steven, Weston Woods Studios Ltd., 1981.)

TABLE B.1
Methods Used for Teaching Punctuation

Method	School
Comprehension work	4, 5, 6, 7
Sentences about pictures (e.g., write one sentence about this picture)	1, 3, 13
Jumbled sentences (e.g., Re-arrange these words to make a sentence: a kite have I little)	8, 9, 13
Sentences on given topics (e.g., write a sentence about yourself)	3, 8, 9
Sentence correction (e.g., what is wrong with this sentence? i go to school)	5
Puzzles (e.g., I have a face. I can tell the time. What am I?)	1

Appendix C

Classroom Groups

Table C1   Sample details   250
Table C2   Categories of talk   251
Definitions of categories and sub-categories for pupil talk   253

TABLE C.1
Details of Each Group for the Twelve Lessons Analysed

	Group Code (indicating school, group and subject)	Composition of Group			Ability of Individual			Rationale for Grouping		
		Number in Group	Boys	Girls	High	Average	Low	Ability	Social	Ability and Social
Number	A(a)N	5	5	—	—	2	3	✓Maths		
	B(a)N	5	—	6	1	4	—		✓	✓✓
	C(a)N	5	3	2	—	1	4			
	C(b)N	5	3	2	3	2	—			
	E(a)N	5	3	2	5	—	—	Language and Reading		
	F(a)N	4	2	2	—	1	3	✓Maths	✓	
	A(a)L	5	5	—	—	2	3			
	B(b)L	3	2	1	1	1	1			
Language	C(a')L	5	3	2	—	2	3			✓
	D(a)L	5	4	1	—	—	5	✓Language		
	D(a')L	5	3	2	2	—	3	✓Mixed		
	F(b)L	5	2	3	2	2	1		✓	

TABLE C.2
Breakdown of all Categories and Sub-Categories for Task Related Talk

Category	Sub-Category	
Instructional Input	Request	Each sub-category is divided into:
	Response	
	Unsolicited	
	(Out Group)	
	Task Specific	
	Task Management	
Sharing Information	Progress Report	Primary Task
	Personalised Discussion	
	Status	
	Reading — to self / to others	
	(Out Group)	
Pupil-to-Pupil		
Materials	Request	Secondary Task
	Response — Cooperative / Argumentative	
	Statement	
	Playing with	
	(Out Group)	
Egocentric	(No sub-categories)	
Talk	Instructional Input	Each Sub-Category is divided into:
	Task Management	
	Procedure	

(Continued)

TABLE C.2
(Continued)

	Category	Sub-Category	
Task Related	Pupil-to-Teacher			
	Reading	Materials	Request
		Status	Response
		(No sub-categories)	Statement
	Instructional Input	Initiates — by talking / by showing	
		Responds — by talking / by showing	Each sub-category is divided into:
	Teacher-to-Pupil		
	Management	Initiates — Task / Behaviour / Feedback	Individual
		Responds — Task / Behaviour / Feedback	Group
			Part Group
	Procedure	Initiates	
		Responds	

DEFINITIONS OF CATEGORIES AND SUB-CATEGORIES
FOR PUPIL TALK

Task Related Pupil-to-Pupil Talk

A. *Instructional input*: Talk relating specifically to a problem, or a need for information in order to complete the task.
    Request: for instructional help, explicit guidance, information.
    Response: to a request for help; peer teaching.
    Unsolicited: peer teaching which has not been requested; help spontaneously offered, occasionally as a response to a request directed to another child.

B. *Sharing information*: Talk which is not specifically related to task completion, but informs others of facts, problems, abilities, etc., related to the performance of the task. Discussion of ongoing work.
    Task Specific: talk that informs others of what the talker himself is doing, writing, thinking about, as he works at the task.
    Task Management: talk in which children organise or manage their task, organise other children involved in the same task, or organise materials needed to perform the task, or consider the ways in which these materials should be used, e.g., "Don't wobble them."
    Progress Report: Talk relating to the number of pages written, work-cards completed, sums finished, etc., generally so that comparisons of progress can be made.
    Personalised Discussion: in which participants take on a role within their talk, or discuss a role within a story, e.g., "I'm not your husband."
    Status: talk concerning a child's abilities, often in comparison with others, to show superiority or inferiority.
    Primary Status: when a child discusses his own status, e.g. "I don't count in my head . . . I just think."
    Secondary Status: when a child discusses another's status, e.g., "Stephen has to count on his fingers."
    Reading: includes a child reading his own work (for example a story) aloud, or reading another child's work aloud, either to himself or to others in the group.

C. *Materials:* Talk relating to materials needed for the task, e.g., pencils, rubbers, practical mathematical equipment.
    Request: for specific materials to be used, shared, passed, handed over, etc. Questions about the need to use materials, which equipment to use, the properties of the materials.

Cooperative Response: when the request is willingly complied with, or an appropriate answer is given.

Argumentative Response: when a dispute arises, when materials will not be shared, etc.

Statement: announcement re materials, e.g., "My pencil's broken."

Playing With: talk when materials related to the task are being used for purposes other than the work in hand.

D. *Egocentric*: Talk which is apparently not intended to evoke any action or response from another.

Within each sub-category a distinction is also made between:

Out Group: when talk is to children from another group or class.

Primary Task: when the child's talk is relevant to the curriculum area in which his task is set, or to the same type of activity, e.g., the child is writing a story and consults others who are also writing stories; or he is working at addition sums along with others in the group.

Secondary Task: when talk relates to a different curriculum area or type of activity from the one on which the child is working, e.g., he is working at English comprehension, but talks about Maths; or he is working at division, but helps another child with an addition sum.

Task Related Pupil-to-Teacher Talk

These definitions are covered by those for Task Related Pupil-to-Pupil talk, but now concern talk between pupil and teacher.

E. *Talk*: Communication between teacher and pupil except reading.
Instructional Input: see category A.
Task Management/Status: see sub-categories of category B.
Materials: see category C.

With each sub-category, a distinction is also made between;

Request: to teacher for help with material, etc; to resolve a dispute, etc.

Response: to teacher about guidance received; response to feedback on task, admonishment for behaviour, etc.

Statement: an announcement to the teacher, related to the task.

F. *Reading*: Reading to the teacher from a text book or reader.

Non Task Related Pupil-to-Teacher Talk

J. *Social*: talk which is not related to the child's task, or essential routine, e.g., "My Dad's ill."

Author Index

Anderson, L. M.,   3, 4, 135, 138, 223, 224
Andreae, J.,   9, 153, 223
Atkinson, R. C.,   4, 223
Ausubel, D. P.,   4, 185, 223

Bassey, M.,   9, 223
Bennett, N.,   9, 153, 154, 223
Berliner, D. C.,   9, 18, 154, 177, 223, 224
Blumenfeld, P. C.,   9, 223
Blundell, D.,   154, 223
Boydell, D.,   153, 223
Bronfenbrenner, U.,   4, 5, 223
Brophy, J.,   214, 223
Bruner, J. S.,   4, 223

Cahen, L.,   9, 154, 177, 224
Cockroft, W. H.,   4, 223
Croll, P.,   153, 224

Dasho, S. J.,   135, 224
Davis, R. B.,   6, 223
Denham, C.,   4, 223
Dishaw, M. H.,   9, 154, 177, 224
Doyle, W.,   5, 6, 7, 219, 223
Duckworth, E.,   4, 223
Duke, D. L.,   224
Dunkin, M. J.,   18, 224

Emmer, E. T.,   135, 138, 224
Evertson, C. M.,   135, 138, 214, 223, 224

Filby, N. N.,   9, 154, 177, 224
Fisher, C. W.,   9, 154, 177, 224
France, N.,   19, 224

Galton, M.,   153, 224
Glaser, R.,   4, 224
Good, T.,   224

Haertel, G. D.,   4, 224
Hegarty, P.,   9, 153, 223
Hewison, J.,   220, 224
Hilgard, E. R.,   223
HMI,   3, 4, 41, 153, 215, 220, 224
Howard, C.,   246
Hughes, J. M.,   120, 224

Jackson, P. W.,   5, 224
Jensen, A. R.,   61, 224

Klahr, D.,   223

Lesgold, A. M.,   4, 224
Lieberman, A.,   4, 223

McNamara, D. R.,   5, 224
McNight, C.,   6, 223
Marliave, R.,   9, 154, 177, 224
Moore, J. E.,   9, 154, 177, 224
Morris, M.,   154, 224

Norman, D. A.,   22, 23, 24, 25, 28, 224
Pellegrino, J. W.,   4, 224
Peterson, P. L.,   223

Plowden,   153, 220, 224
Posner, G. J.,   4, 224

Raph, J.,   4, 224
Robinson, F. G.,   4, 223
Rosenshine, B.,   218, 224
Roth, E.,   160, 224

Schofield, N. N.,   220, 224
Schwebel, M.,   4, 224
Simon, B.,   153, 224
Slavin, R.,   220, 224
Steven, K.,   247
Sullivan, E.,   4, 224

Tikunoff, W. J.,   135, 224
Tizard, J.,   220, 224

Vaughan, P.,   154, 224

Wade, B.,   9, 153, 223
Walberg, H. J.,   4, 223, 224
Ward, B. A.,   135, 224
Webb, N. M.,   167, 224
Weinstein, J.,   4, 224
Wheldall, K.,   154, 224
Wilkinson, B.,   106, 224

Yin Yuk Ng,   154, 224
Young, D.,   19, 224

Subject Index

Accretion. 22, 23

Actual task demands, 28–39

Ambiguity,
of cues and intention, 5–7, 11, 32–34
of teachers' intended task demand, 33–38

Appropriateness,
and expressed interest, 54–56
and level of attention, 54, 218
and perceived ease of task, 56
and pupils' competence, 12–14, 35
and teachers' intention, 13, 14, 17, 33–35, 217–219
indices of, 13
of procedure, 13, 61
of task demand, 42–46, 60, 61, 213
of task management, 13, 17, 217–219

Assessing the degree of match, 41–44, 48, 49, 91

Attainment levels,
and match, 45, 46, 146–151
and patterns of task demand achieved in transfer study, 145, 146
match and mis-match in number and language curricula, 146, 147, 213–216
width of number curriculum, 77–85, 92–94

Attention level,
and appropriateness of task demanded, 54

of target pupils, 54

Behavioural demands, differences between Infant and Junior schools, 134, 135

Classroom,
activity, teachers' accounts, 58
as complex information environment, 5, 58, 61, 62
social context, 153, 154

Classroom groups,
different styles of instructional input and language curriculum, 166–167, 178–183
different styles of instructional input and number curriculum, 164–165, 167–176, 178

Classroom groups (perceived benefits), 153
and Plowden Report, 153, 220
and recent research, 153, 154
size of, 153
study of, 153–183

Classroom groups vs. rows, 154

Classroom group talk categories, 154, 159–163
exploratory study of, 154, 155
inter-group, 159
pupil non-task related, 155, 160, 161
pupil task related, 155–162
pupil task related, ego-centric, 155, 159, 161

257

pupil task related, instructional input, 155–156, 161–167
pupil task related, materials, 155, 158, 159, 161–163
pupil task related, progress report, 155, 158, 162, 163
pupil task related, sharing information, 155–156. 161–163
pupil task related, task management, 155, 157, 162, 163
pupil to pupil, 155–163
pupil to teacher, 155, 159–162
research design for, 154, 155
task related vs. task enhancing, 167
teacher to pupil, 155, 159–162, 166–183
types of and levels of attainment, 162, 163
Classroom learning processes, Doyle's model, 5–7
Classroom management, 58–66, 150, 168, 169, 176–178, 197, 198, 217–219
crisis management, 217–221
Classroom organisation,
differences between Infant and Junior schools in transfer study, 133–135, 137
Classroom practice,
and limited effect of research on teaching and learning, 4, 5, 218, 219
Cockroft report, 4
Cognitive vs. procedural aims of task demanded, 100, 145, 150
Competence,
and appropriateness of task allocated to pupils, 12, 13, 35
identification of pupils', 12, 13, 197–199, 207
interpretive, 6, 7, 11
Complex learning, Norman's theory of, 22–28
Comprehension tasks in the language curriculum, 115

performance on, 119
structuring of, 118, 119
teachers' view, 115–117
Copying, 54
Crisis management style in classrooms, 217–219
Cues and intentions, ambiguity of, 5–7, 11
Curricula, differences between language and number, 100
Curriculum,
change, pupils' resistance to, 6
content, qualitative differences and learning experiences, 21 29–30
differentiation index, number, 83–85
language, 99–128
number, 67–97
organisation and differences between Infant and Junior schools, 134, 135, 137
width and performance of pupils of different levels of attainment, 93, 94

Demand (see task demand)
Diagnosis,
and generation of hypotheses, 197–199, 207
in-service course for teachers in, 9, 10, 20, 185–211
research design for, 186–197
results of, 197–208, 209–211
teachers' comments on relevance, 198, 199
Diagnosis, consequences of failure of, 213–219
Diagnostic interview,
and pupils' perception of allocated task, 12, 139, 211
examples of, 15–17, 43–44, 51, 52, 60–61, 189–191, 193, 194, 196
format of, 13, 15–17
with target pupils, 11, 12–13, 43, 44, 51, 52, 54
Diagnostic interviewing by teachers,

problems of, 185, 186, 197–210, 218, 219
Diagnosis of pupils' knowledge, and matching, 185
  teachers' problems, 169–176, 178, 185, 197, 198, 213–219
Differential task demand, pattern with time in transfer study, 145
Differentiation of curriculum, and teachers' decisions on individualisation, 83–85, 96, 100, 103, 104, 117–118, 213, 216
  language and type of school, 109–113, 145, 216
  number and type of school, 84, 85, 96, 216

Emotional problems, and mis-match, 55–57, 65, 66, 211
Enrichment task demands, appropriateness of, 44
Error production, 51
Error rate, matching, 42, 43, 44
Expressed interest, incidence of, and appropriateness, 54–56

Fieldworkers, selection of, 13

Grammar, emphasis in language curriculum, 111–113, 217

Happiness of target pupils, 53, 54, 132–135
High-attainers,
  and mis-match, 3, 4, 36, 38, 39, 45, 65, 150, 151, 213–215
  performance in language curriculum, 107–109

Incremental task demands,
  appropriateness of, 43–44
  mis-match through over-estimation, 48
  over-estimation and transfer study, 148, 149
Individualisation,
  and infant schools, 85

match and language curriculum, 102–104
  teachers' beliefs in and problems with, 213, 218, 221
  teachers' decisions on, 83–85, 96, 100, 103, 104, 117–118, 213, 216
Infant schools, transfer to junior schools, 9, 10, 19–20, 129–151
Instructional input in classroom groups,
  language curriculum, 166–167, 178–183
  number curriculum, 164–165, 167–176, 178
Interpretive competence, 6, 7

Language concepts, teachers under-estimating of high- and mid- attainers on, 36, 150, 151, 213–215
Language curriculum, 99–128
  writing practice, 100, 110, 217
  methods of developing writing skills, 102, 103
  phonic work, 119–122
  reading, 123–125
  teachers' aims in, 100–102
  teachers' attempts to motivate writing, 102, 103
Learning experiences, qualitative differences,
  in curriculum content, 21, 29–30
  social organisation, 21, 58
Low attainers,
  accuracy of teachers' diagnosis of language competence, 36, 150, 215
  and mis-match, 3, 4, 38, 39, 45, 50, 65, 150, 151, 215
  over-estimation of, 50, 92, 151, 215

Match,
  and introduction of new work, 47, 48
  and the quality of pupil's learning, 41, 50–57, 67, 150, 151

assessing the degree of,   41–44, 48, 49, 91
differences in levels across classrooms,   45, 92
individualisation and language curriculum,   102–104
judgement of,   44, 48–50, 92, 146, 149
mis-diagnosis of competence and quality of learning experience, 35–41, 185–212, 213–219
necessary criteria; cf. appropriateness,   42–46, 91
teachers' views of,   48–50, 149–151
teachers' vs fieldworkers' judgements,   49, 50, 149, 150, 151
Matching study,   9, 10, 28, 41–66, 146–151
research design,   9–19, 41–48
Mis-diagnosis of the progress of high attainers,   39
Mis-match,   3, 4, 37–39
minimising, in number curriculum, 93, 94
Mis-matched tasks, pupils' responses, 51–53

Number curriculum,
accounts of pupil coverage, 77–83
differences in range and depth of coverage between schools,   68–77, 83–85, 93–96, 216
introduction of new ideas,   79, 81
outcomes and matching,   91–94
tailored testing of target pupils, 85–93
teachers' paths through,   67, 68, 77, 85, 94–96
teachers' perception of match, 91, 92
work covered by pupils,   68–77
Number and language curricula, match for different levels of attainment, 146, 147, 213–216

Number tasks, intended demands and attainment levels,   37, 38, 68–69

Observation of target pupils,   11, 12, 14–18, 58–59, 77–83
Over-estimation,
incremental task demands and transfer study,   148, 149
teachers' perceptions and remedies, 63, 92, 149, 215

Performance, pupils' anticipated, 11
Phonic work in the language curriculum, testing of target pupils,   121–122
variations between classes, 199–121
Post-task teacher interview,   11, 13–14, 48, 100
Practice task demands and fluency, 42–43, 50
Praise, absence of, in diagnostic interviews by teachers,   211, 212
Prediction of problems in task performance,   11, 14, 61, 64
Pre-task interview with teacher,   11, 14–15, 31, 64, 100
teacher's intention in task allocation, 11, 14, 31, 100, 188, 191, 194
Primary vs. infant school, and matching, 46, 47, 146–151
Procedural vs. cognitive aims of tasks 100, 145, 150
Procedure, appropriateness of,   13, 61
Pupils' disruptive behaviour in light of new demands,   6
Pupils' perception of teachers' intention in task allocation,   10–12, 15, 16, 57, 60–62, 211
Pupils' understanding of teachers' perception,   64, 65, 185
Pupils' view of new teachers,   132, 133

Qualitative differences in task demands,   21, 23, 24–26

Quality of pupil learning experiences, 3–7, 21, 41, 212
  and matching,   41, 50–57, 150, 151
  and mis-diagnosis of pupils' competence,   35–41, 185–212, 213–219
  management of equipment,   51, 53
Queues,   2, 50, 123, 137, 168, 169, 176–178, 219
Rate of performance vs. understanding, 91
Ratio of incremental to practice tasks, 31, 34, 139, 140, 141, 145, 148, 213, 214
Reading in the language curriculum, 123–125
Rows vs. groups in classrooms,   154
Rules in the classroom,
  and teachers sensitivity over, 137, 138
  unwritten,   1–3, 135, 138
  written,   135–137

Schools: criteria for selection to sample,   45
Schools, type attended and matching, 46, 47, 146–151
Strategic skills, development by and enrichment tasks,   44

Talk in classroom groups, categories, 154, 155, 159–163
Target pupils, choice of,   11
Task cycle,   57, 58, 96
Task demands,   21–39, 138–146
  actual,   28–39
  category system of,   23, 24–28
    enrichment,   23, 25–27, 29, 32, 36–38, 138–146
    incremental,   23–42, 48, 138–149
    practice,   23–50, 63, 138–149, 213
    practice, pre-requisites for,   35, 42–43

restructuring,   22–31, 38, 138–146
  revision,   25–38, 96, 138–149
  confusion between unintended practice and intended incremental, 33–39, 100, 214
  intended procedural objectives, 62, 63
  qualitative differences in,   21, 23, 24–26
Task demands, intended,
  reasons for failure of implementation, 214, 217
  vs. actual,   32–39, 141–146
Teachers,
  failure to perceive under-estimation, 48, 49, 63, 65, 150, 151, 213, 214
  intention and appropriateness of task,   13, 14, 17, 33–35, 217–219
  interviews with junior and infant re. transfer of pupils,   129
  predeliction for quantity of work, 63, 65, 66, 91, 102, 104, 109, 110, 113, 128
  problems over diagnosis of task difficulties,   169–176, 178, 185
Teacher's account of classroom activity,   58
Teacher education, suggestions for, 221
Teacher's intention in task allocation, 10, 11, 13, 14, 28, 32–34, 100, 101, 188, 191, 194, 213
Teachers, sampling,   18, 19
Transfer from infant to junior school, study of,   9, 10, 19–20, 129–151
  arrangements for transfer, 130–132
  differences in classroom organisation, 133–135, 137
  differences in curriculum organisation,   134, 135, 137
  interviews with teachers, re. transfer, 129
  matching and type of task demand, 146–151, 214, 215

over-estimation and incremental task demands,   148, 149

pupil perception of new school, 132–135

pupil perception of new school, after transfer,   133

pupil perception of new school, before transfer,   132, 133

pupil perception of new teacher, 132, 133

pupils' visit prior to transfer, 129, 130, 132

rules in classroom,   137, 138

task demands, differential pattern with time,   145

task demands, pattern of,   138–140, 145

variations in nature and type of records passed from infant to junior,   130, 131

Tuning,   22, 23, 24

Turning to neighbours for help,   54

Under-estimation, teachers' failure to perceive,   48, 49, 63, 65, 150, 151, 213, 214

Writing in the language curriculum, testing of,   102–115